Practical ASP.NET
Web API

Badrinarayanan Lakshmiraghavan

apress·

Practical ASP.NET Web API

ISBN-13 (pbk): 978-1-4302-6175-9

ISBN-13 (electronic): 978-1-4302-6176-6

Trademarked names, logos, and images may appear in this book. Rather than use a trademark symbol with every occurrence of a trademarked name, logo, or image we use the names, logos, and images only in an editorial fashion and to the benefit of the trademark owner, with no intention of infringement of the trademark.

The use in this publication of trade names, trademarks, service marks, and similar terms, even if they are not identified as such, is not to be taken as an expression of opinion as to whether or not they are subject to proprietary rights.

While the advice and information in this book are believed to be true and accurate at the date of publication, neither the authors nor the editors nor the publisher can accept any legal responsibility for any errors or omissions that may be made. The publisher makes no warranty, express or implied, with respect to the material contained herein.

President and Publisher: Paul Manning
Lead Editor: Ewan Buckingham
Technical Reviewer: Fabio Claudio Ferracchiati
Editorial Board: Steve Anglin, Mark Beckner, Ewan Buckingham, Gary Cornell, Louise Corrigan, Morgan Ertel, Jonathan Gennick, Jonathan Hassell, Robert Hutchinson, Michelle Lowman, James Markham, Matthew Moodie, Jeff Olson, Jeffrey Pepper, Douglas Pundick, Ben Renow-Clarke, Dominic Shakeshaft, Gwenan Spearing, Matt Wade, Tom Welsh
Coordinating Editor: Jill Balzano
Copy Editor: James Compton
Compositor: SPi Global
Indexer: SPi Global
Artist: SPi Global
Cover Designer: Anna Ishchenko

Distributed to the book trade worldwide by Springer Science+Business Media New York, 233 Spring Street, 6th Floor, New York, NY 10013. Phone 1-800-SPRINGER, fax (201) 348-4505, e-mail orders-ny@springer-sbm.com, or visit www.springeronline.com. Apress Media, LLC is a California LLC and the sole member (owner) is Springer Science + Business Media Finance Inc (SSBM Finance Inc). SSBM Finance Inc is a Delaware corporation.

For information on translations, please e-mail rights@apress.com, or visit www.apress.com.

Apress and friends of ED books may be purchased in bulk for academic, corporate, or promotional use. eBook versions and licenses are also available for most titles. For more information, reference our Special Bulk Sales–eBook Licensing web page at www.apress.com/bulk-sales.

Any source code or other supplementary materials referenced by the author in this text is available to readers at www.apress.com. For detailed information about how to locate your book's source code, go to www.apress.com/source-code/.

To The White Horse.

Contents at a Glance

Contents

About the Author

Badrinarayanan Lakshmiraghavan has fifteen years of information technology experience in all phases of the software development life cycle, including technology consulting and advisory roles in multiple technologies. He has been programming on the Microsoft technology stack since the days of Visual Basic 3.0.

Badri is currently a senior technology architect with Global Technology Consulting—Microsoft Center of Excellence of Cognizant (NASDAQ: CTSH), a Fortune 500 company. He occasionally blogs at http://lbadri.wordpress.com/. Badri's coordinates are 12.9758° N, 80.2205° E on the third rock from the yellow-dwarf star that lies close to the inner rim of the Orion arm of Milky Way Galaxy.

About the Technical Reviewer

Fabio Claudio Ferracchiati is a senior consultant and a senior analyst/developer using Microsoft technologies. He works for Brain Force (http://www.brainforce.com) in its Italian branch (http://www.brainforce.it). He is a Microsoft Certified Solution Developer for .NET, a Microsoft Certified Application Developer for .NET, a Microsoft Certified Professional, and a prolific author and technical reviewer. Over the past 10 years, he's written articles for Italian and international magazines and coauthored more than 10 books on a variety of computer topics.

Introduction

"I hear...I forget, I see...and I remember, I do...and I understand"

—Confucius

The Hypertext Transfer Protocol (HTTP) is the application-level protocol that powers the World Wide Web. One of the greatest characteristics of HTTP is that it finds support in multiple platforms. HTTP is the lowest common denominator of many platforms and devices. Hence, the primary benefit of creating an HTTP-based service is reachability. A broad range of clients in disparate platforms can consume your HTTP services.

ASP.NET Web API is a framework from Microsoft for building HTTP services. It is not the only possible means for building HTTP services in the .NET technology stack; there is Windows Communication Foundation (WCF) as well, but the ASP.NET Web API framework embraces HTTP instead of fighting against it or abstracting it away. ASP.NET Web API enables you to create HTTP services through the powerful ASP.NET MVC programming model of preferring convention over configuration, which is familiar to many .NET web developers. Some of the best features from ASP. NET MVC, such as routing, model binding, and validation, are all part of ASP.NET Web API as well. ASP.NET Web API also lends itself well to unit testing, in a similar way toASP.NET MVC.

This book, Practical *ASP.NET Web API*, is a practical guide that will help you master the basics of the great ASP. NET Web API framework in a hands-on way. It takes a code-centric approach that will help you grasp the concepts by seeing them in action as you code, run, and debug the projects that you create as you follow the exercises of a chapter.

Though the main focus of the book is the practice, which is the 'how' part of ASP.NET Web API framework development, the 'what' and 'why' parts are implicitly covered to the extent needed for you to understand and appreciate the underlying theoretical concepts demonstrated by the practical code, as you work through the various scenarios. You will see a lot of code, covering all the practical and basic scenarios that are commonly encountered by developers. The recommended approach that will provide the maximum benefit is to follow this book's exercises in sequence and code-along. Although it is a bit of work, I recommend you manually type the code instead of copying and pasting it from the book's download files into the Visual Studio classes you work on. This will help you grasp what you are trying to do, as you work through an exercise. However, if having the completed source code by your side will be of help, you can find the code for the examples shown in this book on the Apress web site, `www.apress.com`. A link can be found on the book's information page under the Source Code/Downloads tab.

If you are looking for a book to just read through and gain an understanding of the ASP.NET Web API framework by simply looking at code listings, this is mostly not your book. While you will see lots of code, this is not a recipe book. Though you will find the code listings in the book useful and relevant for many of the scenarios you face day-to-day, the intention of this book is not to provide you ready-made code that you can copy and paste into the code you are working on in a real-life project and forge ahead. The objective instead is to provide you the hands-on experience of learning the basics of the ASP.NET Web API framework. In short, this book follows the proverb quoted in the epigraph—do, and you will understand.

What You'll Learn

- The basics of HTTP services and debugging through Fiddler.

- Request binding and validation.

- Response formatting and customization to suit client preferences.

- Managing the controller dependencies and unit testing.

- Hosting and security fundamentals.

- Consuming HTTP services from various clients.

- Building a performant web API.

How This Book is Organized

Practical *ASP.NET Web API* is organized into twelve chapters built around hands-on exercises. Each exercise builds on the previous one and for this reason, I highly recommend not only reading the chapters in order but also following the exercises within a chapter in the order presented. You'll find the following chapters in this book.

Chapter 1: Building a Basic Web API

We start off by understanding the differences in building HTTP services using Windows Communication Foundation (WCF) versus ASP.NET Web API at a high level and move on to building our first service, which exposes an in-memory collection over HTTP. We then look at overriding the default behavior of the ASP.NET Web API framework in selecting the action methods based on the HTTP method and finish off the chapter by creating a create-read-update-delete service that plays by the rules of HTTP.

Chapter 2: Debugging and Tracing

The ability to view HTTP traffic, which consists of the request message sent by the client and the response message sent by ASP.NET Web API in response to the request, and the ability to hand-craft requests and submit the same to ASP.NET Web API to view the corresponding response are fundamental requirements for building HTTP services. This chapter covers Fiddler, a great tool for HTTP debugging, and the web browsers' built-in tools to capture and inspect the HTTP traffic. This chapter also covers the tracing feature that comes with the ASP.NET Web API framework.

Chapter 3: Media-Type Formatting CLR Objects

This chapter introduces you to the concept of formatting, which is introduced in the ASP.NET Web API framework. You will understand how the process of content negotiation (conneg) works and learn to override and extend it. You will create media type mappings through a query string and request header, a custom media type mapping, and a custom media formatter, and you'll learn to extend the out-of-box JSON media formatter. Finally, you'll look at controlling what and how members of a type get serialized into HTTP response.

Chapter 4: Customizing Response

Content negotiation is not just about choosing the media type for the resource representation in the response. It is also about the language, character set, and encoding. In Chapter 3, content negotiation is covered from the media type perspective. This chapter explores content negotiation from the perspective of language, character set, and content encoding.

Chapter 5: Binding an HTTP Request into CLR Objects

This chapter introduces the concept of binding, which is borrowed from the ASP.NET MVC framework. Binding in ASP.NET Web API is much broader, with media type formatters also having a role to play. You will learn the three types of binding: model binding, formatter binding, and parameter binding; and you'll learn how to extend the framework by creating custom value providers, custom model binders, custom parameter binders, and custom media-formatters.

Chapter 6: Validating Requests

This chapter covers model validation, a process that is part of model binding, by which ASP.NET Web API runs the validation rules you set against the properties of your model classes. You will use the out-of-box data annotations to enforce the validity of the incoming request and handle the errors raised by model validation. You will also extend the out-of-box validation attribute, create your own validation attribute, and create a validatable object.

Chapter 7: Managing Controller Dependencies

This chapter covers the techniques related to managing one of the most common dependencies an ASP.NET Web API controller takes, which is the dependency on the classes related to persistence infrastructure such as a database. You start off building a controller that depends on Entity Framework and move on to invert the dependencies using the interfaces part of Entity Framework; this is followed by applying the repository pattern and generalizing that pattern into a generic repository. You will also look at mapping domain objects to data transfer objects (DTO) using AutoMapper, injecting dependencies using StructureMap, and writing automated unit tests against the controller by using RhinoMocks as the mocking framework.

Chapter 8: Extending the Pipeline

ASP.NET Web API is a framework. You don't call the framework code but it calls your code, in line with the Hollywood principle. The most fundamental lever that you use to harness the power of ASP.NET Web API framework is the controller, the `ApiController` subclass that you write. In addition, the ASP.NET Web API framework has various points of extensibility built in, for us to hook our code in and extend the processing. This chapter covers the extensibility points of message handlers, filters, and controller selectors.

Chapter 9: Hosting ASP.NET Web API

Though ASP.NET Web API includes ASP.NET in its name, it is not tied to the ASP.NET infrastructure. In fact, ASP.NET Web API is host-independent. This chapter covers the three ways you can host your HTTP services built using ASP.NET Web API: (1) using the ASP.NET infrastructure backed by Internet Information Services (IIS), called web hosting, (2) using any Windows process such as a console application, called self-hosting, and (3) connecting client to the web API runtime, without hitting the network, called in-memory hosting and used mainly for testing purposes.

Chapter 10: Securing ASP.NET Web API

Authentication and authorization are the fundamental building blocks to secure any application, including ASP.NET Web API-powered HTTP services. This chapter covers HTTP basic authentication as an example for implementing the direct authentication pattern and a client obtaining a JSON Web Token (JWT) from an issuing authority and presenting the same to ASP.NET Web API as an example for brokered authentication pattern. This chapter also covers authorization based on roles implemented using `Authorize` filter.

Chapter 11: Consuming ASP.NET Web API

One of the greatest benefits of building HTTP services is the reachability. A broad range of clients in disparate platforms can consume your HTTP service, leveraging the support HTTP enjoys across the platforms and devices. This chapter covers the topic of the client applications consuming your ASP.NET Web API. The coverage is limited to two .NET clients: a console application and a Windows Presentation Foundation (WPF) application, and a JavaScript client running in the context of a browser.

Chapter 12: Building a Performant Web API

Performance, an indication of the responsiveness of an application, can be measured in terms of latency or throughput. Latency is the time taken by an application to respond to an event, while throughput is the number of events that take place in a specified duration of time. Another quality attribute that is often used interchangeably is scalability, which is the ability of an application to handle increased usage load without any (or appreciable) degradation in performance. The topics of performance and scalability are vast and hence this chapter focuses on a few select areas in ASP.NET Web API, namely asynchronous action methods, pushing real-time updates to the client, and web caching.

What You Need to Use This Book

All the code listing and the samples in this book are developed using Visual Studio 2012 Ultimate Edition, targeting the .NET framework 4.5 in Windows 7 and hence Visual Studio 2012 is a must to use this book. Since ASP.NET Web API is a part of ASP.NET MVC 4.0 and it ships with Visual Studio 2012, you will not need any separate installs to get the ASP.NET Web API framework.

For the exercises that involve creating automated unit tests, I used Visual Studio Unit Testing Framework. To work through those exercises, you will need a minimum of the professional edition of Visual Studio to create and run the tests but the ultimate edition is recommended.

In addition to Visual Studio, you will need IIS for web-hosting your web API and Microsoft SQL Server 2012, either the Express edition or preferably the Developer edition, to be used as the persistence store. You will also need the browsers: mostly Internet Explorer 9.0 and Google Chrome in some specific cases. You'll also need the HTTP debugging tool Fiddler (`http://fiddler2.com/`). For the exercises that require external .NET assemblies, you can use NuGet from Codeplex (`http://nuget.codeplex.com/`) to pull those packages into your project. For Chapter 12 on performance, in order to simulate some load, you will need Apache Bench (ab.exe), which is part of Apache HTTP Server.

Who This Book Is For

The book is for every .NET developer who wants to gain a solid and a practical hands-on understanding of the basics of the ASP.NET Web API framework. A good working knowledge of C# and the .NET framework 4.5, familiarity with Visual Studio 2012 are the only pre-requisites to benefit from this book, though a basic knowledge of the ASP.NET MVC framework and the HTTP protocol will be helpful.

CHAPTER 1

■ ■ ■

Building a Basic Web API

A web API is just an application programming interface (API) over the web (that is, HTTP). When the resources of an application can be manipulated over HTTP using the standard HTTP methods of GET, POST, PUT, and DELETE, you can say that the application supports a web API for other applications to use. Because HTTP is platform-agnostic, HTTP services can be consumed by disparate devices across different platforms.

A central concept of HTTP services is the existence of resources that can be identified through a uniform resource identifier (URI). If you equate resources to nouns, then actions on a resource can be equated to verbs and are represented by the HTTP methods such as GET, POST, PUT, and DELETE. For an application that deals with the employees of an organization, each employee is a resource the application deals with.

Let us see how an employee's details can be retrieved with an HTTP service. The URI is http://server/hrapp/employees/12345. It includes the employee ID and serves as an identifier to the resource, which is an employee in this case. Actions on this resource are accomplished through the HTTP verbs. To get the details of an employee, you will perform an HTTP GET on the URI http://server/hrapp/employees/12345. To update this employee, the request will be an HTTP PUT on the same URI. Similarly, to delete this employee, the request will be an HTTP DELETE request, again on the same URI. To create a new employee, the request will be an HTTP POST to the URI without any identifier (http://server/hrapp/employees).

In the case of POST and PUT, the service must be passed the employee data or the resource representation. It is typically XML or JSON that is sent as the HTTP request message body. An HTTP service sends responses in XML or JSON, similar to the request. For example, a GET to http://server/hrapp/employees/12345 results in a response containing JSON representing the employee with an ID of 12345.

HTTP service responds with the HTTP status code indicating success or failure. For example, if the employee with identifier 12345 does not exist, the HTTP status code of 404 - Not found will be returned. If the request is successful, the HTTP status code of 200 - OK will be returned.

The ASP.NET Web API framework enables you to create HTTP-based services through the powerful ASP.NET MVC programming model familiar to many developers. So, we have the URI http://server/hrapp/employees/12345, and a client issues a GET. To respond to this request, we need to write code somewhere that retrieves the employee details for 12345. Obviously, that code has to be in some method in some C# class. This is where the concept of routing comes into play.

The class in this case typically will be one that derives from the ApiController class, part of the ASP.NET Web API framework. All you need to do is to create a subclass of ApiController, say EmployeesController, with a method Get(int id). The ASP.NET Web API framework will then route all the GET requests to this method and pass the employee ID in the URI as the parameter. Inside the method, you can write your code to retrieve the employee details and just return an object of type Employee. On the way out, the ASP.NET Web API framework will handle serialization of the employee object to JSON or XML. The web API is capable of content negotiation: A request can come in along with the choices of the response representation, as preferred by the client. The web API will do its best to send the response in the format requested.

In the case of requests with a message payload such as POST, the method you will need to define will be `Post(Employee employee)` with a parameter of type `Employee`. The ASP.NET Web API framework will deserialize the request (XML or JSON) into the `Employee` parameter object for you to use inside the method. The web API dispatches a request to an action method based on HTTP verbs.

ASP.NET MVC 4 ships as part of Visual Studio 2012 and as an add-on for Visual Studio 2010 SP1. ASP.NET Web API is a part of MVC 4.0. There is a new project template called WebAPI available to create web API projects. You can have both API controllers and MVC controllers in the same project.

1.1 Choosing ASP.NET Web API or WCF

If you have worked with the .NET Framework for any amount of time, you must have encountered the term WCF (Windows Communication Foundation), the one-stop framework for all service development needs in the .NET Framework. Why the new framework of ASP.NET Web API then?

The short answer is that ASP.NET Web API is designed and built from the ground up with only one thing in mind—HTTP—whereas WCF was designed primarily with SOAP and WS-* in mind, and Representational State Transfer (REST) was retrofitted through the WCF REST Starter Kit. The programming model of ASP.NET Web API resembles ASP.NET MVC in being simple and convention-based, instead of requiring you to define interfaces, create implementation classes, and decorate them with several attributes. However, ASP.NET Web API is not supposed to supersede WCF.

It is important to understand the coexistence of WCF and ASP.NET Web API. WCF has been around for a while, and ASP.NET Web API is a new kid on the block, but that does not mean WCF is meant to be replaced by ASP.NET Web API. Both WCF and ASP.NET Web API have their own place in the big picture.

ASP.NET Web API is lightweight but cannot match the power and flexibility of WCF. If you have your service using HTTP as the transport and if you want to move over to some other transport, say TCP, or even support multiple transport mechanisms, WCF will be a better choice. WCF also has great support for WS-*.

However, when it comes to the client base, not all platforms support SOAP and WS-*. ASP.NET Web API–powered HTTP services can reach a broad range of clients including mobile devices. The bottom line: it is all about trade-offs, as is the case with any architecture.

Let's try to understand the differences in programming models by looking at a simple example: an employee service to get an employee of an organization, based on the employee ID. WCF code (see Listing 1-1) is voluminous, whereas ASP.NET Web API code (see Listing 1-2) is terse and gets the job done.

Listing 1-1. Getting an Employee the WCF Way

```
[ServiceContract]
public interface IEmployeeService
{
        [OperationContract]
        [WebGet(UriTemplate = "/Employees/{id}")]
        Employee GetEmployee(string id);
}

public class EmployeeService : IEmployeeService
{
        public Employee GetEmployee(string id)
        {
                return new Employee() { Id = id, Name = "John Q Human" };
        }
}
```

```
[DataContract]
public class Employee
{
        [DataMember]
        public int Id { get; set; }

        [DataMember]
        public string Name { get; set; }

        // other members
}
```

Listing 1-2. Getting an Employee the ASP.NET Web API Way

```
public class EmployeeController : ApiController
{
        public Employee Get(string id)
        {
                return new Employee() { Id = id, Name = "John Q Human" };
        }
}
```

A couple of things are worth mentioning here: First, the web API is exactly the same as a normal MVC controller except that the base class is ApiController. Features of MVC that developers like, such as binding and testability, which are typically achieved through injecting a repository, are all applicable to a web API as well.

If you are experienced with ASP.NET MVC, you may be wondering how different a web API is; after all, the MVC controller's action method can also return JsonResult. With JsonResult action methods, a verb is added to the URI (for example, http://server/employees/get/1234), thereby making it look more like RPC style than REST. Actions such as GET, POST, PUT, and DELETE are to be accomplished through HTTP methods rather than through anything in the URI or query string. ASP.NET Web API also has far superior features, such as content negotiation. ASP.NET MVC's support for JsonResult is only from the perspective of supporting AJAX calls from the JavaScript clients and is not comparable to ASP.NET Web API, a framework dedicated to building HTTP services.

The following are the scenarios where ASP.NET Web API as the back end really shines and brings the most value to the table:

- **Rich-client web applications:** ASP.NET Web API will be a good fit for rich-client web applications that heavily use AJAX to get to a business or data tier. The client application can be anything capable of understanding HTTP; it can be a Silverlight application, an Adobe Flash–based application, or a single-page application (SPA) built using JavaScript libraries such as JQuery, Knockout, and so on, to leverage the power of JavaScript and HTML5 features.

- **Native mobile and non-mobile applications:** ASP.NET Web API can be a back end for native applications running on mobile devices where SOAP is not supported. Because HTTP is a common denominator in all the platforms, even the native applications can use a .NET back-end application through the service façade of a web API. Also, native applications running on platforms other than Windows, such as a Cocoa app running on Mac, can use ASP.NET Web API as the back end.

- **Platform for Internet of Things (IOT):** IOT devices with Ethernet controllers or a Global System for Mobile Communications (GSM) modem, for example, can speak to ASP.NET Web API services through HTTP. A platform built on .NET can receive the data and do business. Not just IOT devices, but other HTTP-capable devices such as radio frequency ID (RFID) readers can communicate with ASP.NET Web API.

ASP.NET Web API is meant for developing web APIs. In other words, although it can technically work, it is not the right candidate for supplementing your ASP.NET web application's AJAX needs, especially when the AJAX use cases are very few.

1.2 Exposing an In-Memory List over HTTP

In this exercise, you will create a simple web API that basically exposes an in-memory List<Employee> over HTTP, for a client application to manipulate the list members. Although this exercise could have relatively limited applicability to a practical web API implementation, it is a stepping stone toward understanding how to use the ASP.NET Web API framework to build your web API.

1. Run Visual Studio and create a new ASP.NET MVC 4 Web Application. Give the project a name of HelloWebApi and click OK, as shown in Figure 1-1.

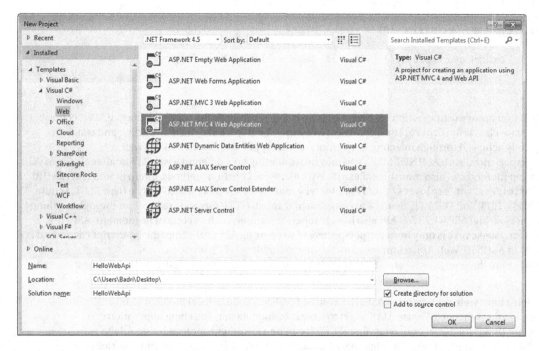

Figure 1-1. *A new ASP.NET MVC 4 web application*

2. Select the Web API template and click OK. You can leave the "Create a unit test project" box unchecked and the Razor option selected in the View Engine dropdown, as shown in Figure 1-2.

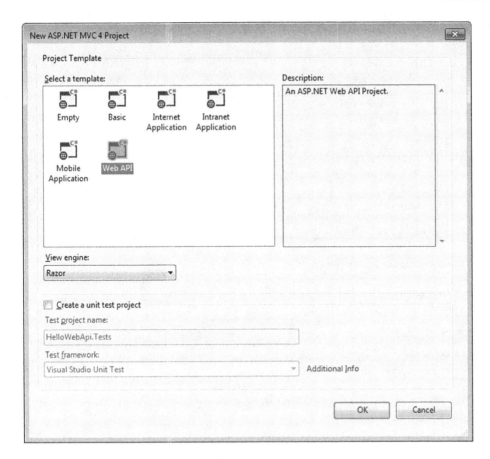

Figure 1-2. *Selecting the Web API Template*

3. Right-click the Controllers folder in the Solution Explorer of Visual Studio. Select Add ➤ Controller and give a name of EmployeesController for the controller. Leave the option Empty API Controller selected in the Template dropdown and click Add, as shown in Figure 1-3. Notice that the generated controller class inherits from ApiController, a class that is part of the ASP.NET Web API framework.

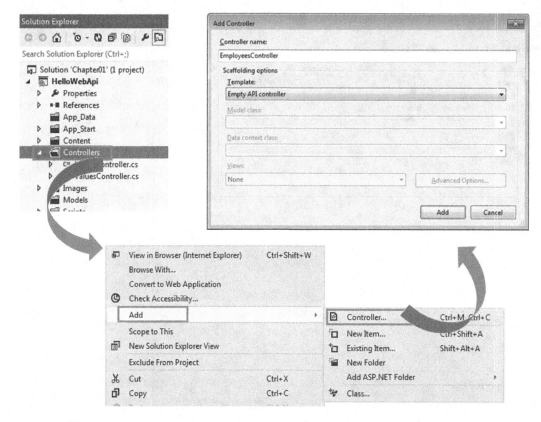

Figure 1-3. *Adding a controller*

4. Right-click the Models folder in the Solution Explorer of Visual Studio. Select Add ➤ Class to add a new class with a name of Employee.

5. Add the code shown in Listing 1-3 to the Employee class.

Listing 1-3. The Employee Class

```
public class Employee
{
    public int Id { get; set; }
    public string FirstName { get; set; }
    public string LastName { get; set; }
}
```

6. Create a new static field at the controller level, as shown in Listing 1-4. This will be the list that our web API exposes over HTTP.

Listing 1-4. The List of Employees

```
public class EmployeesController : ApiController
{
    private static IList<Employee> list = new List<Employee>()
    {
        new Employee()
        {
            Id = 12345, FirstName = "John", LastName = "Human"
        },

        new Employee()
        {
            Id = 12346, FirstName = "Jane", LastName = "Public"
        },

        new Employee()
        {
            Id = 12347, FirstName = "Joseph", LastName = "Law"
        }
    };

    // Action methods go here
}
```

■ **Note** Since you used the `Employee` class, which is in a different namespace than `HelloWebApi.Models` in the controller class, you will need to add a `using` directive. In Visual Studio, the `Employee` references in the preceding code will have a wavy underline in red; right-click any of them and select Resolve ➤ using HelloWebApi.Models. This will add the necessary directive. This is a standard procedure and I will not repeat this step in later exercises, for the sake of brevity.

7. Add five action methods, as shown in Listing 1-5. It is important to use the name as shown in the listing. You will learn more about why you must follow this naming convention in the next exercise.

Listing 1-5. The Action Methods to Get, Post, Put, and Delete Employees

```
// GET api/employees
public IEnumerable<Employee> Get()
{
    return list;
}

// GET api/employees/12345
public Employee Get(int id)
{
    return list.First(e => e.Id == id);
}
```

```csharp
// POST api/employees
public void Post(Employee employee)
{
    int maxId = list.Max(e => e.Id);
    employee.Id = maxId + 1;

    list.Add(employee);
}

// PUT api/employees/12345
public void Put(int id, Employee employee)
{
    int index = list.ToList().FindIndex(e => e.Id == id);
    list[index] = employee;
}

// DELETE api/employees/12345
public void Delete(int id)
{
    Employee employee = Get(id);
    list.Remove(employee);
}
```

8. Build the Visual Studio solution and run it by pressing F5. Internet Explorer, which is the default browser associated with Visual Studio, shows the home page with a URL of http://localhost:55778/. (My ASP.NET Web API project uses port 55778. Your project will use a different one and based on that, Internet Explorer will display a different port in the URL.)

9. In the address bar type http://localhost:<port>/api/employees. Replace *<port>* with the actual port your application runs on.

■ **Note** As you work through the exercises in this book, you will create several new projects, and the port will change every time you create a new ASP.NET MVC project. Remember to replace the port specified in the example code with your application's actual port.

---

10. When Internet Explorer asks if you want to open or save, click Open and choose Notepad as the program to open the file. Notepad will display JSON as shown in Listing 1-6. I have formatted the output for your reading pleasure.

Listing 1-6. JSON Output

```json
[
    {
        "Id":12345,
        "FirstName":"John",
        "LastName":"Human"
    },
    {
```

```
        "Id":12346,
        "FirstName":"Jane",
        "LastName":"Public"
    },
    {
        "Id":12347,
        "FirstName":"Joseph",
        "LastName":"Law"
    }
]
```

11. You can also get the details of a specific employee by performing an HTTP GET on http://localhost:55778/api/employees/12345. In this case, you get the JSON output shown in Listing 1-7.

Listing 1-7. JSON Output for an Individual Employee

```
{
    "Id":12345,
    "FirstName":"John",
    "LastName":"Human"
}
```

12. If you see the preceding two JSON outputs, you have just created your first web API and exposed the in-memory list of employees to the outside world over HTTP!

Currently, we have tested only the HTTP GET but we will test the other methods in the upcoming exercises.

■ **Note** The steps outlined in this exercise are the fundamental steps to create a basic ASP.NET Web API project. In the rest of the exercises throughout this book, I will not repeat these steps, but you will need to perform them as and when required to get your project to a point where you can start working on the steps of a specific exercise. Once you have set up a project, you can reuse it for multiple exercises, and there is no need to create a new project for every exercise.

1.3 Choosing Configuration over Convention

In this exercise, you will override the default behavior of the ASP.NET Web API framework in selecting the action method of the controller based on the HTTP method. The default convention is to give the action method the same name as the HTTP method or to name the method so that it starts with the HTTP method. For example, I used Get in the previous exercise to handle HTTP GET. So the action method can be GetEmployee, or GetAllEmployees, or GetEmployeeById.

Similarly, the action methods of Post, Put, and Delete will respectively handle HTTP POST, PUT, and DELETE. Of course, an action method with a weird name such as PutTheLimeInTheCokeYouNut can still be matched by the ASP.NET Web API framework to handle HTTP PUT because the method name begins with Put, which corresponds to HTTP PUT. To override this convention, you can apply the AcceptVerbs attribute or use the equivalent shorthand notation of HttpGet, HttpPost, HttpPut, HttpDelete, and so on.

1. Comment out all the action methods in the EmployeesController class that we created in Exercise 1.2, retaining only the static list. The controller class after this change will look like Listing 1-8.

    Listing 1-8. The EmployeesController Class with Action Methods Commented Out

    ```
    public class EmployeesController : ApiController
    {
        private static IList<Employee> list = new List<Employee>()
        {
            new Employee()
            {
                Id = 12345, FirstName = "John", LastName = "Human"
            },

            new Employee()
            {
                Id = 12346, FirstName = "Jane", LastName = "Public"
            },

            new Employee()
            {
                Id = 12347, FirstName = "Joseph", LastName = "Law"
            }
        };

        // Following action methods are commented out
    }
    ```

2. Add the RetrieveEmployeeById method to the EmployeesController class, as shown in Listing 1-9. Listing 1-9 shows two action methods that do not follow the naming convention mapped to the required HTTP method through the usage of AcceptVerbs and HttpGet attributes. You can copy and paste one of the methods but not both, for the obvious reason that the code will not compile with duplicate method names.

    Listing 1-9. Using AcceptVerbs

    ```
    [AcceptVerbs("GET")]
    public Employee RetrieveEmployeeById(int id)
    {
            return list.First(e => e.Id == id);
    }

    [HttpGet]
    public Employee RetrieveEmployeeById(int id)
    {
            return list.First(e => e.Id == id);
    }
    ```

3. Build the Visual Studio solution and run it by pressing F5. Internet Explorer, which is the default browser associated with Visual Studio, shows the home page.

4. In the address bar, type `http://localhost:55778/api/employees/12345`. When Internet Explorer asks if you want to open or save, click Open and choose Notepad as the program to open the file. Notepad displays JSON, the same as in the previous exercise. The only difference now is the action method that handles the GET request; it is now the `RetrieveEmployeeById` method and not the `Get` method.

5. You can use custom names for action methods handling other verbs as well. See Listing 1-10 for the `UpdateEmployee` method that handles PUT. You do not need to copy and paste this code into the `EmployeesController` that you are working on, since you will not test PUT methods until the next chapter.

Listing 1-10. Action Method Handling PUT

```
[HttpPut]
public void UpdateEmployee(int id, Employee employee)
{
        int index = list.ToList().FindIndex(e => e.Id == id);
        list[index] = employee;
}
```

It is possible to switch the selection of an action method from the HTTP style, which is along the lines of REST, to the RPC style, which is based on the action method, as specified in the URI. This is same way that ASP.NET MVC selects action methods.

6. Comment out the `RetrieveEmployeeById` action method you added earlier. At this point, the `EmployeesController` class will have only the static field `list` and will be same as the code shown in Listing 1-8. The following code simply repeats Listing 1-8 for your easy reference.

```
public class EmployeesController : ApiController
{
    private static IList<Employee> list = new List<Employee>()
    {
        new Employee()
        {
            Id = 12345, FirstName = "John", LastName = "Human"
        },

        new Employee()
        {
            Id = 12346, FirstName = "Jane", LastName = "Public"
        },

        new Employee()
        {
            Id = 12347, FirstName = "Joseph", LastName = "Law"
        }
    };

    // All action methods are commented out
}
```

7. Add the methods shown in Listing 1-11 to EmployeesController. The listing shows the code for implementing two RPC-style methods. The URIs corresponding to RpcStyleGet and GetEmployeeRpcStyle action methods are respectively http://localhost:55778/api/employees/rpcstyleget and http://localhost:55778/api/employees/getemployeerpcstyle/12345.

Listing 1-11. Action Methods RPC Style

```
[HttpGet]
public IEnumerable<Employee> RpcStyleGet()
{
    return list;
}

public Employee GetEmployeeRpcStyle(int id)
{
    return list.First(e => e.Id == id);
}
```

8. Of course, for this RPC-style selection of an action method to work, you have to make an entry in the WebApiConfig.cs file under App_Start folder, as shown in Listing 1-12. Make sure the code in bold type is added before the existing MapHttpRoute, as shown in the listing.

Listing 1-12. Configuring RPC-Style Action Methods

```
public static class WebApiConfig
{
    public static void Register(HttpConfiguration config)
    {
        config.Routes.MapHttpRoute(
            name: "RpcApi",
            routeTemplate: "api/{controller}/{action}/{id}",
            defaults: new { id = RouteParameter.Optional }
        );

        config.Routes.MapHttpRoute(
            name: "DefaultApi",
            routeTemplate: "api/{controller}/{id}",
            defaults: new { id = RouteParameter.Optional }
        );
    }
}
```

9. Build the Visual Studio solution and run it by pressing F5. Internet Explorer displays the home page.

10. Type `http://localhost:55778/api/employees/getemployeerpcstyle/12345` in the
    address bar of the browser. When Internet Explorer asks if you want to open or save, click
    Open and choose Notepad as the program to open the file. Notepad displays JSON, just as
    in the previous exercise. The only difference now is that the action method that handles
    the GET request is `GetEmployeeRpcStyle`, which is part of the URI route data. Review the
    URI you used. It is no longer in the REST style. The action method is also part of the URI
    and is in RPC-style.

11. Now that you have tested RPC-style action methods, remove the RPC-style mapping from
    the `WebApiConfig` class, as shown in Listing 1-13. The code shown with strikethrough is
    what you will delete from the `WebApiConfig` class.

    Listing 1-13. WebApiConfig Class with RPC-style Mapping Removed

    ```
    public static class WebApiConfig
    {
        public static void Register(HttpConfiguration config)
        {
            config.Routes.MapHttpRoute(
                name: "RpcApi",
                routeTemplate: "api/{controller}/{action}/{id}",
                defaults: new { id = RouteParameter.Optional }
            );

            config.Routes.MapHttpRoute(
                name: "DefaultApi",
                routeTemplate: "api/{controller}/{id}",
                defaults: new { id = RouteParameter.Optional }
            );
        }
    }
    ```

Now, you will change the default route template to see how ASP.NET Web API works.

12. Change the `WebApiConfig` class under `App_Start` folder to modify the route template,
    as shown in Listing 1-14.

    Listing 1-14. WebApiConfig Class with Default Route Template Modified

    ```
    public static class WebApiConfig
    {
        public static void Register(HttpConfiguration config)
        {
            config.Routes.MapHttpRoute(
                name: "DefaultApi",
                routeTemplate: "webapi/{controller}/{id}",
                defaults: new { id = RouteParameter.Optional }
            );
        }
    }
    ```

13. Build the Visual Studio solution. Type `http://localhost:55778/api/employees` in the address bar of the browser.

14. You will see the message "The resource cannot be found." Basically, ASP.NET Web API is not able to route your GET request to the correct controller and action method.

15. Type `http://localhost:55778/webapi/employees` in the address bar of the browser.

16. It starts working. So, it is clear that the route template defined in the `Register` method of `WebApiConfig.cs` file under `App_Start` folder is important for the framework to choose the controller and the action method. By default, the route template comes with `api`, which is a literal path segment, and two placeholder variables, `{controller}` and `{id}`. Because a project created using the Web API template can have both API controllers and MVC controllers, the `api` literal path segment is used by default to avoid collisions with MVC routing.

17. Change the `WebApiConfig` class under `App_Start` folder, as shown in Listing 1-15. The literal `Webapi` is changed to `api`, and a new placeholder variable `orgid` with a constraint is introduced.

Listing 1-15. WebApiConfig Class with a New Variable in Route Template

```
public static class WebApiConfig
{
    public static void Register(HttpConfiguration config)
    {
        config.Routes.MapHttpRoute(
                        name: "DefaultApi",
                        routeTemplate: "api/{orgid}/{controller}/{id}",
                        defaults: new { id = RouteParameter.Optional },
                        constraints: new { orgid = @"\d+" }
                );
        );
    }
}
```

18. Rebuild the solution and press F5 to run it. Type `http://localhost:55778/api/employees` in the address bar of the browser. You'll see the message `404 —The webpage cannot be found`.

19. Type `http://localhost:55778/api/123/employees` in the address bar of the browser. It starts to work again. Notice the additional segment with a value of 123 in the URI.

20. In `EmployeesController`, comment out all the action methods, retaining only the static field. Add a new action method, as shown in Listing 1-16.

Listing 1-16. EmployeesController with Action Method Receiving OrgID

```
public Employee Get(int orgid, int id)
{
    return list.First(e => e.Id == id);
}
```

21. Add a breakpoint to this action method. Rebuild the solution and run the project by pressing F5.

22. Type `http://localhost:55778/api/123/employees/12345` in the address bar of the browser.

23. When the execution breaks, inspect the parameters: `orgid` and `id`. They are both mapped to 123 and 12345 respectively.

24. Type `http://localhost:55778/api/abc/employees/12345` in the address bar of the browser.

You get a 404 —The webpage cannot be found. So, by adding a new {orgid} variable and adding a constraint, we have made sure the URI must include a new URI segment immediately after api and that it must be a number. When we define an action parameter matching the placeholder variable name, the URI path is mapped to the action parameter.

25. Restore the `WebApiConfig` class to its out-of-box state, like so:

```
public static class WebApiConfig
{
    public static void Register(HttpConfiguration config)
    {
        config.Routes.MapHttpRoute(
            name: "DefaultApi",
            routeTemplate: "api/{controller}/{id}",
            defaults: new { id = RouteParameter.Optional }
        );
    }
}
```

1.4 Playing by the Rules of HTTP

In this exercise, you will create a web API that plays by the rules of HTTP. It is natural for a developer to assume that the CRUD operations create, read, update, and delete correspond to the HTTP methods POST, GET, PUT, and DELETE. Equating GET with reading and DELETE with deleting are correct, but POST for creating and PUT for updating are not fully accurate.

GET is guaranteed not to cause any side effects and is said to be *nullipotent*; nothing happens to the system's state, even when it is called multiple times or not called at all. In other words, the system state will be the same for all the following scenarios: (1) the method was not called at all, (2) the method was called once, and (3) the method was called multiple times. PUT and DELETE are *idempotent*; the effect to the system state will be the same as that of the first call, even when they are called multiple times subsequently. There is no stopping, for example, if you implement the logic that changes the state of the system in the action method handling GET. It is not only a deviation from the standards, it is also an inferior implementation from a security standpoint.

▪ **Note** The HTTP specification (`http://www.w3.org/Protocols/rfc2616/rfc2616-sec9.html#sec9.1`) calls GET a "safe" method. It also mentions GET under idempotent methods, because a nullipotent method is also idempotent. I use the term nullipotent because it clearly indicates that GET must be "safe"; that is, there must not be any side-effects.

The usage of the appropriate HTTP status codes is another important aspect of building HTTP-compliant services. By default, 200 – OK is returned, indicating success. 401 – Not authorized is sent when a user requests an action on a resource that requires the user to be authenticated and that user has either not provided the credentials or provided invalid credentials. Sending a 200 – OK and a message in the response body that authentication failed is not something an HTTP-compliant service will do.

In this exercise, I show you the standard way of implementing the CRUD action methods in your HTTP-compliant ASP.NET Web API.

1.4.1 Retrieving Resource(s)

The HTTP GET method is useful for retrieving resource representations. For example, http://server/api/employees lists all employees, while http://server/api/employees/12345 retrieves a specific employee (12345 is the identifier of the employee).

GET methods have no request body. The response body is a JSON/XML representation of the resource requested—either a list of employees or a specific employee. ASP.NET Web API has out-of-box formatters for JSON and XML, but it is not hard to create a custom formatter. I'll cover custom formatters in Chapter 3 and Chapter 5. It is very important not to implement logic in a GET method that changes the state of the system, because HTTP GET is nullipotent.

1. Comment out all the action methods in EmployeesController from the previous exercise. At this point, the EmployeesController class will have only the static field list and will be same as the code shown in Listing 1-8 earlier. The following code is just a repeat of Listing 1-8 for your easy reference.

```
public class EmployeesController : ApiController
{
    private static IList<Employee> list = new List<Employee>()
    {
        new Employee()
        {
            Id = 12345, FirstName = "John", LastName = "Human"
        },

        new Employee()
        {
            Id = 12346, FirstName = "Jane", LastName = "Public"
        },

        new Employee()
        {
            Id = 12347, FirstName = "Joseph", LastName = "Law"
        }
    };

    // All action methods are commented out
}
```

2. Add a new action method to handle GET, as shown in the Listing 1-17. It retrieves one specific employee based on the ID. If there is no employee matching the ID, 404 - Not Found status code is returned.

Listing 1-17. Retrieval of a Specific Employee by ID

```
public Employee Get(int id)
{
    var employee = list.FirstOrDefault(e => e.Id == id);

    if(employee == null)
    {
        throw new HttpResponseException(HttpStatusCode.NotFound);
    }

    return employee;
}
```

3. Rebuild the solution and make a GET request by typing a URI in the address bar of Internet Explorer. The URI should contain an employee ID for which there is no corresponding resource, such as http://localhost:55778/api/employees/45678.

404 - Not Found is returned, and Internet Explorer shows the same with the message that The webpage cannot be found.

It is possible to retrieve a list of employees matching a condition. For example, you can filter the employees based on the department to which they belong. In this case, the department is sent in the query string: http://localhost:port/api/employees?department=2. ASP.NET Web API matches the query parameter (department) to the parameter on the action method. If the department in the request is not a valid department number, the 422 - Unprocessable Entity status code is returned. This is not a standard HTTP status code but is defined in the HTTP extension for WebDAV. It is acceptable to send the status code 400 - Bad Request as well.

4. To the Employee model class, add a new property, as shown in Listing 1-18.

Listing 1-18. Employee Class with Department

```
public class Employee
{
        public int Id { get; set; }
        public string FirstName { get; set; }
        public string LastName { get; set; }

        public int Department { get; set; }
}
```

5. Modify the IList<Employee> list in EmployeesController, as shown in Listing 1-19, to populate the Department property.

Listing 1-19. Employee List with Departments

```
private static IList<Employee> list = new List<Employee>()
{
    new Employee()
    {
        Id = 12345, FirstName = "John", LastName = "Human", Department = 2
    },
```

```
new Employee()
{
    Id = 12346, FirstName = "Jane", LastName = "Public", Department = 3
},

new Employee()
{
    Id = 12347, FirstName = "Joseph", LastName = "Law", Department = 2
}
};
```

6. Add the action method shown in Listing 1-20 to EmployeesController.

Listing 1-20. Retrieval of Employees by Department

```
public IEnumerable<Employee> GetByDepartment(int department)
{
    int[] validDepartments = {1, 2, 3, 5, 8, 13};

    if (!validDepartments.Any(d => d == department))
    {
        var response = new HttpResponseMessage()
        {
            StatusCode = (HttpStatusCode)422, // Unprocessable Entity
            ReasonPhrase = "Invalid Department"
        };

        throw new HttpResponseException(response);
    }

    return list.Where(e => e.Department == department);
}
```

7. Rebuild the solution and make a GET request by typing the URI
   http://localhost:55778/api/employees?department=2 in the address bar of
   Internet Explorer.

The resulting JSON will include only John and Joseph.

It is possible to apply multiple conditions based on parameters. For example, http://localhost:port/api/
employees?department=2&lastname=Smith can be used to filter for all Smiths in department number 2. The action
method in this case can have two parameters, department and lastName. An alternative is to use a model class that
represents the input, as shown in Listing 1-21. For ASP.NET Web API to bind the query parameters to the complex
type Filter, you must use the FromUri attribute. You'll learn more about this in Chapter 5.

8. Comment out all the action methods in EmployeesController and add the action method
   shown in Listing 1-21.

Listing 1-21. Retrieving an Employee by Applying Two Conditions

```
public IEnumerable<Employee> Get([FromUri]Filter filter)
{
    return list.Where(e => e.Department == filter.Department &&
                                    e.LastName == filter.LastName);
}
```

9. Create a class named `Filter`, under the Models folder. The code should be as shown in Listing 1-22.

   Listing 1-22. The Filter Class

   ```
   public class Filter
   {
       public int Department { get; set; }
       public string LastName { get; set; }
   }
   ```

10. Rebuild the solution and make a GET request by typing the URI `http://localhost:55778/api/employees?department=2&lastname=Human` in the address bar of Internet Explorer. Pay attention to the upper case 'H'.

Now, the resulting JSON will include only John.

1.4.2 Creating a Resource with a Server-Generated Identifier

A resource such as an employee can be created by an HTTP POST to the URI `http://localhost:port/api/employees`. There is no ID that is specified in the URI. In this case, the request body contains the JSON/XML representation of the resource being added, which is the new employee. The response body will be a JSON/XML representation of the resource, the new employee who was just added into the system. The difference between the request and the response representations is that the employee ID that was generated by the system is present in the response representation, while it is absent in the request. Hence, this type of resource creation is analogous to INSERT SQL statements on tables with the primary key generated by the database engine, with the client having no say on what the new ID can be.

In Exercise 1.2, we returned the `Employee` type. In response to this, the ASP.NET Web API framework returned a `200 - OK` status code, and we did not have control over the status code that must be returned. By returning an object of type `HttpResponseMessage`, we can have better control over what is returned to the client, including the HTTP status code. In the case of resource creation using POST, returning the HTTP status code of `201 - Created` and the URI of the new resource created in the `location` response header as shown in Listing 1-23 will better conform to HTTP/1.1 than sending a blanket `200 - OK` status code.

Listing 1-23. Creating an Employee using HTTP POST

```
public HttpResponseMessage Post(Employee employee)
{
    int maxId = list.Max(e => e.Id);
    employee.Id = maxId + 1;

    list.Add(employee);

    var response = Request.CreateResponse<Employee>(HttpStatusCode.Created, employee);

    string uri = Url.Link("DefaultApi", new { id = employee.Id });
    response.Headers.Location = new Uri(uri);
    return response;
}
```

You will need a tool like Fiddler to create a POST request and view the response. For the purpose of this exercise, Listing 1-24 shows the response message for POST. If you are already familiar with Fiddler, you can issue a POST and inspect the response. I'll cover Fiddler in Chapter 2.

Listing 1-24. Response Status Code and Headers

HTTP/1.1 201 Created
Date: Mon, 26 Mar 2013 07:35:07 GMT
Location: http://localhost:55778/api/employees/12348
Content-Type: application/json; charset=utf-8

■ **Note**   To create a resource using HTTP POST, you must use a URI without the ID, for example,
http://localhost:port/api/employees. Requesting a POST on a URI with an ID, for example
http://localhost:port/api/employees/12348, where 12348 is an ID that does not exist, must be rejected with
a 404 - Not Found. See Exercise 1.4.5.

1.4.3 Creating a Resource with a Client-Supplied Identifier

A resource such as an employee can be created by an HTTP PUT to the URI http://localhost:port/api/
employees/12348, where the employee with an ID of 12348 does not exist until this PUT request is processed.
In this case, the request body contains the JSON/XML representation of the resource being added, which is the
new employee. The response body can be a JSON/XML representation of the resource, the new employee that was
just added into the system. But in this case the response body can be omitted, since there will not be any difference
between the request and the response resource representations. Listing 1-25 shows the code to create employee
using PUT.

Listing 1-25. Creating an Employee using HTTP PUT

```
public HttpResponseMessage Put(int id, Employee employee)
{
    if (!list.Any(e => e.Id == id))
    {
        list.Add(employee);

        var response = Request.CreateResponse<Employee>
                                        (HttpStatusCode.Created, employee);

        string uri = Url.Link("DefaultApi", new { id = employee.Id });
        response.Headers.Location = new Uri(uri);
        return response;
    }

    return Request.CreateResponse(HttpStatusCode.NoContent);
}
```

This type of resource creation using PUT is applicable for scenarios where the client decides the key or the ID for
the resource. Hence, this type of resource creation is analogous to INSERT SQL statements that specify the primary key.

■ **Note** To test POST, PUT, and DELETE, you will need a tool like Fiddler, covered in Chapter 2.

1.4.4 Overwriting a Resource

A resource can be overwritten using HTTP PUT. This operation is generally considered the same as updating the resource, but there is a difference. To issue a PUT request, you must send the representation of the resource in the request in its entirety. Partial updates are *not* allowed. For example, this SQL statement:

```
UPDATE employee SET last_name = 'Schindler' where employee_id = 12345
```

updates only one field in the record. This type of functionality must not be supported by PUT, which is analogous to deleting a record and reinserting it, in the SQL world.

A PUT request is issued to an URI, for example `http://localhost:port/api/employees/12345`, where the employee with an ID of 12345 already exists in the system. Listing 1-26 shows the action method handling PUT to overwrite a resource.

Listing 1-26. Overwriting an Employee using HTTP PUT

```csharp
public HttpResponseMessage Put(int id, Employee employee)
{
    int index = list.ToList().FindIndex(e => e.Id == id);
    if (index >= 0)
    {
        list[index] = employee; // overwrite the existing resource
        return Request.CreateResponse(HttpStatusCode.NoContent);
    }
    else
    {
        list.Add(employee);

        var response = Request.CreateResponse<Employee>
                                        (HttpStatusCode.Created, employee);

        string uri = Url.Link("DefaultApi", new { id = employee.Id });
        response.Headers.Location = new Uri(uri);
        return response;
    }
}
```

1.4.5 Updating a Resource

A resource such as an employee in our example can be updated by an HTTP POST to the URI `http://server/api/employees/12345`, where the employee with an ID of 12345 already exists in the system. Listing 1-27 shows the action method handling POST to update an employee. If an employee of the ID same as the incoming ID is not present, the request is rejected with a 404 - Not Found status code.

Listing 1-27. Updating an Employee using HTTP POST

```
public HttpResponseMessage Post(int id, Employee employee)
{
    int index = list.ToList().FindIndex(e => e.Id == id);

    if (index >= 0)
    {
        list[index] = employee;

        return Request.CreateResponse(HttpStatusCode.NoContent);
    }

    return Request.CreateResponse(HttpStatusCode.NotFound);
}
```

1.4.6 Partially Updating (Patching) a Resource

HTTP POST can support partial updates to a resource. But there is a separate PATCH method. Request for Comments (RFC) 5789 "PATCH Method for HTTP" adds this new HTTP method, PATCH, to modify an existing HTTP resource.

In applying partial updates, an issue is that since the ASP.NET Web API framework deserializes the resource representation in the request to an object parameter, it is not easy to differentiate between the case where a specific field is present but null and where it is absent.

For example, suppose the Employee type has a property, Age, that is defined as an int? (nullable integer). If you do not want this property to be updated, you can leave the property out of the request representation and it will remain null in the deserialized object parameter. If you want to reset the age from a value to null, then you will want the property to be null but present in the request representation, but in this case also, the deserialized object parameter will have the Age property as null. So the above two cases cannot be differentiated, and a partial update using POST is a bit complex to achieve.

Fear not! Microsoft ASP.NET Web API OData package ships with a dynamic proxy Delta<T>. This will keep track of the differences between the object that ASP.NET Web API deserialized based on the resource representation in the request and the object stored in your persistence store. In this exercise, you will use Delta<T> in an action method handling HTTP PATCH.

1. Right-click References in the Visual Studio Solution Explorer and select Manage NuGet Packages.

2. Search for odata. You will see Microsoft ASP.NET Web API OData package. Install this into your project, as shown in Figure 1-4. The version and the last published date may be different by the time you read this book.

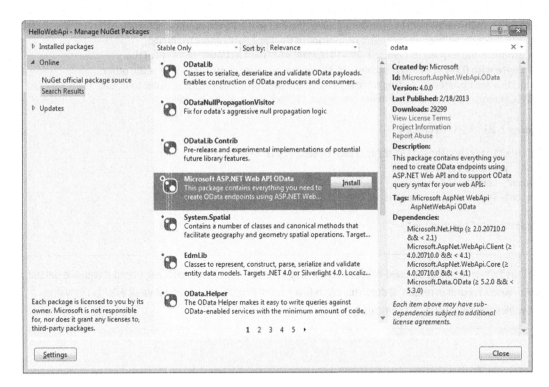

Figure 1-4. *Installing Microsoft ASP.NET Web API OData Package*

3. This brings in the System.Web.Http.OData namespace that contains Delta<T>.

4. Implement an action method in EmployeesController, as shown in Listing 1-28. The second parameter of the action method takes in an object of type Delta<Employee>. The Delta<Employee> object is a dynamic lightweight proxy for the Employee object. It allows you to set any property of the Employee object, but it also tracks the properties that are set. When the Patch method is called, it copies across only those properties that are set when the ASP.NET Web API framework deserialized the resource representation in the request.

Listing 1-28. Patching an Employee using HTTP PATCH

```
public HttpResponseMessage Patch(int id, Delta<Employee> deltaEmployee)
{
    var employee = list.FirstOrDefault(e => e.Id == id);
    if (employee == null)
    {
        throw new HttpResponseException(HttpStatusCode.NotFound);
    }

    deltaEmployee.Patch(employee);

    return Request.CreateResponse(HttpStatusCode.NoContent);
}
```

5. Since I use an in-memory list as the data source, the call to the Patch method is sufficient to partially update the corresponding properties of the Employee object in the list. For example, the request in Listing 1-29 will update only the LastName property of the employee with ID of 12345 to Longbottom. Of course, you can verify that none of the other properties are updated by setting a breakpoint in the property setters, but in order to issue a PATCH request, you will need to use a tool like Fiddler, covered in Chapter 2.

Listing 1-29. A PATCH Request

```
PATCH http://localhost:55778/api/employees/12345 HTTP/1.1
Host: localhost:55778
Content-Length: 25
Content-Type: application/json

{"LastName":"Longbottom"}
```

■ **Caution** Delta<T> was meant to be used with ODataMediaTypeFormatter. In this exercise, I used it with the default JsonMediaTypeFormatter. For this reason, it does run into a few issues, notably that it cannot work with Int32 values. Also, it does not work with collections and complex types.

1.4.7 Deleting a Resource

Similar to PUT, DELETE is idempotent as well. After the first request to delete a resource, which is successful, if there are subsequent DELETE requests to the same resource, we will have a problem in finding the resource in subsequent requests. Should we send 200 - OK for first request and 404 - Not Found for subsequent requests? 204 - No Content can be uniformly sent for the first as well as subsequent requests, as shown in Listing 1-30. ASP.NET Web API ensures the status code of 204 - No Content is returned, since the return type of the action method is void.

Listing 1-30. Deleting an Employee

```
public void Delete(int id)
{
    Employee employee = Get(id);
    list.Remove(employee);
}
```

■ **Note** If you do not delete the resource immediately but only mark it for deletion for some other process to pick it up and delete at a later point in time, do not send 200 - OK or 204 - No Content as the status code in the response to DELETE request. Instead, send 202 - Accepted.

Summary

The ASP.NET Web API framework enables you to create HTTP-based services through the powerful ASP.NET MVC programming model familiar to developers. The programming model of ASP.NET Web API is similar to ASP.NET MVC in that it is simple and convention-based.

In this chapter, you first created a simple web API that exposes an in-memory list over HTTP, for a client application to manipulate the list members. Then you overrode the default behavior of the ASP.NET Web API framework in selecting the action method of a controller based on the HTTP method. The default convention is to name the action method either same as the HTTP method or starting with the HTTP method name. To override this convention, you applied the `AcceptVerbs` attribute. You also created RPC-style action methods instead of the default REST-style action methods.

Finally, you created a web API that plays by the rules of HTTP. It is natural for a developer to assume the CRUD operations create, read, update, and delete correspond to the HTTP methods POST, GET, PUT, and DELETE. You saw that it's correct to equate GET for reading and DELETE for deleting, but POST for creating and PUT for updating are not fully accurate. A resource can be created as well as modified by both POST and PUT. A resource can be created by an HTTP POST to the URI without the ID. A resource can also be created by an HTTP PUT to the URI with the ID. If the employee with the specified ID does not already exist, the new resource is created with the client-specified ID. So, the former method of using an HTTP POST is analogous to INSERT SQL statements on tables with the primary key generated by the database engine and the latter case is analogous to INSERT SQL with the primary key specified by the caller.

A resource can be overwritten using HTTP PUT. This operation is generally regarded as updating the resource but there is a difference. To issue a PUT request, you must send the representation of the resource in the request in its entirety. Partial updates are not allowed. PUT is analogous to deleting a record and re-inserting it, in the SQL world. HTTP POST can support partial updates to a resource. But there is a separate PATCH method. Request for Comments (RFC) 5789 "PATCH Method for HTTP" adds this new HTTP method, PATCH, to modify an existing HTTP resource.

In the next chapter, you will see how to test the POST, PUT and DELETE methods that you created in this chapter, using the web debugging tool Fiddler. Also, you will learn how to implement tracing for your code as well as for the framework code.

CHAPTER 2

■ ■ ■

Debugging and Tracing

The ability to view HTTP traffic, which consists of the request message sent by the client and the response message sent by the server in response to the request, is a fundamental requirement for developing HTTP services. Equally important is the ability to hand-craft requests, submit them to ASP.NET Web API, and view the corresponding response from ASP.NET Web API. Fiddler is a great tool that helps you in both these needs. As you'll see, web browsers also come with built-in tools to capture and inspect the HTTP traffic.

Another key aspect of debugging ASP.NET Web API is tracing. ASP.NET Web API supports tracing of your code as well as of the framework code. Tracing the framework code is essential for understanding what goes on behind the scenes as ASP.NET Web API handles a request, calls your code at the right moment, and sends back a response.

2.1 Using Fiddler for Web Debugging

Fiddler is a web debugging proxy. It is a useful tool for capturing and analyzing both HTTP and HTTPS traffic between the computer running Fiddler and the outside. Fiddler also has a feature to build a complete request with headers, send it to an HTTP endpoint such as the web API, and inspect the response returned by the web API. It is virtually impossible to develop a production-grade web API without using a debugger like Fiddler. You can get Fiddler from `http://www.fiddler2.com/get-fiddler`. Fiddler lists the requests captured in the pane on the left (see Figure 2-1).

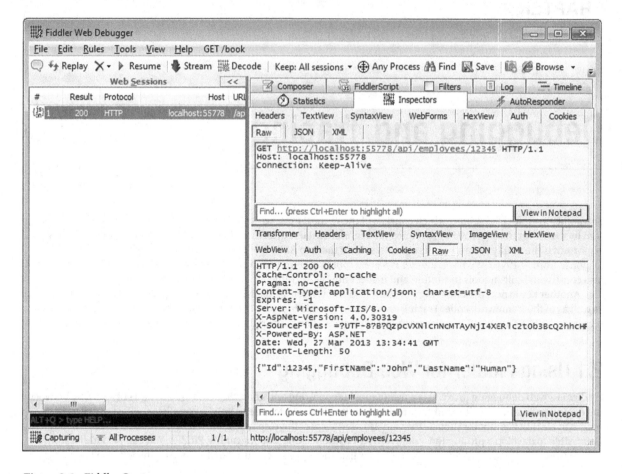

Figure 2-1. *Fiddler Capture*

When a specific request is selected, the Inspectors tab on the right pane shows the request on the top and the corresponding response on the bottom. The Composer tab allows the requests to be hand-crafted and submitted with the HTTP method of your choice.

The older versions of Fiddler do not capture the traffic from the localhost. Common workarounds are to use the identifier localhost with a dot suffix followed by fiddler (http://localhost.fiddler:<port>), use the machine name instead of localhost, add an entry to the C:\Windows\System32\drivers\etc\hosts file for 127.0.0.1, and use that. The following list details how Fiddler can be configured to capture the traffic with different types of applications.

> **Internet Explorer:** When the Fiddler tool is launched, it registers itself as the system proxy. For this reason, requests from the applications that use WinInet such as Internet Explorer are automatically intercepted by Fiddler. No setting or configuration changes are needed.

> **Other browsers like Firefox:** Fiddler can be configured as the web proxy with the browser to start intercepting the requests. Fiddler runs on port 8888, so the proxy can be configured as localhost:8888 or 127.0.0.1:8888.

Non-browser applications such as a .NET Framework WPF application: Typically, these applications use the WebClient for HTTP communication. The Proxy property of the WebClient must be set to an instance of the WebProxy with the host as localhost and port as 8888 like this:

```
Proxy = new WebProxy("localhost", 8888)..
```

ASP.NET web application: If you need to look at the HTTP client requests made by your code in an ASP.NET application, or by a third-party library you are using in your ASP.NET application, it is possible to configure Fiddler as the proxy in the web.config file, as shown in Listing 2-1.

Listing 2-1. Web.config Configuring Fiddler as Proxy

```
<configuration>
        <system.net>
            <defaultProxy>
                    <proxy usesystemdefault="False" bypassonlocal="True"
                                    proxyaddress="http://127.0.0.1:8888" />
            </defaultProxy>
        </system.net>
</configuration>
```

2.2 Capturing Console App Traffic through Fiddler

In this exercise, you will create a simple console application that uses the WebClient class to talk to the ASP.NET Web API that was created in Exercise 1.2. You will configure Fiddler as the proxy so that the request generated by the console app and the response sent by ASP.NET Web API are available for us to analyze.

1. Download Fiddler and install it, if you have not already done so.

2. Create a console application with a name of **TestConsoleApp** and add the code from Listing 2-2. Add a using directive to the top of the Program class, like so:

```
using System.Net;
```

Listing 2-2. A Console Client Application

```
using System.Net;

class Program
{
    static void Main(string[] args)
    {
        string uri = "http://localhost.fiddler:55778/api/employees/12345";

        using (WebClient client = new WebClient())
        {
            client.DownloadString(uri);
        }
    }
}
```

3. Notice that the URI used is http://localhost.fiddler:55778/api/employees/12345. Fiddler does not capture the traffic on localhost, especially when your client is making the HTTP requests using System.Net (as is the case with WebClient). Remember to replace the port 55778 specified in the example code with the actual port the application you created in Exercise 1.2 runs on.

4. Launch Fiddler and make sure it captures the traffic from all processes by clicking the status bar next to Capturing and selecting All Processes. See Figure 2-2.

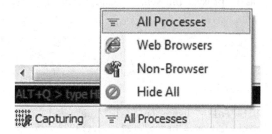

Figure 2-2. *Fiddler capturing all processes*

5. Open the project corresponding to Exercise 1.2 in Visual Studio. Open the EmployeesController class and make sure the class is same as shown in Listing 1-4 and Listing 1-5. The code is reproduced in the following listing for your easy reference.

```
public class EmployeesController : ApiController
{
    private static IList<Employee> list = new List<Employee>()
    {
        new Employee()
        {
            Id = 12345, FirstName = "John", LastName = "Human"
        },

        new Employee()
        {
            Id = 12346, FirstName = "Jane", LastName = "Public"
        },

        new Employee()
        {
            Id = 12347, FirstName = "Joseph", LastName = "Law"
        }
    };

    // GET api/employees
    public IEnumerable<Employee> Get()
    {
        return list;
    }
```

```
// GET api/employees/12345
public Employee Get(int id)
{
    return list.First(e => e.Id == id);
}

// POST api/employees
public void Post(Employee employee)
{
    int maxId = list.Max(e => e.Id);
    employee.Id = maxId + 1;

    list.Add(employee);
}

// PUT api/employees/12345
public void Put(int id, Employee employee)
{
    int index = list.ToList().FindIndex(e => e.Id == id);
    list[index] = employee;
}

// DELETE api/employees/12345
public void Delete(int id)
{
    Employee employee = Get(id);
    list.Remove(employee);
}
}
```

6. Press F5 in Visual Studio and let the project corresponding to Exercise 1.2 run. This will ensure that IIS Express is running.

7. Run the console application.

8. Go to Fiddler and select the session captured in the left pane. Go to the Inspectors tab on the right to look at the raw request and response.

2.3 Capturing HTTPS Traffic in Fiddler

Fiddler can capture and even decrypt HTTPS traffic. Fiddler acts as a man-in-the-middle and generates certificates on the fly to decrypt HTTPS traffic.

1. To enable Fiddler to capture HTTPS traffic, select Tools ➤ Fiddler Options and select the Decrypt HTTPS traffic check box as shown in Figure 2-3.

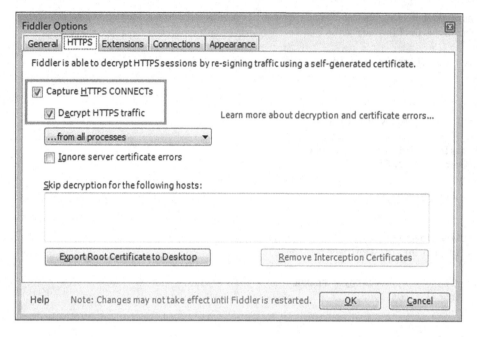

Figure 2-3. *Fiddler options*

2. When you select the Decrypt HTTP traffic check box, Fiddler asks you whether to add the root certificate it generates to the trusted CA list in your machine.

3. Select No and click OK. Fiddler is now all set to capture and decrypt HTTPS traffic.

4. To see Fiddler in action capturing the HTTPS traffic, go to https://www.google.com in Internet Explorer, with Fiddler running.

5. As part of the capture, Fiddler sends the public key of a certificate it has just generated to Internet Explorer, as if it is the certificate from www.google.com.

6. Internet Explorer promptly displays the message "There is a problem with this website's security certificate."

7. Go to the site without heeding Internet Explorer's warning. Internet Explorer displays the page.

8. Now go to Fiddler. You can see the traffic it has captured in all clear text, although sent over HTTPS.

9. Internet Explorer does show the URL bar in red, since it suspects some foul play with the certificate it received. If you look at the certificate error, it shows that the certificate is issued to www.google.com, but it was issued by DO_NOT_TRUST_Fiddler_Root, which is not a CA that Internet Explorer trusts (see Figure 2-4). This is how a browser alerts an end user about a man-in-the-middle attack, if someone tries to eavesdrop by tampering with the certificate in HTTPS.

Certificate Information

This certificate cannot be verified up to a trusted
certification authority.

Issued to:	www.google.com

Issued by:	DO_NOT_TRUST_FiddlerRoot

Valid from 9/ 21/ 2012 **to** 9/ 20/ 2022

Figure 2-4. *Certificate error*

2.4 Composing and Submitting Requests in Fiddler

In this exercise, you will hand-craft an HTTP request and submit it to an ASP.NET Web API. In Exercise 1.2, we created a web API that supports GET, PUT, POST, and DELETE, but we tested only GET using a browser. In this recipe, we will test the other methods.

1. Run the project corresponding to Exercise 1.2 in Visual Studio.

2. Set a breakpoint in the Post action method.

3. Run Fiddler and go to the Composer tab on the right. From the drop-down showing HTTP methods, select POST.

4. Enter http://localhost:55778/api/employees for the URI. Remember to replace the port 55778 specified in the example code with the actual port the application you created in Exercise 1.2 runs on.

5. Copy and paste the request, as shown in Listing 2-3. Paste the headers (first two lines) in Request Headers and the JSON in the Request Body text box.

   Listing 2-3. POST Request

   ```
   Host: localhost:55778
   Content-Type: application/json

   {"Id":12348,"FirstName":"Philip","LastName":"Hughes"}
   ```

6. Click the Execute button.

7. Visual Studio hits the break point. Inspect the parameter. ASP.NET Web API should have created the parameter Employee object based on the JSON in the request body, as shown in Figure 2-5.

```
public void Post(Employee employee)
{
    int maxId = list.Max(e => e.
    employee.Id = maxId + 1;

    list.Add(employee);
}
```

employee {HelloWebApi.Models.Employee}
FirstName Q ▾ "Philip"
Id   12348
LastName Q ▾ "Hughes"

Figure 2-5. *Execution Breaking in the Action Method in Visual Studio*

■ **Note**   The Content-Type request header is important; without it the Employee parameter of the action method will be null.

8.   Press F5 and let the execution complete. Fiddler displays an entry in the captured sessions, as shown in Figure 2-6.

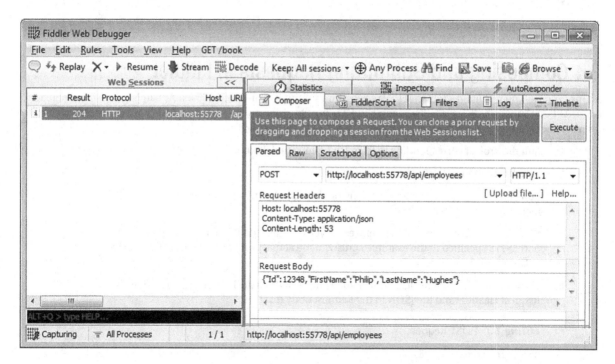

Figure 2-6. *Fiddler Composer*

9.   Select the entry to view the response sent by our web API. Since the Post method returns void, the HTTP status code of 204 - No Content is sent back.

10.   The Request Headers textbox in Figure 2-6 shows the Content-Length header, which we did not enter (see Listing 2-3). Fiddler automatically calculates the length based on the request body and plugs that in.

11. Similarly, try making a PUT request to `http://localhost:55778/api/employees/12348` with a message body of `{"Id":12348,"FirstName":"Phil","LastName":"Hughes"}`. If you now make a GET to `http://localhost:55778/api/employees/12348`, it will return the resource representation with the first name changed to Phil. You can try a DELETE request as well to the URI `http://localhost:55778/api/employees/12348`.

12. To make a PATCH request, select PATCH from the method drop down and give the request body of `{"FirstName":"Jon"}`. Give the URI as `http://localhost:55778/api/employees/12345`. This will update only the `FirstName` property of the corresponding Employee object from John to Jon.

HTTP MESSAGE ANATOMY

The two endpoints of any communication based on HTTP are a server and a client. The client sends a request message to the server; the server processes the request and sends a response message back to the client and these steps constitute an HTTP transaction.

An HTTP request begins with the request line as its first line. The request line starts with the HTTP method, followed by a space followed by the URI of the resource requested, a space, and then the HTTP version. The request line is terminated by a Carriage Return (CR) and a Line Feed (LF) character. Following the request line are the request headers. The header fields are colon-separated key-value pairs, terminated by a CRLF, just like the request line. The end of the header fields is indicated by an empty field—two consecutive CRLF pairs. Finally, following the request headers is the optional request body. Depending on the HTTP method used, the request body could be present or absent. Putting all these pieces of the HTTP request together, here is what a typical request message looks like.

Request Line

```
GET /home.html HTTP/1.1
```

Request Headers

```
Accept: text/html
User-Agent: Mozilla/5.0 (compatible; MSIE 9.0; Windows NT6.1; Trident/5.0)
Host: server.com
[Blank line indicating the end of request headers]
```

The HTTP response has the status line as its first line. The status line starts with the HTTP version, followed by a space, the status code, another space, and then the reason phrase. The HTTP response status code is a three-digit number. The Request line is terminated by a CRLF. The response body has the representation of the resource, as defined by the Content-Type header. For ASP.NET Web API, this is typically JSON or XML. Putting all these pieces of the HTTP response together, here is what a typical response message looks like, with some of the headers removed for brevity.

Status Line

```
HTTP/1.1 200 OK
```

Response Headers

```
Date: Thu, 27 Sep 2013 09:00:19 GMT
Cache-Control: no-cache
Content-Type: application/json; charset=utf-8
Content-Length: 122
```

Response Body

```
[{"Id":12345,"Name":"John Q Law","Department":"Enforcement"},
{"Id":45678,"Name":"Jane Q Taxpayer","Department":"Revenue"}]
```

2.5 Using F12 Developer Tools in Internet Explorer

In this exercise, you will use the Network tab in the F12 Developer Tools of Internet Explorer to view the HTTP requests originating from IE and the corresponding response messages.

1. Open Internet Explorer 9+ and press the F12 key.

2. Go to the Network tab and click Start Capturing.

3. Enter `http://localhost:55778/api/employees/12345` in the address bar and press Enter. Remember to replace the port 55778 with the actual port that the application you created in Exercise 1.2 runs on.

4. IE now shows the capture. Select the capture and click Go To Detailed View, as shown in Figure 2-7.

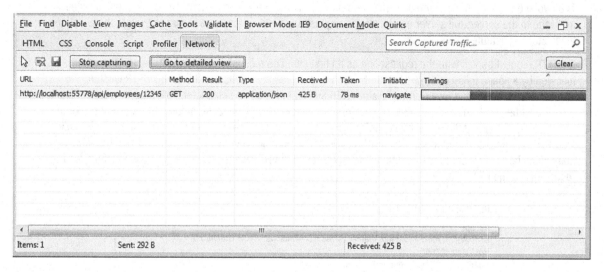

Figure 2-7. *The IE Developer Tools Network tab*

5. IE displays the request headers, request body, response headers, response body, and so on as different tabs, as shown in Figure 2-8.

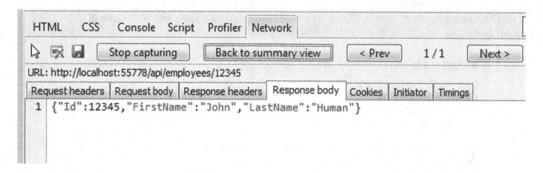

Figure 2-8. *IE Developer Tools—Detailed View*

This capacity will be very handy if you develop single-page applications (SPAs) with JavaScript libraries such as JQuery consuming ASP.NET Web API.

2.6 Using Developer Tools in Chrome

In this exercise, you will use the developer tools of the Chrome browser to view the HTTP requests originating from Chrome and the corresponding response messages.

1. Open Chrome and press Ctrl+Shift+I. The Developer Tools option is available from the Tools menu as well.

2. Navigate to `http://localhost:55778/api/employees/12345`. Remember to replace the port 55778 with the actual port that the application you created in Exercise 1.2 runs on.

3. Chrome displays the capture in the Network tab, as shown in Figure 2-9.

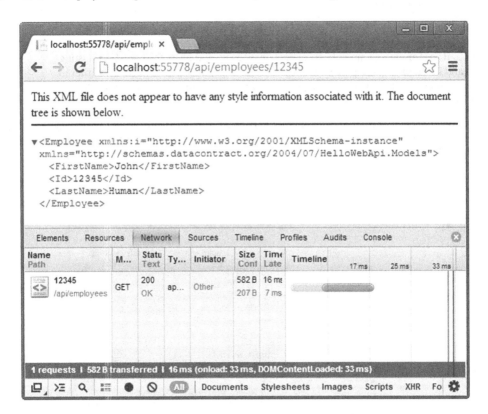

Figure 2-9. *The Chrome Developer Tools*

4. You can click within the capture to see the details.

■ **Note**   It is interesting to observe that Chrome shows the response as XML, while Internet Explorer shows the response as JSON. Key to this difference in behavior is the Accept request header sent by these browsers. IE sends Accept: text/html, application/xhtml+xml, */*. Chrome sends Accept: text/html,application/ xhtml+xml,application/xml;q=0.9,*/*;q=0.8. Because Chrome asked for application/xml, that's what it gets. Since IE asked for only HTML or XHTML, ASP.NET Web API has sent the response in the default MIME type, which is application/json. You'll learn more about this topic of content negotiation in Chapter 3.

2.7 Enabling ASP.NET Web API Tracing

In this exercise, you will enable ASP.NET Web API tracing using System.Diagnostics. You will use the NuGet package Microsoft ASP.NET Web API Tracing.

1. Run Visual Studio and open the project corresponding to Exercise 1.2. Alternatively, you can create a new ASP.NET MVC 4 project with the Web API template, add a new ApiController with a name of EmployeesController, and paste the code from Listing 1-4 and Listing 1-5 of Chapter 1. (This code is also reproduced in Exercise 2.2 earlier in this chapter for your easy reference.) If you create a new project, remember to add the Employee model class to it as well.

2. Click on Tools ➤ Library Package Manager ➤ Package Manager Console. In the Package Manager Console, as shown in Figure 2-10, enter Install-Package Microsoft.AspNet. WebApi.Tracing and press Enter.

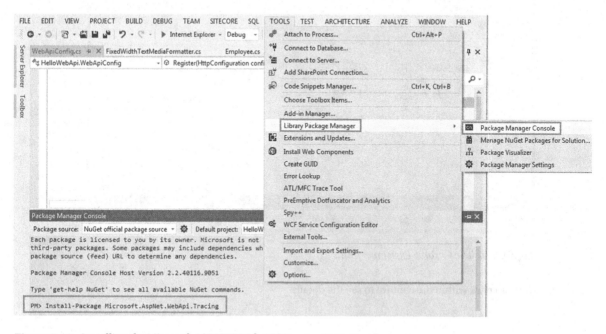

Figure 2-10. *Installing the Microsoft ASP.NET Web API Tracing NuGet package*

3. In the Register method of WebApiConfig, in the App_Start folder, add the following line of code:

   ```
   config.EnableSystemDiagnosticsTracing();
   ```

4. Rebuild the solution and run the project by pressing F5. Clear the Output window of Visual Studio by right-clicking it and selecting Clear All.

5. In the Internet Explorer window that opens up, type the URI http://localhost:55778/api/employees/12345 in the address bar. Remember to replace the port 55778 with the actual port your application runs on.

6. Review the trace lines that are now written into the Output window. Trace provides a good insight into how ASP.NET Web API goes about handling the GET request.

```
iisexpress.exe Information: 0 : Request, Method=GET, Url=http://localhost:55778/api/employees/12345,
Message='http://localhost:55778/api/employees/12345'
iisexpress.exe Information: 0 : Message='Will use same 'JsonMediaTypeFormatter' formatter',
Operation=JsonMediaTypeFormatter.GetPerRequestFormatterInstance
iisexpress.exe Information: 0 : Message='Will use same 'XmlMediaTypeFormatter' formatter',
Operation=XmlMediaTypeFormatter.GetPerRequestFormatterInstance
iisexpress.exe Information: 0 : Message='Will use same 'FormUrlEncodedMediaTypeFormatter'
formatter', Operation=FormUrlEncodedMediaTypeFormatter.GetPerRequestFormatterInstance
iisexpress.exe Information: 0 : Message='Will use same 'JQueryMvcFormUrlEncodedFormatter'
formatter', Operation=JQueryMvcFormUrlEncodedFormatter.GetPerRequestFormatterInstance
iisexpress.exe Information: 0 : Message='Employees', Operation=DefaultHttpControllerSelector.
SelectController
iisexpress.exe Information: 0 : Message='HelloWebApi.Controllers.EmployeesController',
Operation=DefaultHttpControllerActivator.Create
iisexpress.exe Information: 0 : Message='HelloWebApi.Controllers.EmployeesController',
Operation=HttpControllerDescriptor.CreateController
iisexpress.exe Information: 0 : Message='Selected action 'Get(Int32 id)'',
Operation=ApiControllerActionSelector.SelectAction
iisexpress.exe Information: 0 : Message='Parameter 'id' bound to the value '12345'',
Operation=ModelBinderParameterBinding.ExecuteBindingAsync
iisexpress.exe Information: 0 : Message='Model state is valid. Values: id=12345',
Operation=HttpActionBinding.ExecuteBindingAsync
iisexpress.exe Information: 0 : Message='Action returned 'HelloWebApi.Models.Employee'',
Operation=ReflectedHttpActionDescriptor.ExecuteAsync
iisexpress.exe Information: 0 : Message='Will use same 'JsonMediaTypeFormatter' formatter',
Operation=JsonMediaTypeFormatter.GetPerRequestFormatterInstance
iisexpress.exe Information: 0 : Message='Selected formatter='JsonMediaTypeFormatter',
content-type='application/json; charset=utf-8'', Operation=DefaultContentNegotiator.Negotiate
iisexpress.exe Information: 0 : Operation=ApiControllerActionInvoker.InvokeActionAsync,
Status=200 (OK)
iisexpress.exe Information: 0 : Operation=EmployeesController.ExecuteAsync, Status=200 (OK)
iisexpress.exe Information: 0 : Response, Status=200 (OK), Method=GET,
Url=http://localhost:55778/api/employees/12345, Message='Content-type='application/json;
charset=utf-8', content-length=unknown'
iisexpress.exe Information: 0 : Operation=JsonMediaTypeFormatter.WriteToStreamAsync
iisexpress.exe Information: 0 : Operation=EmployeesController.Dispose
```

■ **Note**   Tracing is not enabled by default, and this exercise showed you how to enable it. If you have installed the tooling refresh of Visual Studio 2012 ASP.NET and Web Tools 2012.2, tracing is enabled by default when you create your project from Web API project template.

2.8 Creating a Custom Trace Writer

In this exercise, you will create a custom trace writer that writes XML elements. A custom trace writer must implement the System.Web.Http.Tracing.ITraceWriter interface.

1. Run Visual Studio and open the project corresponding to Exercise 1.2. If you have opted to create a new project instead of using the project from Exercise 1.2, open it.

2. Create a new class WebApiTracer implementing ITraceWriter, as shown in Listing 2-4. There is an ITraceWriter interface in the Newtonsoft.Json.Serialization namespace as well as in System.Web.Http.Tracing. We need the latter. Make sure you include the using System.Web.Http.Tracing; directive.

Listing 2-4. A Custom Trace Writer

```
using System;
using System.IO;
using System.Net.Http;
using System.Text;
using System.Web.Http.Tracing;
using System.Xml;

public class WebApiTracer : ITraceWriter
{
    public void Trace(HttpRequestMessage request,
                        string category,
                            TraceLevel level,
                                Action<TraceRecord> traceAction)
    {
        if (level != TraceLevel.Off)
        {
            TraceRecord rec = new TraceRecord(request, category, level);
            traceAction(rec);
            WriteXmlElement(rec);
        }
    }

    private void WriteXmlElement(TraceRecord rec)
    {
        using (Stream xmlFile = new FileStream(@"C:\path\log.xml", FileMode.Append))
        {
            using (XmlTextWriter writer = new XmlTextWriter(xmlFile, Encoding.UTF8))
            {
                writer.Formatting = Formatting.Indented;
                writer.WriteStartElement("trace");
```

```
                writer.WriteElementString("timestamp", rec.Timestamp.ToString());
                writer.WriteElementString("operation", rec.Operation);
                writer.WriteElementString("user", rec.Operator);

                if (!String.IsNullOrWhiteSpace(rec.Message))
                {
                    writer.WriteStartElement("message");
                    writer.WriteCData(rec.Message);
                    writer.WriteEndElement();
                }

                writer.WriteElementString("category", rec.Category);
                writer.WriteEndElement();
                writer.WriteString(Environment.NewLine);
                writer.Flush();
            }
        }
    }
}
```

3. Visual Studio shows a wavy red underline for the types that need using directives. You can right-click each one and choose the namespace to resolve it. Listing 2-4 shows the required using directives preceding the class definition.

4. To implement ITraceWriter, you must implement the Trace method. The logic of the Trace method is as follows.

   a. Create a new TraceRecord object.

   b. Invoke the caller's traceAction, passing the TraceRecord object.

   c. Write XML out based on the TraceRecord object with details filled in by the caller.

   d. I use C:\path\log.xml in Listing 2-4 as a placeholder. You will need to adjust this path to get the XML file created in a valid path in your computer.

5. To plug the trace writer in, add a line of code in the Register method of WebApiConfig under App_Start folder, like so:

```
config.Services.Replace(typeof(ITraceWriter), new WebApiTracer());
```

Make sure this line appears after the line config.EnableSystemDiagnosticsTracing(); that you added in Exercise 2.7. This sequence is important to ensure that the WebApiTracer class you just created replaces all the existing services for the ITraceWriter service type.

6. ITraceWriter is from the namespace System.Web.Http.Tracing. So you will need to add a using directive to the WebApiConfig class, like so:

```
using System.Web.Http.Tracing;
```

7. Rebuild the solution and issue a request to the web API (it can be any request).

8. Open the XML file and review the contents.

You will see that an XML element is created for each trace record. Currently, our trace writer is tracing only the framework code.

2.9 Tracing Entry and Exit

In this exercise, you will create a custom trace writer that writes trace records with the time taken for each operation. The ASP.NET Web API pipeline writes traces at the beginning and end of an operation. By finding the difference between the timestamps of the beginning and end trace records, you can find the time taken by that operation. This is a handy way to quickly check the performance in production. Of course, you will need to enable the tracing in production for this. Generally, tracing is switched on for a short duration, and once the sufficient data is collected, it is switched off again. No production server will have tracing enabled all the time.

In this exercise, we will store TraceRecord objects in a modified version of a ring buffer. We will keep it simple and not use the head and tail pointers typically used with a ring buffer; instead, we will use only one pointer, which resets back to the index 0 once it is past the last element of the buffer. The older entries are evicted to make room for the newer ones. The buffer will be read by an ApiController that returns the trace information as StringContent, after computing TimeSpan differences.

1. Create a new trace writer with a name of EntryExitTracer, as shown in Listing 2-5. The trace writer just stores the TraceRecord object with details in a ring buffer, which is our custom implementation.

Listing 2-5. The EntryExitTracer Class

```
using System.Net.Http;
using System.Web.Http.Tracing;

public class EntryExitTracer : ITraceWriter
{
    public void Trace(HttpRequestMessage request,
                            string category,
                                    TraceLevel level,
                                            Action<TraceRecord> traceAction)
    {
        if (level != TraceLevel.Off)
        {
            TraceRecord rec = new TraceRecord(request, category, level);
            traceAction(rec);

            RingBufferLog.Instance.Enqueue(rec);
        }
    }
}
```

2. Create a new RingBufferLog class, as shown in Listing 2-6. It is a singleton class, and it stores the TraceRecord objects in a fixed-size array. The basic idea is to ensure that only TraceRecord objects of a fixed size are stored, and the older items are evicted to make way for the newer items. When an item is queued, it moves the pointer by one and stores the item in that position. If the pointer reaches the end of the array, it is reset to 0. Since multiple threads can queue, we use lock to handle concurrency. PeekAll returns the buffer content, and DequeueAll drains the buffer.

Listing 2-6. The Ring Buffer for Storing TraceLog

```
using System.Collections.Generic;
using System.Linq;
using System.Web.Http.Tracing;

public class RingBufferLog
{
    private const int BUFFER_SIZE = 1000;

    TraceRecord[] buffer;
    int pointer = 0;
    private readonly object myPrecious = new object();

    private static RingBufferLog instance = new RingBufferLog();

    private RingBufferLog()
    {
        buffer = new TraceRecord[BUFFER_SIZE];
        ResetPointer();
    }

    public IList<TraceRecord> DequeueAll()
    {
        lock (myPrecious)
        {
            ResetPointer();

            var bufferCopy = new List<TraceRecord>(buffer.Where(t => t != null));

            for (int index = 0; index < BUFFER_SIZE; index++)
            {
                buffer[index] = null;
            }

            return bufferCopy;
        }
    }

    public IList<TraceRecord> PeekAll()
    {
        lock (myPrecious)
        {
            var bufferCopy = new List<TraceRecord>(buffer.Where(t => t != null));
```

```
        return bufferCopy;
    }
}

private void ResetPointer()
{
    pointer = BUFFER_SIZE - 1;
}

private void MovePointer()
{
    pointer = (pointer + 1) % BUFFER_SIZE;
}

public void Enqueue(TraceRecord item)
{
    lock (myPrecious)
    {
        MovePointer();
        buffer[pointer] = item;
    }
}

public static RingBufferLog Instance
{
    get
    {
        return instance;
    }
}
}
```

3. To plug the trace writer in, add a line of code in the `Register` method of `WebApiConfig` under App_Start folder, as shown in Listing 2-7. You can comment out the previous lines or simply leave them in. By adding the line shown in bold type as the last line, you are replacing all the existing services for the `ITraceWriter` service type with that of `EntryExitTracer`.

Listing 2-7. The Register Method in WebApiConfig

```
public static class WebApiConfig
{
    public static void Register(HttpConfiguration config)
    {
        config.Routes.MapHttpRoute(
            name: "DefaultApi",
            routeTemplate: "api/{controller}/{id}",
            defaults: new { id = RouteParameter.Optional }
        );
```

```
                        //config.EnableSystemDiagnosticsTracing();
                        //config.Services.Replace(typeof(ITraceWriter), new WebApiTracer());

                        config.Services.Replace(
                                            typeof(System.Web.Http.Tracing.ITraceWriter),
                                               new EntryExitTracer());
                    }
            }
```

4. Add a new ApiController with a name of TracesController. Add an action method to handle GET, as shown in Listing 2-8. The logic implemented in the action method consists of the following steps:

   a. Retrieve all the TraceRecord entries from the buffer.

   b. For each record of Kind of TraceKind.Begin, try to find the corresponding TraceKind.End record.

   c. If there is one, calculate the difference in the TimeStamp values and display the time taken. Do the matching based on the Operation, Operator, Category, and RequestId values.

   d. Keep track of the indent level to format the string, which is returned back to the caller as Content-Type: text/plain.

   e. This implementation just peeks into the entries. The DequeueAll method of the buffer is not called by this controller. In a production environment, the entries must be dequeued to clear the memory taken by the TraceRecord objects, probably from a DELETE action method (not implemented here though).

Listing 2-8. An API Controller to Display Trace Entries

```
using System;
using System.Linq;
using System.Net.Http;
using System.Text;
using System.Web.Http;
using System.Web.Http.Tracing;

public class TracesController : ApiController
{
    public HttpResponseMessage Get()
    {
        StringBuilder content = new StringBuilder();

        var entries = RingBufferLog.Instance.PeekAll();
        if (entries != null && entries.Count > 0)
        {
            int indent = 0;

            foreach (var entry in entries)
            {
                if (!String.IsNullOrEmpty(entry.Operation) &&
                        !String.IsNullOrEmpty(entry.Operator) &&
                            !String.IsNullOrEmpty(entry.Category))
```

```
        {
            if (entry.Kind == TraceKind.Begin)
            {
                var end = entries.FirstOrDefault(e =>
                                        entry.RequestId.Equals(e.RequestId) &&
                                        entry.Operator.Equals(e.Operator) &&
                                        entry.Operation.Equals(e.Operation) &&
                                        entry.Category.Equals(e.Category) &&
                                        e.Kind == TraceKind.End);
                string millis = String.Empty;

                if (end != null)
                    millis =
                        (end.Timestamp - entry.Timestamp).TotalMilliseconds.ToString();

                content.Append('\t', indent);
                content.AppendFormat("BGN {0} {1} {2} {3}\n",
                                    entry.RequestId, entry.Operator,
                                    entry.Operation, millis);

                indent++;
            }
            else
            {
                indent--;

                content.Append('\t', indent);
                content.AppendFormat("END {0} {1} {2}\n",
                                    entry.RequestId, entry.Operator, entry.Operation);
            }
        }
    }

    return new HttpResponseMessage()
    {
        Content = new StringContent(content.ToString())
    };
}
}
```

5. Rebuild the solution and make a few requests to EmployeesController.

6. Make a GET request to http://localhost:55778/api/traces from Internet Explorer.
Remember to replace the port 55778 with the actual port that the application runs on.
It displays the trace with time in milliseconds, as shown in Figure 2-11.

Figure 2-11. *Trace output*

2.10 Tracing from Your Code

In this exercise, you will use the trace writer to write trace output from your code.

1. Modify the Register method of WebApiConfig in the App_Start folder, as shown in Listing 2-9. We are basically going back to the WebApiTracer.

   Listing 2-9. The Register method of WebApiConfig

   ```
   public static class WebApiConfig
   {
       public static void Register(HttpConfiguration config)
       {
           config.Routes.MapHttpRoute(
               name: "DefaultApi",
               routeTemplate: "api/{controller}/{id}",
               defaults: new { id = RouteParameter.Optional }
           );

           config.Services.Replace(typeof(ITraceWriter), new WebApiTracer());
       }
   }
   ```

2. Comment out the code in the EmployeesController class and add the code from Listing 2-10. The TraceWriter.Info method is the shorthand equivalent of the Trace method. The Get action method uses them both just for illustration.

Listing 2-10. The Get Action Method Writing Trace

```csharp
using System;
using System.Collections.Generic;
using System.Linq;
using System.Web.Http;
using System.Web.Http.Tracing;
using HelloWebApi.Models;

public class EmployeesController : ApiController
{
    private readonly ITraceWriter traceWriter = null;

    public EmployeesController()
    {
        this.traceWriter = GlobalConfiguration.Configuration.Services.GetTraceWriter();
    }

    private static IList<Employee> list = new List<Employee>()
    {
        new Employee()
        {
            Id = 12345, FirstName = "John", LastName = "Human"
        },

        new Employee()
        {
            Id = 12346, FirstName = "Jane", LastName = "Public"
        },

        new Employee()
        {
            Id = 12347, FirstName = "Joseph", LastName = "Law"
        }
    };

    public Employee Get(int id)
    {
        var employee = list.FirstOrDefault(e => e.Id == id);

        if (traceWriter != null)
            traceWriter.Info(Request, "EmployeesController", String.Format("Getting employee {0}", id));

        if (traceWriter != null)
            traceWriter.Trace(
                Request, "System.Web.Http.Controllers", System.Web.Http.Tracing.TraceLevel.Info,
                    (traceRecord) =>
```

```
            {
                traceRecord.Message =
                String.Format("Getting employee {0}", id);

                traceRecord.Operation = "Get(int)";
                traceRecord.Operator = "EmployeeController";
            });

    return employee;
}
}
```

3. Rebuild the solution and make a GET request from Internet Explorer to the URI
    http://localhost:55778/api/employees/12345.

4. Open log.xml and search for the string **Getting Employee**. There will be two entries
    corresponding to the two trace statements we have in Listing 2-10.

```xml
<trace>
  <timestamp>4/13/2013 3:47:49 AM</timestamp>
  <operation />
  <level>Info</level>
  <operator />
  <request_id>07cc7d16-90ff-401f-bf1a-2df4a4072423</request_id>
  <message><![CDATA[Getting employee 12345]]></message>
  <category>EmployeesController</category>
</trace>

<trace>
  <timestamp>4/13/2013 3:47:49 AM</timestamp>
  <operation>Get(int)</operation>
  <level>Info</level>
  <operator>EmployeeController</operator>
  <request_id>07cc7d16-90ff-401f-bf1a-2df4a4072423</request_id>
  <message><![CDATA[Getting employee 12345]]></message>
  <category>System.Web.Http.Controllers</category>
</trace>
```

It is possible to write begin and end trace from your code as well, just as the framework does. We'll do that in the
following steps.

5. Revert to the EntryExitTracer by modifying the Register method of WebApiConfig under
    App_Start folder as shown in Listing 2-11.

    Listing 2-11. The Register Method of WebApiConfig

```
public static class WebApiConfig
{
    public static void Register(HttpConfiguration config)
    {
        config.Routes.MapHttpRoute(
            name: "DefaultApi",
```

```
                routeTemplate: "api/{controller}/{id}",
                defaults: new { id = RouteParameter.Optional }
        );

        config.Services.Replace(typeof(System.Web.Http.Tracing.ITraceWriter),
                                    new EntryExitTracer());
    }
}
```

6. Add the action method for GET, as shown in Listing 2-12, to the EmployeesController shown in Listing 2-10. This action method previously returned the list of employees defined as a field at the controller level. It still does that, but now inside the TraceBeginEnd method. I have added a delay of one second just for illustration.

Listing 2-12. The Get Action Method Tracing the Entry and Exit

```
public IEnumerable<Employee> Get()
{
    IEnumerable<Employee> employees = null;

    if (traceWriter != null)
    {
        traceWriter.TraceBeginEnd(
            Request,
            TraceCategories.FormattingCategory,
            System.Web.Http.Tracing.TraceLevel.Info,
            "EmployeesController",
            "Get",
            beginTrace: (tr) =>
            {
                tr.Message = "Entering Get";
            },
            execute: () =>
            {
                System.Threading.Thread.Sleep(1000); // Simulate delay
                employees = list;
            },
            endTrace: (tr) =>
            {
                tr.Message = "Leaving Get";
            },
            errorTrace: null);
    }

    return employees;
}
```

7. Rebuild the solution and make a GET request from Fiddler or Internet Explorer to the URI `http://localhost:55778/api/employees`. Remember to replace the port 55778 with the actual port that the application runs on.

8. Make another GET request from Fiddler or Internet Explorer to the URI `http://localhost:55778/api/traces`. You will see the begin and end trace appearing for the Get method, like so:

```
BGN 7b577bf9-4e5d-4539-b15a-3d4c629e4de2 EmployeesController Get 1000.0572
END 7b577bf9-4e5d-4539-b15a-3d4c629e4de2 EmployeesController Get
```

2.11 Tracing Request and Response Messages

In this exercise, you will use the trace writer to log the request and response messages. I use a message handler for this purpose; you'll learn more about message handlers in Chapter 8. A message handler runs both before and after the action method is executed; the request handling part runs before the action method starts executing, and the response handling part runs after the action method has generated the response. This behavior is similar to an action filter, but message handlers run for all the requests in a route (a pre-route handler) or for all requests (a global handler). The important difference is that a message handler runs much earlier in the ASP.NET Web API pipeline.

1. Create a message handler as shown in Listing 2-13 by adding a new class to the project with a name of `TracingHandler`. I initialize new `HttpMessageContent` instances of the request and response objects and call `ReadAsStringAsync` to get the corresponding message, which you'll write to the trace.

Listing 2-13. Tracing Message Handler

```
using System;
using System.Net.Http;
using System.Threading;
using System.Threading.Tasks;
using System.Web.Http;

public class TracingHandler : DelegatingHandler
{
    protected override async Task<HttpResponseMessage> SendAsync(
                                              HttpRequestMessage request,
                                              CancellationToken cancellationToken)
    {
        HttpMessageContent requestContent = new HttpMessageContent(request);
        string requestMessage = await requestContent.ReadAsStringAsync();

        var response = await base.SendAsync(request, cancellationToken);

        HttpMessageContent responseContent = new HttpMessageContent(response);
        string responseMessage = await responseContent.ReadAsStringAsync();

        GlobalConfiguration.Configuration.Services.GetTraceWriter()
                .Trace(request, "System.Web.Http.MessageHandlers",
                                              System.Web.Http.Tracing.TraceLevel.Info,
                    (t) =>
```

```
        {
            t.Message = String.Format(
                                "\n{0}\n{1}\n", requestMessage, responseMessage);
        });

    return response;
}
}
```

2. Revert to the WebApiTracer by modifying the Register method of WebApiConfig under App_Start folder, as shown in Listing 2-14. Also in that method, add the message handler to the handlers collection. If you have multiple message handlers in your project, ensure that this is the first handler that appears in the handlers collection.

Listing 2-14. The Register method of WebApiConfig

```
public static class WebApiConfig
{
    public static void Register(HttpConfiguration config)
    {
        config.Routes.MapHttpRoute(
            name: "DefaultApi",
            routeTemplate: "api/{controller}/{id}",
            defaults: new { id = RouteParameter.Optional }
        );

        config.Services.Replace(typeof(ITraceWriter), new WebApiTracer());

        config.MessageHandlers.Add(new TracingHandler());
    }
}
```

3. Rebuild the solution and make a GET request from Fiddler or Internet Explorer to the URI http://localhost:55778/api/employees/12345.

4. Open log.xml and you will find an entry like this one:

```
<trace>
    <timestamp>4/13/2013 5:13:11 AM</timestamp>
    <operation />
    <level>Info</level>
    <operator />
    <request_id>69bfa407-a2ba-4d0b-8843-8773e2da699f</request_id>
    <message>
    <![CDATA[
        GET /api/employees/12345 HTTP/1.1
        Host: localhost:55778
        User-Agent: Fiddler

        HTTP/1.1 200 OK
        Content-Type: application/json; charset=utf-8
```

```
        {"Id":12345,"FirstName":"John","LastName":"Human"}
    ]]>
    </message>
    <category>System.Web.Http.MessageHandlers</category>
</trace>
```

Summary

The ability to view the request message coming into your ASP.NET Web API and the response message sent by your web API is fundamental for developing HTTP services. Another important need is to hand-craft requests by manipulating headers and the body content and submit them to ASP.NET Web API and view the corresponding response.

Fiddler, a web debugging proxy, is a useful tool to capture and analyze HTTP and HTTPS traffic between the computer running Fiddler and the outside. Fiddler also has a feature to build a complete request with headers, send it to an HTTP endpoint such as the web API, and inspect the response returned by the web API. By default, traffic from any WinInet stack, such as that of Internet Explorer, is automatically captured by Fiddler. For others, Fiddler can be configured as proxy. For classes such as `WebClient` that are part of the `System.Net` namespace, a special URL (`http://localhost.fiddler:<port>`) can be used so that Fiddler captures the traffic. Fiddler can also capture and even decrypt HTTPS traffic. Fiddler acts as a man-in-the-middle and generates certificates on the fly to decrypt HTTPS traffic.

Apart from Fiddler, the browsers come with tools to capture and inspect the HTTP traffic originating from them. You saw that Internet Explorer has F12 Developer Tools and Chrome has Developer Tools too, for the purpose of allowing an end user (or a developer) to view the traffic. As we reviewed the developer tools of IE and Chrome, we observed that ASP.NET Web API is capable of sending response messages in both XML and JSON. Chrome shows the web API response as XML, while Internet Explorer shows the response as JSON. In the next chapter, we will explore this topic of content negotiation further.

Another key aspect of debugging ASP.NET Web API is tracing. ASP.NET Web API supports tracing of your code as well as the framework code. Tracing the framework code is essential to understand what goes on behind the scene as ASP.NET Web API handles a request, calls your code at the right moment, and sends back a response.

The NuGet package Microsoft ASP.NET Web API Tracing enables tracing using `System.Diagnostics`. Here you learned how to can create your own custom tracer by implementing the `System.Web.Http.Tracing.ITraceWriter` interface.

CHAPTER 3

■ ■ ■

Media-Type Formatting CLR Objects

From the ASP.NET Web API perspective, *serialization* is the process of translating a .NET Common Language Runtime (CLR) type into a format that can be transmitted over HTTP. The format is either JSON or XML, out of the box. A media type formatter, which is an object of type MediaTypeFormatter, performs the serialization in the ASP.NET Web API pipeline. Consider a simple action method handling GET in an ApiController:

```
public Employee Get(int id)
{
        return list.First(e => e.Id == id);
}
```

This method returns a CLR object of type Employee. In order for the data contained in this object to be returned to the client in the HTTP response message, the object must be serialized. The MediaTypeFormatter object in the ASP.NET Web API pipeline performs this serialization. It serializes the object returned by the action method into JSON or XML, which is then written into the response message body. The out-of-box media formatters that produce JSON and XML are respectively JsonMediaTypeFormatter and XmlMediaTypeFormatter, both deriving from MediaTypeFormatter. The process through which the MediaTypeFormatter is chosen is called *content negotiation*, commonly shortened to *conneg*.

A resource can have one or more representations. When you issue a GET to retrieve a resource, such as the employee with ID 12345, the response message contains the representation of the resource, which is a specific employee in this case. The Web API indicates how the resource is represented in the response through the Content-Type response header. The Accept request header can be used by a client to indicate the set of preferred representations for the resource in the response.

Out of the box, the ASP.NET Web API framework supports two media or content types: JSON and XML. If you send a request with Accept: application/json, the response message will be JSON and Content-Type will be application/json. Similarly, if you send a request with Accept: application/xml, the response message will be XML. You can also specify a quality value indicating the relative preference. The range is 0–1, with 0 being unacceptable and 1 being the most preferred. The default value is 1. For example, if you send the request header Accept: application/json; q=0.8, application/xml;q=0.9, the response message will be XML, because application/xml has a quality value of 0.9, which is higher than the quality value of 0.8 specified for application/json.

3.1 Listing the Out-of-Box Media Formatters

In this exercise, you will list the media type formatters that come out of the box with ASP.NET Web API.

1. You can use the project from Exercise 1.2 or create a new ASP.NET MVC 4 project with a name of HelloWebApi using Web API template.

2. If you create a new project, add the Employee class from the project corresponding to Exercise 1.2 into your new project under the Models folder. The following code listing shows the Employee class, for your easy reference.

```
public class Employee
{
    public int Id { get; set; }
    public string FirstName { get; set; }
    public string LastName { get; set; }
    public int Department { get; set; }
}
```

3. Modify the Register method in WebApiConfig in the App_Start folder, as shown in Listing 3-1, to see the output it produces (also shown in Listing 3-1). You can see this output in the Output window of Visual Studio, as you press F5 and run the application.

Listing 3-1. Listing Media Formatters

```
using System;
using System.Diagnostics;
using System.Web.Http;
using HelloWebApi.Models;

public static class WebApiConfig
{
    public static void Register(HttpConfiguration config)
    {
        config.Routes.MapHttpRoute(
            name: "DefaultApi",
            routeTemplate: "api/{controller}/{id}",
            defaults: new { id = RouteParameter.Optional }
        );

        foreach (var formatter in config.Formatters)
        {
            Trace.WriteLine(formatter.GetType().Name);
            Trace.WriteLine("\tCanReadType: " + formatter.CanReadType(typeof(Employee)));
            Trace.WriteLine("\tCanWriteType: " + formatter.CanWriteType(typeof(Employee)));
            Trace.WriteLine("\tBase: " + formatter.GetType().BaseType.Name);
            Trace.WriteLine("\tMedia Types: " + String.Join(", ", formatter.
                                                     SupportedMediaTypes));
        }

    }

}
```

```
// Output
JsonMediaTypeFormatter
        CanReadType: True
        CanWriteType: True
        Base: MediaTypeFormatter
        Media Types: application/json, text/json
XmlMediaTypeFormatter
        CanReadType: True
        CanWriteType: True
        Base: MediaTypeFormatter
        Media Types: application/xml, text/xml
FormUrlEncodedMediaTypeFormatter
        CanReadType: False
        CanWriteType: False
        Base: MediaTypeFormatter
        Media Types: application/x-www-form-urlencoded
JQueryMvcFormUrlEncodedFormatter
        CanReadType: True
        CanWriteType: False
        Base: FormUrlEncodedMediaTypeFormatter
        Media Types: application/x-www-form-urlencoded
```

From the serialization point of view, the last two media type formatters can be ignored, since they cannot write any type. The first two, JsonMediaTypeFormatter and XmlMediaTypeFormatter, are the important ones. They are the media formatters that produce JSON and XML resource representations in the response.

3.2 Understanding Conneg

This exercise demonstrates how the process of content negotiation works. Content negotiation is the process by which ASP.NET Web API chooses the formatter to use and the media type for the response message.

The System.Net.Http.Formatting.DefaultContentNegotiator class implements the default conneg algorithm in the Negotiate method that it implements, as part of implementing the IContentNegotiatior interface. This method accepts three inputs:

1. The type of the object to serialize

2. The collection of media formatters

3. The request object (HttpRequestMessage)

The Negotiate method checks the following four items before deciding on the media formatter to use, in descending order of precedence:

1. Media type mapping: Every MediaTypeFormatter has a collection of MediaTypeMapping values. A MediaTypeMapping allows you to map the request or response messages that have certain characteristics to a media-type. There are four out-of-box media type mappings: QueryStringMapping, UriPathExtensionMapping, RequestHeaderMapping, and MediaRangeMapping. These respectively map a query string parameter, URI path extension, request header, and media range to a media type. As an example, defining a QueryStringMapping with a parameter name of fmt and a value of json and media-type of application/json will let ASP.NET Web API choose JsonMediaTypeFormatter, if the query string has a field fmt with a value of json, such as this: http://localhost:<port>/api/employees/12345?fmt=json.

2.   Media type as specified in the Accept request header.

3.   Media type as specified in the Content-Type request header.

4.   If there is no match so far, the conneg algorithm goes through the MediaTypeFormatter objects defined in the config and checks if a formatter can serialize the type by calling the CanWriteType method. The first formatter that can serialize the type is chosen.

Try the following steps to see for yourself how ASP.NET Web API conneg works.

1.   You can use the project from Exercise 1.2 or create a new ASP.NET MVC 4 project (Web API template). If it does not already exist, add a new ApiController with a name of EmployeesController and implement an action-method-handling GET, as shown in Listing 3-2. Also copy the Employee class into the Models folder of your new project.

Listing 3-2. An ApiController With an Action-Method-Handling GET

```
using System.Collections.Generic;
using System.Linq;
using System.Web.Http;
using HelloWebApi.Models;

public class EmployeesController : ApiController
{
    private static IList<Employee> list = new List<Employee>()
    {
        new Employee()
        {
            Id = 12345, FirstName = "John", LastName = "Human"
        },

        new Employee()
        {
            Id = 12346, FirstName = "Jane", LastName = "Public"
        },

        new Employee()
        {
            Id = 12347, FirstName = "Joseph", LastName = "Law"
        }
    };

    // GET api/employees/12345
    public Employee Get(int id)
    {
        return list.First(e => e.Id == id);
    }
}
```

2.   Fire up Fiddler and go to the Composer tab. Issue a GET request for http://localhost:55778/api/employees/12345, specifying Accept: application/json in the Request Headers text box. Remember to replace the port 55778 with the port that the application runs on. The Web API response you get will be JSON.

Request	GET http://localhost:55778/api/employees/12345 HTTP/1.1 Accept: application/json Host: localhost:55778
Response	HTTP/1.1 200 OK Content-Type: application/json; charset=utf-8 {"Id":12345,"FirstName":"John","LastName":"Human"}

3. Issue a GET request for http://localhost:55778/api/employees/12345, specifying Accept: application/xml in the Request Headers text box. Now, the Web API response is XML.

Request	GET http://localhost:55778/api/employees/12345 HTTP/1.1 Content-Type: application/xml Host: localhost:55778

Response	HTTP/1.1 200 OK
	Content-Type: application/xml; charset=utf-8
	
	<Employee xmlns:i="http://www.w3.org/2001/XMLSchema-instance"
	
	xmlns="http://schemas.datacontract.org/2004/07/HelloWebApi.Models">
	      <FirstName>John</FirstName>
	      <Id>12345</Id>
	      <LastName>Human</LastName>
	</Employee>

4. Issue a GET request for http://localhost:55778/api/employees/12345, specifying Accept: application/xml;q=0.2, application/json;q=0.8 in the Request Headers text box. The Web API response is JSON, since application/json has the quality factor of 0.8, which is greater than 0.2 for XML.

Request	GET http://localhost:55778/api/employees/12345 HTTP/1.1 Accept: application/xml;q=0.2, application/json;q=0.8 Host: localhost:55778
Response	HTTP/1.1 200 OK Content-Type: application/json; charset=utf-8 ...

5. Issue a GET request for http://localhost:55778/api/employees/12345, specifying Content-Type: application/xml in the Request Headers text box. Do not include the Accept header. The Web API response is XML. Even though there is no message body for the request, we specified a Content-Type. Since there is no Accept header for conneg to choose the media type, it resorted to Content-Type.

Request	GET http://localhost:55778/api/employees/12345 HTTP/1.1 Content-Type: application/xml Host: localhost:55778
Response	HTTP/1.1 200 OK Content-Type: application/xml; charset=utf-8 ...

6. Issue a GET request for http://localhost:55778/api/employees/12345, without specifying either the Accept header or the Content-Type header. The Web API response is JSON. Because conneg cannot determine the media type based on the Accept header or the Content-Type header, it just goes through the list of the MediaTypeFormatter objects, in the same way that we looped in Listing 3-1. The order in which the MediaTypeFormatter objects are listed in Listing 3-1 is significant because it determines the order in which ASP.NET Web API picks up the default formatter to serialize. The first media type formatter in the list is JsonMediaTypeFormatter. Since this media type formatter can serialize the Employee type (notice the true returned by CanWriteType in Listing 3-1), the Web API chooses it and responds with JSON.

Request	GET http://localhost:55778/api/employees/12345 HTTP/1.1 Host: localhost:55778
Response	HTTP/1.1 200 OK Content-Type: application/json; charset=utf-8 ...

7. Modify the WebApiConfig class in the App_Start folder to add the statement

    ```
    config.Formatters.RemoveAt(0);
    ```

    as shown in Listing 3-3. This removes JsonMediaTypeFormatter, which is the first formatter in the Formatters collection.

Listing 3-3. Removing a Media Formatter

```
public static class WebApiConfig
{
    public static void Register(HttpConfiguration config)
    {
        config.Routes.MapHttpRoute(
            name: "DefaultApi",
            routeTemplate: "api/{controller}/{id}",
            defaults: new { id = RouteParameter.Optional }
        );

        config.Formatters.RemoveAt(0);

        foreach (var formatter in config.Formatters)
        {
            Trace.WriteLine(formatter.GetType().Name);
            Trace.WriteLine("\tCanReadType: " + formatter.CanReadType(typeof(Employee)));
            Trace.WriteLine("\tCanWriteType: " + formatter.CanWriteType(typeof(Employee)));
```

```
            Trace.WriteLine("\tBase: " + formatter.GetType().BaseType.Name);
            Trace.WriteLine("\tMedia Types: " + String.Join(", ", formatter.
                                                    SupportedMediaTypes));
        }
    }
}
```

8. Issue a GET request for http://localhost:55778/api/employees/12345 without
    specifying either the Accept or the Content-Type header. Now ASP.NET Web API sends
    back an XML response by default, since JsonMediaTypeFormatter is no longer first in the
    list; instead, XmlMediaTypeFormatter is now first. If you repeat the GET explicitly asking
    for JSON with the Accept: application/json header, even then you will get only the XML
    representation of the Employee object.

Request	GET http://localhost:55778/api/employees/12345 HTTP/1.1 Accept: application/json Host: localhost:55778
Response	HTTP/1.1 200 OK Content-Type: application/xml; charset=utf-8 ...

9. In WebApiConfig in the App_Start folder, immediately after the code you added in the
    previous step, add the same code again: config.Formatters.RemoveAt(0);. This removes
    the second formatter from the Formatters collection, which is XmlMediaTypeFormatter.

10. Issue a GET request for http://localhost:55778/api/employees/12345. The Web API
    now responds with a 406 - Not Acceptable status code. By removing both the formatters,
    we have left the API with no formatter option to serialize Employee type and hence the 406
    status code.

Request	GET http://localhost:55778/api/employees/12345 HTTP/1.1 Host: localhost:55778
Response	HTTP/1.1 406 Not Acceptable Content-Length: 0

11. Modify the WebApiConfig class to delete both the lines we added to remove the first
    formatter from the collection:

```
config.Formatters.RemoveAt(0);
```

3.3 Requesting a Content Type through the Query String

In the previous exercise, you saw conneg in action. One piece that was missing, however, was the media type
mapping, which occupies the top slot in the order of precedence. If the conneg algorithm finds a matching media
type based on this mapping, and if the corresponding media type formatter is capable of serializing the type, no more
matching is done. The matching media type based on the media type mapping will be used as the media type for the
response message. In this exercise, you will see how to request a content type through media type mapping based on a
query string.

1. Make a change to the Register method of WebApiConfig in the App_Start folder, as shown in Listing 3-4.

   Listing 3-4. Media Type Mapping Based on Query String

```
using System;
using System.Diagnostics;
using System.Net.Http.Formatting;
using System.Net.Http.Headers;
using System.Web.Http;
using HelloWebApi.Models;

public static class WebApiConfig
{
    public static void Register(HttpConfiguration config)
    {
        config.Routes.MapHttpRoute(
            name: "DefaultApi",
            routeTemplate: "api/{controller}/{id}",
            defaults: new { id = RouteParameter.Optional }
        );

        config.Formatters.JsonFormatter.MediaTypeMappings.Add(
                new QueryStringMapping("frmt", "json",
                    new MediaTypeHeaderValue("application/json")));

        config.Formatters.XmlFormatter.MediaTypeMappings.Add(
                new QueryStringMapping("frmt", "xml",
                    new MediaTypeHeaderValue("application/xml")));

        foreach (var formatter in config.Formatters)
        {
            Trace.WriteLine(formatter.GetType().Name);
            Trace.WriteLine("\tCanReadType: " + formatter.CanReadType(typeof(Employee)));
            Trace.WriteLine("\tCanWriteType: " + formatter.CanWriteType(typeof(Employee)));
            Trace.WriteLine("\tBase: " + formatter.GetType().BaseType.Name);
            Trace.WriteLine("\tMedia Types: " + String.Join(", ", formatter.
                                                    SupportedMediaTypes));
        }

    }
}
```

2. We have now mapped the query string of field frmt with a value of json to the media type application/json and xml to the media type application/xml.

3. Issue a GET request for `http://localhost:55778/api/employees/12345?`**`frmt=json`**
    specifying `Accept: application/xml` in the Request Headers text box. As always,
    remember to replace the port 55778 with the actual port that the application runs on. Pay
    attention to the query string that is part of the URI. The Web API response is JSON, even
    though we have specified `application/xml` in the `Accept` header. The conneg algorithm
    has chosen `application/json` based on the query string media type mapping, which takes
    precedence over the `Accept` header.

Request	`GET http://localhost:55778/api/employees/12345?`**`frmt=json`** `HTTP/1.1`
	`Accept: application/xml`
	`Host: localhost:55778`

Response	`HTTP/1.1 200 OK`
	`Content-Type: application/json; charset=utf-8`
	
	`{"Id":12345,"FirstName":"John","LastName":"Human"}`

4. Issue a GET request for `http://localhost:55778/api/employees/12345?`**`frmt=xml`**,
    specifying `Accept: application/json` in the Request Headers text box. The response
    will be XML this time. Whether or not the `Accept` header is present, the response is always
    XML because of the order of precedence.

Request	`GET http://localhost:55778/api/employees/12345?`**`frmt=xml`** `HTTP/1.1`
	`Accept: application/json`
	`Host: localhost:55778`

Response	`HTTP/1.1 200 OK`
	`Content-Type: application/xml; charset=utf-8`
	`...`

3.4 Requesting a Content Type through the Header

In this exercise, you will see how a content type can be requested through the media type mapping based on the
request header.

1. Add the code shown in Listing 3-5 to the `Register` method of `WebApiConfig` in the
    `App_Start` folder, following the lines we added in Exercise 3.3.

Listing 3-5. Media Type Mapping Based on Request Header

```
config.Formatters.JsonFormatter
        .MediaTypeMappings.Add(
                new RequestHeaderMapping(
                        "X-Media", "json",
                                StringComparison.OrdinalIgnoreCase, false,
                                        new MediaTypeHeaderValue("application/json")));
```

2. Issue a GET request for `http://localhost:55778/api/employees/12345`, specifying two
    request headers, `Accept: application/xml` and `X-Media: json`, in the Request Headers
    text box. The Web API response is JSON, even though we have specified `application/xml`
    in the `Accept` header. The conneg algorithm has chosen `application/json` based on the
    header media type mapping, which takes precedence over the `Accept` header.

Request	GET http://localhost:55778/api/employees/12345 HTTP/1.1 Accept: application/xml **X-Media: json** Host: localhost:55778
Response	HTTP/1.1 200 OK Content-Type: application/json; charset=utf-8 {"Id":12345,"FirstName":"John","LastName":"Human"}

3. Issue a GET request for http://localhost:55778/api/employees/12345?frmt=xml, specifying X-Media: json in the Request Headers text box. The response is still JSON.

Request	GET http://localhost:55778/api/employees/12345?**frmt=xml** HTTP/1.1 Accept: application/xml **X-Media: json** Host: localhost:55778
Response	HTTP/1.1 200 OK Content-Type: application/json; charset=utf-8 {"Id":12345,"FirstName":"John","LastName":"Human"}

3.5 Implementing a Custom Media Type Mapping

In this exercise, you will create a custom media type mapping class that derives from MediaTypeMapping to map the IP address of the client to a media type. For all the requests coming from the local machine with loopback address of ::1 (IPv6), JSON will be the media type, regardless of the values in the Accept and Content-Type headers.

1. Add a reference to the System.ServiceModel assembly to your project by right-clicking References under your project in Visual Studio Solution Explorer and selecting Add Reference.

2. Add a new class IPBasedMediaTypeMapping, as shown in Listing 3-6.

Listing 3-6. Custom Media Type Mapping

```
using System;
using System.Net.Http;
using System.Net.Http.Formatting;
using System.Net.Http.Headers;
using System.ServiceModel.Channels;
using System.Web;

public class IPBasedMediaTypeMapping : MediaTypeMapping
{
    public IPBasedMediaTypeMapping() :
                                    base(new MediaTypeHeaderValue("application/json")) { }
```

```
public override double TryMatchMediaType(HttpRequestMessage request)
{
    string ipAddress = String.Empty;

    if (request.Properties.ContainsKey("MS_HttpContext"))
    {
        var httpContext = (HttpContextBase)request.Properties["MS_HttpContext"];
        ipAddress = httpContext.Request.UserHostAddress;
    }
    else if (request.Properties.ContainsKey(RemoteEndpointMessageProperty.Name))
    {
        RemoteEndpointMessageProperty prop;
        prop = (RemoteEndpointMessageProperty)
                    request.Properties[RemoteEndpointMessageProperty.Name];
        ipAddress = prop.Address;
    }

    //::1 is the loopback address in IPv6, same as 127.0.0.1 in IPv4
    // Using the loopback address only for illustration
    return "::1".Equals(ipAddress) ? 1.0 : 0.0;
}
}
```

3. Add it to the media type mappings collection of the JSON media type formatter in the Register method of WebApiConfig in the App_Start folder, as shown in Listing 3-7.

    Listing 3-7. Registering the Custom Media Type Mapping

```
config.Formatters.JsonFormatter
            .MediaTypeMappings.Add(new IPBasedMediaTypeMapping());
```

4. Issue a GET request using Fiddler, from the machine running Web API, for http://localhost:55778/api/employees/12345, specifying Accept: application/xml in the Request Headers text box. Remember to replace the port 55778 with the actual port that the application runs on. The Web API response is JSON, even though we have specified application/xml in the Accept header. The conneg algorithm has chosen application/json based on the IP address that is mapped to application/json.

Request	GET http://localhost:55778/api/employees/12345 HTTP/1.1 Accept: application/xml Host: localhost:55778
Response	HTTP/1.1 200 OK Content-Type: application/json; charset=utf-8 {"Id":12345,"FirstName":"John","LastName":"Human"}

---

5. I have chosen an IP address only for illustration. You can create the mapping to literally anything on the request, including headers, and you can implement any complex logic that is based on the multiple parameters of the request to choose the media type.

6. Undo all the changes we have made so far to the WebApiConfig class and restore it to the out-of-box state, as shown in Listing 3-8.

Listing 3-8. The Default WebApiConfig Class

```
public static class WebApiConfig
{
    public static void Register(HttpConfiguration config)
    {
        config.Routes.MapHttpRoute(
            name: "DefaultApi",
            routeTemplate: "api/{controller}/{id}",
            defaults: new { id = RouteParameter.Optional }
        );
    }
}
```

3.6 Overriding Conneg and Returning JSON

In this exercise, you will override conneg and let ASP.NET Web API use the media formatter that you specify
to serialize the resource. The key is to manually return HttpResponseMessage after setting the Content to
ObjectContent<T>, specifying the media formatter. In the following example, you will specify that the Employee object
must always be serialized as JSON using JsonMediaTypeFormatter, regardless of what conneg comes up with.
The formatter you specify here takes precedence over the formatter determined by conneg.

    1.   Modify the GET action method in EmployeesController, as shown in Listing 3-9.

        Listing 3-9. Overriding Conneg

```
public HttpResponseMessage Get(int id)
{
    var employee = list.FirstOrDefault(e => e.Id == id);

    return new HttpResponseMessage()
    {
        Content = new ObjectContent<Employee>(employee,

                                        Configuration.Formatters.JsonFormatter)
    };
}
```

    2.   Rebuild the solution and make a GET request to http://localhost:55778/api/
employees/12345. Regardless of the Accept and Content-Type headers, you will always get
JSON back.

3.7 Piggybacking on Conneg

In this exercise, you will manually run conneg, similar to the way the ASP.NET Web API framework runs, and take
action based on what conneg comes up with. Here is a scenario where manual conneg will be handy. Suppose your
web API is consumed by multiple external client applications, over which you have no control. You support multiple
media types, and you charge the web API consumers based on the egress traffic (response message size). One
consumer has asked you to blacklist a specific media type, say XML. One way to meet this requirement is by removing
the XmlMediaTypeFormatter altogether, as we did in Exercise 3.2. But this will not be desirable when other consumers
do need XML. Another option is to hard-code a specific formatter other than that of XML, as we did in Exercise 3.6.

But the drawback in that case is that the customer would still want the ability to conneg between the available options other than XmlMediaTypeFormatter. A simple solution to meet this need will be to manually run conneg after removing the media type formatters that support the blacklisted media type. Modify the Get action method, as shown in Listing 3-10.

Listing 3-10. Piggybacking on Conneg

```
public HttpResponseMessage Get(int id)
{
    // hard-coded for illustration but for the use case described,
    // the blacklisted formatter might need to be retrieved from
    // a persistence store for the client application based on some identifier
    var blackListed = "application/xml";

    var allowedFormatters = Configuration.Formatters
                                .Where(f => !f.SupportedMediaTypes
                                     .Any(m => m.MediaType
                                         .Equals(blackListed,
                                             StringComparison.OrdinalIgnoreCase)));

    var result = Configuration.Services
                        .GetContentNegotiator()
                            .Negotiate(
                                typeof(Employee), Request, allowedFormatters);
    if (result == null)
        throw new HttpResponseException(System.Net.HttpStatusCode.NotAcceptable);

    var employee = list.First(e => e.Id == id); // Assuming employee exists

    return new HttpResponseMessage()
    {
        Content = new ObjectContent<Employee>(
                        employee,
                            result.Formatter,
                                result.MediaType)
    };
}
```

3.8 Creating a Custom Media Formatter

ASP.NET Web API comes with two out-of-the-box media formatters: JsonMediaTypeFormatter and XmlMediaTypeFormatter, for JSON and XML media types, respectively. They both derive from MediaTypeFormatter. It is possible to create your own media formatter to handle other media types. To create a media formatter, you must derive from the MediaTypeFormatter class or the BufferedMediaTypeFormatter class. The BufferedMediaTypeFormatter class also derives from the MediaTypeFormatter class, but it wraps the asynchronous read and write methods inside synchronous blocking methods. Deriving from the BufferedMediaTypeFormatter class and implementing your custom media formatter is easier, because you do not have to deal with asynchrony, but the downside is that the methods are blocking and can create performance bottlenecks in performance-demanding applications that lend themselves well for asynchrony.

One of the benefits of using HTTP service is reachability. The consumer of your service can be from any platform. In a typical enterprise, a variety of technologies both new and legacy co-exist and work together to meet the demands of the business. Though XML or JSON parsing is available in most platforms, there are times when you will want to go back to the last century and create a fixed-width text response for specific client applications such as one running in mainframe. A fixed-width text file contains fields in specific positions within each line. These files are the most common in mainframe data feeds going both directions, because it is easier to load them into a mainframe dataset for further processing. In this exercise, you will create a fixed-width text response by creating a custom media formatter, for the client application running in a mainframe to perform a GET and load the response into a dataset.

The fixed-width text response we create will take this format: Employee ID will be 6 digits and zero-prefixed, followed by the first name and the last name. Both the names will have a length of 20 characters padded with trailing spaces to ensure the length. Thus, a record for an employee John Human with ID of 12345 will be 012345John<followed by 16 spaces>Human<followed by 15 spaces>.

1. You can use an existing ASP.NET Web API project or create a new one.

2. If it does not already exist, create a new model class Employee, as shown in Listing 3-11.

Listing 3-11. The Employee Class – The Basic Version with Three Properties

```
public class Employee
{
        public int Id { get; set; }
        public string FirstName { get; set; }
        public string LastName { get; set; }
}
```

3. Create a new ApiController with the name EmployeesController and add the action method shown in Listing 3-10 earlier. In the example I use some hard-coded data to return, for the purpose of illustration. If you use the EmployeesController class from an existing project, ensure that the controller class has the static list and the Get action method, as shown in Listing 3-12.

Listing 3-12. The Action Method to Get Employee Data

```
public class EmployeesController : ApiController
{
    private static IList<Employee> list = new List<Employee>()
    {
        new Employee()
        {
            Id = 12345, FirstName = "John", LastName = "Human"
        },

        new Employee()
        {
            Id = 12346, FirstName = "Jane", LastName = "Public"
        },

        new Employee()
        {
            Id = 12347, FirstName = "Joseph", LastName = "Law"
        }
    };
```

```
    // GET api/employees
    public IEnumerable<Employee> Get()
    {
        return list;
    }
}
```

4. Create a new class `FixedWidthTextMediaFormatter`, deriving from `MediaTypeFormatter`, as shown in Listing 3-13.

   a. In the constructor, add UTF-8 and UTF-16 to the `SupportedEncodings` collection. By doing so, you can support two charsets for the clients to choose from.

   b. Add the media type of `text/plain` to the `SupportedMediaTypes` collection. This will let conneg pick our formatter when a client asks for this media type.

   c. We will not support requests coming in as fixed-width text for this exercise, so return `false` in the `CanReadType` method.

   d. For serialization, we support only a list of employees (`IEnumerable<Employee>`). You will check for this list in the `CanWriteType` method.

   e. The `WriteToStreamAsync` method does the actual serialization by formatting a string in accordance with the width specifications for the fields. Call the `SelectCharacterEncoding` method from the `MediaTypeFormatter` base class to get the most appropriate encoding and use it to create the `StreamWriter`.

Listing 3-13. A Custom Media Type Formatter Class

```
using System;
using System.Collections.Generic;
using System.IO;
using System.Net;
using System.Net.Http;
using System.Net.Http.Formatting;
using System.Net.Http.Headers;
using System.Text;
using System.Threading.Tasks;
using HelloWebApi.Models;

public class FixedWidthTextMediaFormatter : MediaTypeFormatter
{
    public FixedWidthTextMediaFormatter()
    {
        SupportedEncodings.Add(Encoding.UTF8);
        SupportedEncodings.Add(Encoding.Unicode);

        SupportedMediaTypes.Add(new MediaTypeHeaderValue("text/plain"));
    }

    public override bool CanReadType(Type type)
    {
        return false;
    }
```

```csharp
public override bool CanWriteType(Type type)
{
    return typeof(IEnumerable<Employee>)
                                    .IsAssignableFrom(type);
}

public override async Task WriteToStreamAsync(
                        Type type,
                            object value,
                                Stream stream,
                                    HttpContent content,
                                        TransportContext transportContext)
{
    using (stream)
    {
        Encoding encoding = SelectCharacterEncoding(content.Headers);

        using (var writer = new StreamWriter(stream, encoding))
        {
            var employees = value as IEnumerable<Employee>;
            if (employees != null)
            {
                foreach (var employee in employees)
                {
                    await writer.WriteLineAsync(
                                String.Format("{0:000000}{1,-20}{2,-20}",
                                            employee.Id,
                                                employee.FirstName,
                                                    employee.LastName));
                }

                await writer.FlushAsync();
            }
        }
    }
}
```

■ **Note** There is no real need for this fixed-width formatter to derive from MediaTypeFormatter; you can equally well derive from BufferedMediaTypeFormatter. Here I derive from MediaTypeFormatter and use the asynchronous methods with await only for the purpose of illustration. Using asynchronous methods for CPU-bound operations has no benefit and creates only overhead.

---

5. Register the formatter in the Register method of WebApiConfig in the App_Start folder, as shown in Listing 3-14.

Listing 3-14. Adding the Formatter to the Collection

```
config.Formatters.Add(
                new FixedWidthTextMediaFormatter());
```

6. Rebuild the solution and make a GET request to `http://localhost:55778/api/` `employees` from the Composer tab of Fiddler. Remember to include `Accept: text/plain`, to indicate to the Web API that you would like the fixed-width format.

Request	GET `http://localhost:55778/api/employees` HTTP/1.1 Host: localhost:55778 **Accept: text/plain**
Response	HTTP/1.1 200 OK Content-Type: text/plain; charset=utf-8 Date: Wed, 03 Apr 2013 05:39:17 GMT Content-Length: 144 012345John Human 012346Jane Public 012347Joseph Law

7. Make a GET to `http://localhost:55778/api/employees` from Internet Explorer by typing the URI in the address bar. The content downloaded is JSON. The reason for this behavior is that IE specified `Accept: text/html, application/xhtml+xml, */*`. Because of the `*/*`, ASP.NET Web API picks up the first formatter in the collection that can serialize `IEnumerable<Employee>`. This happens to be `JsonMediaTypeFormatter` and not our custom formatter, which we added to the end of the formatters collection.

8. It is possible to conneg based on query string, as we saw in Exercise 3.3. In the preceding steps, we simply added the formatter into the formatter collection. It is also possible to specify media type mapping and then add it to the `Formatters` collection. Comment out the line you added to the `WebApiConfig` class:

```
config.Formatters.Add(new FixedWidthTextMediaFormatter());
```

9. Add the code shown in Listing 3-15 to the `Register` method of `WebApiConfig` in the App_Start folder.

Listing 3-15. Adding Media Type Mapping

```
var fwtMediaFormatter = new FixedWidthTextMediaFormatter();

fwtMediaFormatter.MediaTypeMappings.Add(
    new QueryStringMapping("frmt", "fwt",
        new MediaTypeHeaderValue("text/plain")));

config.Formatters.Add(fwtMediaFormatter);
```

10. With this change, if you request a GET for `http://localhost:55778/api/` `employees?frmt=fwt` from Internet Explorer, ASP.NET Web API will return the response in text/plain. This technique of using query string media type mapping will be especially handy when the client does not have the ability to add the `Accept` header to the request message.

3.9 Extending an Out-of-Box Media Formatter

In this exercise you will piggyback on an out-of-box media formatter, in this case `JsonMediaTypeFormatter`, and extend its functionality. JavaScript Object Notation (JSON), as the name indicates, is based on the JavaScript language for representing objects. For example, consider the following JSON:

```
{"Id":12345,"FirstName":"John","LastName":"Human"}
```

It is nothing but the JSON representation of the resource, which is an employee of ID 12345. By wrapping the preceding JSON with a function call around it—that is, by padding it—we can have JSON interpreted as object literals in JavaScript. For example, by wrapping the preceding JSON with a function named `callback`, we can have the payload evaluated as JavaScript, as shown in Listing 3-16. If you copy-and-paste this code into a view of an ASP. NET MVC application, for example, and navigate to the corresponding URI, an alert box with the data from JSON is displayed.

Listing 3-16. Using Padded JSON

```
@section scripts{
<script type="text/javascript">
    $(document).ready(function () {
            callback({ "Id": 12345, "FirstName": "Johny", "LastName": "Human" });
    });

    callback = function (employee) {
        alert(employee.Id + ' ' + employee.FirstName + ' ' + employee.LastName);
    };
</script>
}
```

This technique is used to get around the restriction imposed by browsers called the *same-origin policy*. This policy allows JavaScript running on the web page originating from a site (defined by a combination of scheme, hostname, and port number) to access the methods and properties of another page originating from the same site but prevents access to pages originating from different sites. For example, the URI for an employee resource that we have been using all along is `http://localhost:55778/api/employees/12345`. If you try to access this from the JavaScript running in a page from another ASP.NET MVC application, say `http://localhost:30744/Home/Index`, the browser will not allow the call. This is in accordance with the same-origin policy.

One of the ways to get around this restriction is to make use of the leniency shown towards `<script>` tags to get the script content from anywhere. Consider the following JavaScript tag:

```
<script type="text/javascript" src="http://localhost:55778/api/employees/12345"></script>
```

This can be used from `http://localhost:30744/Home/Index`. JSON will be retrieved, but the problem is that the downloaded JSON can only be evaluated as a JavaScript block. To interpret the data as object literals, a variable assignment is needed, and because we wrap a function call around it and have the function already defined in the `/Home/Index` view, the data becomes a JavaScript literal and the function with the same name as that of the wrapping function can access the data. That is exactly what I showed you in Listing 3-14.

Now, I'll show you the steps by which browsers enforce the same-origin policy, so you'll understand how we can get around the restriction by using JSONP. Most importantly, I'll show you how to extend `JsonMediaTypeFormatter`, the formatter responsible for producing the JSON, to produce JSONP. Remember that ASP.NET Web API can only produce JSON out of the box. For this purpose, we do not write a custom formatter from scratch. We just extend the existing one because we need to only create the wrapping. The actual JSON payload generation is something we do not want to worry about, and so we let `JsonMediaTypeFormatter` take care of that.

The objective of this exercise is only to demonstrate subclassing an out-of-box formatter, not to solve the same-origin policy restriction. That policy is there for security reasons. You will not want to allow the script executing in a page to which you have browsed to access pages from sites you do not trust or will never go to. When you must work around the restriction, there are better techniques available, such as Cross-Origin Resource Sharing (CORS). I have covered CORS in another Apress book, *Pro ASP.NET Web API Security* (Apress, 2013). Also, there is a great resource available in the form of Thinktecture.IdentityModel that supports CORS. In fact, that will be part of ASP.NET Web API VNext. At the time of writing of this book, this functionality is available in the System.Web.Cors namespace in the nightly builds.

1. As with other exercises, you can create a new ASP.NET Web API project and implement an action method to handle GET or use the project from Exercise 1.2.

2. I assume the URI for the employee resource with ID of 12345 is http://localhost:55778/api/employees/12345. If you run in a different port, you will need to adjust the port number.

3. Create a new ASP.NET MVC project in the same solution. The name does not matter, so use any name of your liking, say **TestMvcApplication**. You can choose the Web API template or other MVC templates as well. We just need an MVC controller. Ensure that Razor is selected as the view engine when you create the new project.

4. Go to the Home/Index view and replace the generated code with the code shown in Listing 3-17. Remember to replace the port 55778 with the actual port that your ASP.NET Web API application runs on.

Listing 3-17. The Home/Index View

```
@section scripts{
<script type="text/javascript">
    $(document).ready(function () {
        $('#search').click(function () {
            $('#employee').empty();

            $.getJSON("http://localhost:55778/api/employees/12345", function (employee) {
                var content = employee.Id + ' ' + employee.FirstName + ' ' + employee.LastName;
                $('#employee').append($('<li/>', { text: content }));
            });
        });
    });
</script>
}
<div>
        <div>
                <h1>Employees Listing</h1>
                <input id="search" type="button" value="Get" />
        </div>
        <div>
                <ul id="employee" />
        </div>
</div>
```

5. In the Solution Explorer of Visual Studio, right-click the TestMvcApplication project and select Debug ➤ Start New Instance. This will open up Internet Explorer. Assuming your MVC application runs on port 30744, the URI will be http://localhost:30744.

6. If you click Get, nothing happens; the Ajax call does not go through. The browser is enforcing the same-origin policy. The page that is part of the domain localhost:30744 is not allowed to access a resource in localhost:55778.

7. Now that we are on this view, change the URI used by getJSON to http://localhost:55778/api/employees/12345?frmt=jsonp&callback=?. It will not work yet either, but as we go through the remaining steps of this exercise, we will get it working.

8. Create a new class JsonpMediaTypeFormatter, deriving from JsonMediaTypeFormatter, as shown in Listing 3-18, in the ASP.NET Web API project. The media type that the formatter will support is application/javascript. The name of the wrapper function will be made available to us in the request as a query string parameter with a name of callback. In the code I've made sure the media types and media type mappings from the base class are not inherited, by clearing out these collections. I do not intend this formatter to handle application/json. I leave that to the out-of-box JsonMediaTypeFormatter. I add a new media type query string mapping so that a client can explicitly ask for JSONP. This should explain why we changed the URI in the previous step to http://localhost:55778/api/employees/12345?frmt=jsonp&callback=?. We do not supply the wrapping function name, because jQuery will do that dynamically at run time. We only need to have a placeholder in the form of a question mark.

Listing 3-18. The JsonpMediaTypeFormatter Class (Incomplete)

```
using System;
using System.IO;
using System.Linq;
using System.Net;
using System.Net.Http;
using System.Net.Http.Formatting;
using System.Net.Http.Headers;
using System.Text;
using System.Threading.Tasks;
using System.Web;

public class JsonpMediaTypeFormatter : JsonMediaTypeFormatter
{
    private const string JAVASCRIPT_MIME = "application/javascript";

    private string queryStringParameterName = "callback";
    private string Callback { get; set; }
    private bool IsJsonp { get; set; }

    public JsonpMediaTypeFormatter()
    {
        // Do not want to inherit supported media types or
        // media type mappings of JSON
        SupportedMediaTypes.Clear();
        MediaTypeMappings.Clear();

        // We have our own!
        SupportedMediaTypes.Add(new MediaTypeHeaderValue(JAVASCRIPT_MIME));
```

```
                    MediaTypeMappings.Add(new QueryStringMapping(
                                          "frmt", "jsonp", JAVASCRIPT_MIME));
       }

       // other members go here
}
```

9. Override the CanReadType method and return false to indicate that our formatter cannot be used for deserialization of any types, as shown in Listing 3-19.

Listing 3-19. The CanReadType Method

```
public override bool CanReadType(Type type)
{
            return false;
}
```

10. Override the GetPerRequestFormatterInstance method, as shown in Listing 3-20. The DefaultContentNegotiator calls this method after it selects a formatter. This method gives us the opportunity to inspect the HttpRequestMessage object. It checks for two things: (1) the HTTP method and (2) the name of the wrapping function passed by jQuery in the query string. The code wraps the JSON response with this callback function name. Here is the most important point. Since we need the callback function to be available to the other two methods of the class, we must store the callback at the class level, making it stateful. The out-of-box formatters are stateless, and the same instance can handle multiple requests. Since this formatter is stateful, we return a new instance every time. Only if the HTTP method is GET and there is a callback function name available to us will the IsJsonp property of the new formatter instance be set to true.

Listing 3-20. The GetPerRequestFormatterInstance Method

```
public override MediaTypeFormatter GetPerRequestFormatterInstance(
                                   Type type,
                                        HttpRequestMessage request,
                                             MediaTypeHeaderValue mediaType)
{
    bool isGet = request != null && request.Method == HttpMethod.Get;

    string callback = String.Empty;

    if (request.RequestUri != null)
    {
        callback = HttpUtility.ParseQueryString(
                                 request.RequestUri.Query)
                                      [queryStringParameterName];
    }

    // Only if this is an HTTP GET and there is a callback do we consider
    // the request a valid JSONP request and service it. If not,
    // fallback to JSON
    bool isJsonp = isGet && !String.IsNullOrEmpty(callback);
```

```
        // Returning a new instance since callback must be stored at the
        // class level for WriteToStreamAsync to output. Our formatter is not
        // stateless, unlike the out-of-box formatters.
        return new JsonpMediaTypeFormatter() { Callback = callback, IsJsonp = isJsonp };
    }
```

11. Override the SetDefaultContentHeaders method, as shown in Listing 3-21. By the time execution comes to our media formatter, the DefaultContentNegotiator has already chosen the formatter, and the media type we support (application/javascript) will be set in the Content-Type response header. However, when we must fall back to regular JSON, as when the HTTP method is not GET or the callback function is not passed, we must override this behavior and restore the Content-Type to application/json. That is exactly what this method does. DefaultMediaType corresponds to application/json, and we get this by virtue of inheritance. In addition to setting the media type, we ensure that the charset chosen by DefaultContentNegotiator is set in the Content-Type header, provided the charset is one that we support. If it is not, we choose the first of the available encodings. Note that the encoding supported by our class and the base class need not be the same. We can add a new encoding specifically for JSONP. You'll learn more about charset encoding in Chapter 4.

Listing 3-21. The SetDefaultContentHeaders Method

```
public override void SetDefaultContentHeaders(Type type,

HttpContentHeaders headers,

MediaTypeHeaderValue mediaType)
{
    base.SetDefaultContentHeaders(type, headers, mediaType);

    if (!this.IsJsonp)
    {
        // Fallback to JSON content type
        headers.ContentType = DefaultMediaType;

        // If the encodings supported by us include the charset of the
        // authoritative media type passed to us, we can take that as the charset
        // for encoding the output stream. If not, pick the first one from
        // the encodings we support.
        if (this.SupportedEncodings.Any(e => e.WebName.Equals(mediaType.CharSet,
                                        StringComparison.OrdinalIgnoreCase)))
            headers.ContentType.CharSet = mediaType.CharSet;
        else
            headers.ContentType.CharSet = this.SupportedEncodings.First().WebName;
    }

}
```

12. Override the WriteToStreamAsync method, as shown in Listing 3-22. For JSONP, we write the callback wrapping function to the stream first and call the base class method to let it write the JSON, followed by the closing bracket. If we need to fall back to JSON, we write nothing additional to the stream and leave it fully to the base class. It's important point here to use the correct encoding that was selected in the previous step to create the StreamWriter instance. Otherwise, what is sent back in the Content-Type header may not match how the response is encoded, especially when an encoding other than the default is picked by the DefaultContentNegotiator based on the user request.

Listing 3-22. The WriteToStreamAsync Method

```
public override async Task WriteToStreamAsync(Type type, object value,
                                              Stream stream,
                                                  HttpContent content,
                                                  TransportContext transportContext)
{
    using (stream)
    {
        if (this.IsJsonp) // JSONP
        {
            Encoding encoding = Encoding.GetEncoding
                                        (content.Headers.ContentType.CharSet);

            using (var writer = new StreamWriter(stream, encoding))
            {
                writer.Write(this.Callback + "(");
                await writer.FlushAsync();

                await base.WriteToStreamAsync(type, value, stream, content,
                                                            transportContext);

                writer.Write(")");
                await writer.FlushAsync();
            }
        }
        else // fallback to JSON
        {
            await base.WriteToStreamAsync(type, value, stream, content,
                                                        transportContext);
            return;
        }
    }
}
```

13. Add the media formatter to the formatters collection in the Register method of WebApiConfig in the App_Start folder:

```
config.Formatters.Add(new JsonpMediaTypeFormatter());
```

14. Since `JsonpMediaTypeFormatter` does not handle application/json, there is no need to insert this as the first formatter in the collection. Because we have implemented a query string media type mapping for application/javascript, passing frmt=jsonp in the query string in addition to the callback will ensure that the `DefaultContentNegotiator` picks up our JSONP formatter.

15. With all these changes in place, rebuild the solution and go to `http://localhost:30744` (the MVC application's home page). Click on Get. It should now pull the employee data and display it. By making a GET to `http://localhost:55778/api/employees/12345?frmt=jsonp&callback=?`, we request the JSONP representation of the employee resource with ID 12345. Since it is JavaScript, the same-origin policy restrictions do not apply. jQuery's getJSON does the rest, and we are able to read the employee data.

ACCEPT HEADER AND AJAX (XMLHTTPREQUEST)

The query string media type mapping will not be needed for all browsers. For example, I use Internet Explorer 9.0.8112. When compatibility view is disabled, it correctly sends the Accept header in the request as Accept: application/javascript, */*;q=0.8. By sending application/javascript, it makes sure our formatter of JsonpMediaTypeFormatter is chosen by DefaultContentNegotiator.

Run Internet Explorer and go to `http://localhost:30744`. Now press F12. In the Developer Tools, select the Network tab and choose Start Capturing ➤ Get. In the capture, go to detailed view and select the Request Headers tab to see the Accept header. I covered the F12 Developer Tools in Chapter 2.

In browsers that do not send the required Accept header, frmt=jsonp must be sent in the query string. When you enable compatibility view with Internet Explorer, it starts sending Accept: */* so that DefaultContentNegotiator will choose JsonMediaTypeFormatter (without a *p*) by default. By passing frmt=jsonp in the query string, we ensure that our formatter is chosen regardless of the Accept header.

3.10 Controlling Which Members Are Serialized

By default, `JsonMediaTypeFormatter` and `XmlMediaTypeFormatter` use the Json.NET library and `DataContractSerializer` class, respectively, to perform serialization.

- The public fields and properties are serialized by default with both Json.NET and `DataContractSerializer`.

- The read-only properties (properties with only the getter) are serialized by Json.NET but not by `DataContractSerializer`. The Compensation property of the Employee class shown in Listing 3-21 earlier is an example of this.

- The private, protected, and internal members are not serialized in either case.

3.10.1 Blacklisting Members

To prevent a property or field from being serialized, apply the `IgnoreDataMember` attribute. This works with both Json. NET and `DataContractSerializer`. To have only Json.NET ignore, apply the `JsonIgnore` attribute, as shown in Listing 3-23. To use `IgnoreDataMember`, add a reference to the `System.Runtime.Serialization` assembly.

Listing 3-23. The Employee Class with Json.NET Attributes

```csharp
using System;
using System.Runtime.Serialization;
using Newtonsoft.Json;

public class Employee
{
    public int Id { get; set; }

    public string FirstName { get; set; }

    public string LastName { get; set; }

    public decimal Compensation
    {
        get
        {
            return 5000.00M;
        }
    }

    [JsonIgnore] // Ignored only by Json.NET
    public string Title { get; set; }

    [IgnoreDataMember] // Ignored by both Json.NET and DCS
    public string Department { get; set; }
}
```

3.10.2 Whitelisting Members

To prevent all the members from being serialized by default, apply the DataContract attribute at the class level. Then apply the DataMember attribute to only those members (including the private ones) that you want to be serialized. This approach works with both Json.NET and DataContractSerializer. See Listing 3-24.

Listing 3-24. The Employee Class with DataContract

```csharp
[DataContract]
public class Employee
{
    [DataMember]
    public int Id { get; set; }

    public string FirstName { get; set; } // Does not get serialized

    [DataMember]
    public string LastName { get; set; }

    [DataMember]
    public decimal Compensation
    {
        // Serialized with json.NET but fails with an exception in case of
```

```
        // DataContractSerializer, since set method is absent
        get
        {
            return 5000.00M;
        }
    }
}
```

3.11 Controlling How Members Are Serialized

ASP.NET Web API uses Json.NET and DataContractSerializer for serializing CLR objects into JSON and XML, respectively. For XML, you can use XMLSerializer instead of DataContractSerializer by setting the UseXmlSerializer property to true, as shown in the following line of code:

```
config.Formatters.XmlFormatter.UseXmlSerializer = true;
```

XMLSerializer gives you more control over the resulting XML. This is important if you must generate the XML in accordance with an existing schema. DataContractSerializer is comparatively faster and can handle more types but gives you less control over the resulting XML.

Json.NET and DataContractSerializer (specifically XMLSerializer) both have lots of knobs and switches to control the serialization output. I cover only a small subset here. You will need to refer to the respective documentation for more information.

3.11.1 Controlling Member Names

By default, the names of the members are used as-is while creating the serialized representation. For example, a property with name LastName and value of Human gets serialized as <LastName>Human</LastName> in case of XML and "LastName":"Human" in case of JSON. It is possible to change the names. In the case of Json.NET, we do this using JsonProperty with a PropertyName, as shown in Listing 3-25. In the case of DataContractSerializer, DataMember can be used but will have no effect unless DataContract is used at the class level, which forces you to apply the DataMember attribute for all the individual members.

Listing 3-25. The Employee Class with Member Names Customized for Serialization

```
public class Employee
{
    [JsonProperty(PropertyName="Identifier")]
    public int Id { get; set; }

    public string FirstName { get; set; }

    [DataMember(Name="FamilyName")] // No effect unless DataContract used
    public string LastName { get; set; }
}
```

3.11.2 Prettifying JSON

In C#, the general coding standard is to use Pascal-casing for property names. In JavaScript and hence JSON, the standard is camel-casing. You can retain the C# standards and yet have the JSON camel-cased. It is also possible to get the JSON indented. Add the code shown in Listing 3-26 to the Register method of WebApiConfig in the App_Start folder.

Listing 3-26. Camel-Casing and Indenting JSON

```
config.Formatters.JsonFormatter
                      .SerializerSettings.Formatting = Formatting.Indented;

config.Formatters.JsonFormatter
                      .SerializerSettings.ContractResolver = new
                                           CamelCasePropertyNamesContractResolver();
```

With this, if you make a GET to `http://localhost:55778/api/employees`, the resulting JSON is well-formatted!

```
[
  {
    "id": 12345,
    "firstName": "John",
    "lastName": "Human"
  },
  {
    "id": 12346,
    "firstName": "Jane",
    "lastName": "Public"
  },
  {
    "id": 12347,
    "firstName": "Joseph",
    "lastName": "Law"
  }
]
```

3.12 Returning Only a Subset of Members

Often you'll need to return only a subset of the properties of a class; this exercise shows how to do that. Take the case of the Employee class shown in Listing 3-27.

Listing 3-27. The Employee Class with Five Properties

```
public class Employee
{
    public int Id { get; set; }

    public string FirstName { get; set; }

    public string LastName { get; set; }

    public decimal Compensation { get; set; }

    public int Department { get; set; }
}
```

Suppose you need to return only two properties, say Id and a new property called Name, which is nothing but FirstName and LastName concatenated. One option is to create a new type and then create and return instances of that type. Another option, which I show here, is to use anonymous types.

One of the great features of C# is the ability to create new types on the fly using anonymous types. They are essentially compiler-generated types that are not explicitly declared. Anonymous types typically are used in the select clause of a query expression to return a subset of the properties from each object in the source sequence.

To try anonymous types for yourself, create a new ApiController, as shown in Listing 3-28.

Listing 3-28. Employees Controller Returning Anonymous Type

```
public class EmployeesController : ApiController
{
    private static IList<Employee> list = new List<Employee>()
    {
        new Employee()
        {
            Id = 12345, FirstName = "John", LastName = "Human"
        },

        new Employee()
        {
            Id = 12346, FirstName = "Jane", LastName = "Public"
        },

        new Employee()
        {
            Id = 12347, FirstName = "Joseph", LastName = "Law"
        }
    };

    public HttpResponseMessage Get()
    {
        var values = list.Select(e => new
                        {
                            Identifier = e.Id,
                            Name = e.FirstName + " " + e.LastName
                        });

        var response = new HttpResponseMessage(HttpStatusCode.OK)
        {
            Content = new ObjectContent(values.GetType(),
                                    values,
                                        Configuration.Formatters.JsonFormatter)
        };

        return response;
    }
}
```

This code explicitly returns `ObjectContent` from the `Get` action method, using the anonymous type that we create in the select clause. The important point to note here is that `XmlFormatter` cannot handle anonymous types. We pass the `JsonFormatter` while creating the `ObjectContent` instance and make sure conneg result is not used and any formatter other than `JsonFormatter` is not picked for serialization. Here is the JSON output:

```
[
  {
    "Identifier": 12345,
    "Name": "John Human"
  },
  {
    "Identifier": 12346,
    "Name": "Jane Public"
  },
  {
    "Identifier": 12347,
    "Name": "Joseph Law"
  }
]
```

Summary

From the perspective of ASP.NET Web API, serialization is the process of translating a .NET Common Language Runtime (CLR) type into a format that can be transmitted over HTTP. The format is either JSON or XML, out of the box. A media type formatter, which is an object of type `MediaTypeFormatter`, performs the serialization in the ASP.NET Web API pipeline. The out-of-box media formatters that produce JSON and XML are respectively `JsonMediaTypeFormatter` and `XmlMediaTypeFormatter`, both deriving from `MediaTypeFormatter`.

It is possible to create your own media formatter to handle media types other than JSON and XML. To create a media formatter, you must derive from the `MediaTypeFormatter` class or the `BufferedMediaTypeFormatter` class. The `BufferedMediaTypeFormatter` class also derives from the `MediaTypeFormatter` class, but it wraps the asynchronous read and write methods inside synchronous blocking methods.

The process through which the `MediaTypeFormatter` is chosen is called *Content Negotiation*. The `System.Net.Http.Formatting.DefaultContentNegotiator` class implements the default content negotiation algorithm in the `Negotiate` method that it implements, as part of implementing the `IContentNegotiatior` interface. In the world of HTTP, a resource can have one or more representations. The Web API indicates how a resource is represented in the response through the `Content-Type` response header. The `Accept` request header can be used by a client to indicate the set of preferred representations for the resource in the response. The `Accept` request header and media type mappings are important in the process of content negotiation.

ASP.NET Web API uses Json.NET and `DataContractSerializer` for serializing CLR objects into JSON and XML respectively. For XML, you can opt for `XMLSerializer` instead of `DataContractSerializer` by setting the `UseXmlSerializer` property to true. `XMLSerializer` gives you more control over how you want the resulting XML to be. This is important if you must generate the XML in accordance with an existing schema. `DataContractSerializer` is comparatively faster and can handle more types but gives you less control over the resulting XML.

■ ■ ■

CHAPTER 4

Customizing Response

Request for Comments (RFC) 2616 defines content negotiation *as "the process of selecting the best representation for a given response when there are multiple representations available."* RFC also states *"this is not called **format negotiation**, because the alternate representations may be of the same media type, but use different capabilities of that type, be in different languages, etc."* The term *negotiation* is used because the client indicates its preferences. A client sends a list of options with a quality factor specified against each option, indicating the preference level. It is up to the service, which is Web API in our case, to fulfill the request in the way the client wants, respecting the client preferences. If Web API cannot fulfill the request the way the client has requested, it can switch to a default or send a 406 - Not Acceptable status code in the response. There are four request headers that play a major part in this process of content negotiation:

1. Accept, which is used by a client to indicate the preferences for the media types for the resource representation in the response, such as JSON (application/json) or XML (application/xml).

2. Accept-Charset, which is used by a client to indicate the preferences for the character sets, such as UTF-8 or UTF-16.

3. Accept-Encoding, which is used by a client to indicate the preferences for the content encoding, such as gzip or deflate.

4. Accept-Language, which is used by a client to indicate the preferences for the language, such as en-us or fr-fr.

Content negotiation is not just about choosing the media type for the resource representation in the response. It is also about the language, character set, and encoding. Chapter 3 covered content negotiation related to the media type, in which the Accept header plays a major role. This chapter covers content negotiation related to language, character set, and encoding.

4.1 Negotiating Character Encoding

Simply put, character encoding denotes how characters—letters, digits and other symbols—are represented as bits and bytes for storage and communication. The HTTP request header Accept-Charset can be used by a client to indicate how the response message can be encoded. ASP.NET Web API supports UTF-8 and UTF-16 out of the box. The following are the steps to see the process of character-set negotiation in action.

1. Create a new ASP.NET MVC 4 project with a name of HelloWebApi using the Web API template.

2. Add the Employee class, as shown in Listing 4-1, to the Models folder.

Listing 4-1. The Employee Class

```
public class Employee
{
    public int Id { get; set; }
    public string FirstName { get; set; }
    public string LastName { get; set; }
}
```

3. Modify the Register method in WebApiConfig, in the App_Start folder, as shown in Listing 4-2.

Listing 4-2. Supported Encodings

```
public static class WebApiConfig
{
    public static void Register(HttpConfiguration config)
    {
        config.Routes.MapHttpRoute(
            name: "DefaultApi",
            routeTemplate: "api/{controller}/{id}",
            defaults: new { id = RouteParameter.Optional }
        );

        foreach (var encoding in config.Formatters.JsonFormatter.SupportedEncodings)
        {
            System.Diagnostics.Trace.WriteLine(encoding.WebName);
        }
    }
}
```

4. Rebuild the solution and press F5 to run the application from Visual Studio. You will see that the code prints utf-8 followed by utf-16 in the Output window of Visual Studio. UTF-8 and UTF-16 are the character encodings supported by ASP.NET Web API out of the box. UTF-8 is the default.

5. Add a new empty API controller with the name EmployeesController to your Web API project, as shown in Listing 4-3. You can directly copy and paste the Japanese characters into the class file and compile.

Listing 4-3. The EmployeesController Class

```
using System.Collections.Generic;
using System.Linq;
using System.Web.Http;
using HelloWebApi.Models;

public class EmployeesController : ApiController
{
    private static IList<Employee> list = new List<Employee>()
    {
```

```
        new Employee()
        {
            Id = 12345, FirstName = "John", LastName = "ようこそいらっしゃいました。"
        },

        new Employee()
        {
            Id = 12346, FirstName = "Jane", LastName = "Public"
        },

        new Employee()
        {
            Id = 12347, FirstName = "Joseph", LastName = "Law"
        }
    };

    public Employee Get(int id)
    {
        return list.First(e => e.Id == id);
    }
}
```

6. Fire up Fiddler and send a GET request from the Composer tab to the URI
   http://localhost:55778/api/employees/12345. Remember to replace the port 55778
   with the actual port that your application runs on.

7. The response returned is shown in Listing 4-4. Some of the headers are removed
   for brevity.

   Listing 4-4. Web API Response Showing Default Character Encoding

   ```
   HTTP/1.1 200 OK
   Content-Type: application/json; charset=utf-8
   Date: Fri, 29 Mar 2013 03:51:11 GMT
   Content-Length: 87

   {"Id":12345,"FirstName":"John","LastName":"ようこそいらっしゃいました。"}
   ```

8. ASP.NET Web API has returned the content encoded in UTF-8, which is the first element in
   the SupportedEncodings collection that we looped through and printed the members
   in Listing 4-2.

9. Change the request in the Request Headers text box as shown in Listing 4-5 and
   click Execute.

   Listing 4-5. Web API Request Asking for UTF-16

   ```
   Host: localhost:55778
   Accept-charset: utf-16
   ```

10. Web API returns the response shown in Listing 4-6. Some of the headers are removed for
    brevity. This time, the response is encoded in UTF-16. Because of this, the content-length
    has increased from 87 to 120.

Listing 4-6. Web API Response Encoded in UTF-16

```
HTTP/1.1 200 OK
Content-Type: application/json; charset=utf-16
Date: Fri, 29 Mar 2013 03:52:20 GMT
Content-Length: 120

{"Id":12345,"FirstName":"John","LastName":"ようこそいらっしゃいました。"}
```

11. Change the request in the Request Headers text box as shown in Listing 4-7 and click Execute.

Listing 4-7. Web API Request Asking for DBCS Character Encoding of Shift JIS

```
Host: localhost:55778
Accept-charset: shift_jis
```

12. Web API returns the response shown in Listing 4-8. Some of the headers are removed for brevity. Since Shift JIS is not supported out of the box, ASP.NET Web API reverts to the default encoding, which is UTF-8. This is negotiation in action.

Listing 4-8. Web API Response When Client Requested Shift JIS

```
HTTP/1.1 200 OK
Content-Type: application/json; charset=utf-8
Date: Fri, 29 Mar 2013 03:57:55 GMT
Content-Length: 87

{"Id":12345,"FirstName":"John","LastName":"ようこそいらっしゃいました。"}
```

4.2 Supporting DBCS Character Encoding (Shift JIS)

In this exercise, you will add support for a double-byte character set (DBCS) such as Shift JIS. The term *DBCS* refers to a character encoding where each character is encoded in two bytes. DBCS is typically applicable to oriental languages like Japanese, Chinese, Korean, and so on. Shift JIS (shift_JIS) is a character encoding for the Japanese language. Code page 932 is Microsoft's extension of Shift JIS.

Why bother with DBCS like Shift JIS when Unicode is there? The answer is that there are still legacy systems out there that do not support Unicode. Also, believe it or not, there are database administrators who are not willing to create Unicode databases, and there are still old and outdated IT administration policies that prohibit creation of databases in Unicode to save storage cost, even though storage prices have fallen to such a degree that this cost-saving point becomes moot. But there are still applications out there that do not handle Unicode!

1. Modify the Register method of the WebApiConfig class in the App_Start folder, as shown in Listing 4-9. The new line to be added is shown in bold type.

Listing 4-9. Enabling Shift JIS

```
using System.Text;
using System.Web.Http;

public static class WebApiConfig
{
```

```
    public static void Register(HttpConfiguration config)
    {
        config.Routes.MapHttpRoute(
            name: "DefaultApi",
            routeTemplate: "api/{controller}/{id}",
            defaults: new { id = RouteParameter.Optional }
        );

        config.Formatters.JsonFormatter
                        .SupportedEncodings
                            .Add(Encoding.GetEncoding(932));

        foreach (var encoding in config.Formatters.JsonFormatter.SupportedEncodings)
        {
            System.Diagnostics.Trace.WriteLine(encoding.WebName);
        }
    }
}
```

2. This code adds Shift JIS support to ASP.NET Web API on a per-formatter basis; it adds Shift JIS support only to `JsonFormatter`. It uses the `Encoding.GetEncoding` method to get the `Encoding` object corresponding to the code page of 932, which is Shift JIS.

3. Rebuild the solution in Visual Studio.

4. Retry the previous Shift JIS request. Change the request in the Request Headers text box, as shown in Listing 4-7 earlier, and click Execute. The following are the headers to be copy-pasted, for your easy reference.

```
Host: localhost:55778
Accept-charset: shift_jis
```

5. Web API returns the response shown in Listing 4-10. Some of the headers are removed for brevity. Now, the charset in the response is shown as `shift_jis`. Also, the content length is only 73 now, even less than we got with UTF-8.

Listing 4-10. Web API Response Encoded in Shift JIS

```
HTTP/1.1 200 OK
Content-Type: application/json; charset=shift_jis
Date: Fri, 29 Mar 2013 04:19:36 GMT
Content-Length: 73

{"Id":12345,"FirstName":"John","LastName":"ようこそいらっしゃいました。"}
```

6. Modify the static `list` in `EmployeesController` to update the last name of the employee with ID 12345 from ようこそいらっしゃいました。 to **Human**, as shown in Listing 4-11.

Listing 4-11. EmployeesController Modified to Remove Japanese Characters

```
public class EmployeesController : ApiController
{
    private static IList<Employee> list = new List<Employee>()
    {
        new Employee()
        {
            Id = 12345, FirstName = "John", LastName = "Human"
        },

        new Employee()
        {
            Id = 12346, FirstName = "Jane", LastName = "Public"
        },

        new Employee()
        {
            Id = 12347, FirstName = "Joseph", LastName = "Law"
        }
    };

    // Rest of the code goes here
}
```

4.3 Negotiating Content Encoding (Compression)

Content coding is the encoding transformation applied to an entity. It is primarily used to allow a response message to be compressed. The main objective of HTTP compression is to make better use of available bandwidth. Of course, this is achieved with a tradeoff in processing power. The HTTP response message is compressed before it is sent from the server, and the client indicates, in the request, its preference for the compression schema to be used. A client that does not support compression can opt out of it and receive an uncompressed response. The most common compression schemas are gzip and deflate. HTTP/1.1 specifies identity, which is the default encoding to denote the use of no transformation. These values are case-insensitive.

A client sends the compression schema values along with an optional quality factor value in the Accept-Encoding request header. The server (Web API) tries to satisfy the request to the best of its ability. If Web API can successfully encode the content, it indicates the compression schema in the response header Content-Encoding. Based on this, a client can decode the content. The default identity is used only in the request header of Accept-Encoding and not in the response Content-Encoding. Sending identity in Content-Encoding is same as sending nothing. In other words, the response is not encoded.

Table 4-1 shows a few sample Accept-Encoding request headers and the corresponding response details for an ASP.NET Web API that supports gzip and deflate compression schema in that order of preference.

Table 4-1. *Content Coding*

Accept-Encoding	Content-Encoding	Explanation
Accept-Encoding: gzip, deflate	Gzip	Both gzip and deflate default to a quality factor of 1. Since Web API prefers gzip, it will be chosen for content encoding.
Accept-Encoding: gzip;q=0.8, deflate	Deflate	deflate defaults to a quality factor of 1, which is greater than gzip.
Accept-Encoding: gzip, deflate;q=0	gzip	The client indicates deflate must not be used but gzip can be.
Accept-Encoding:	No encoding and Content-Encoding header will be absent.	Per HTTP/1.1, identity has to be used, and it means no encoding.
Accept-Encoding: *	gzip	The client indicates that Web API can use any encoding it supports.
Accept-Encoding: identity; q=0.5, *;q=0	No encoding and Content-Encoding header will be absent.	By specifying *; q=0, the client is indicating it does not like any encoding schemes. Since identity is also specified, Web API does not perform any encoding.
Accept-Encoding: zipper, *	gzip	The client prefers zipper, but Web API is not aware of any such scheme and does not support it. Since the client has specified the * character as well, Web API uses gzip.
Accept-Encoding: *;q=0	No encoding and Content-Encoding header will be absent. Status code will be 406 - Not Acceptable.	The client is specifically refusing all schemas, and by not including identity, it has left Web API no other choice but to respond with a 406.
Accept-Encoding: DeFlAtE	deflate	The client is basically asking for deflate but uses a mixture of upper- and lowercase letters. Field values are case-insensitive, as per HTTP/1.1.

The following exercise demonstrates the steps involved in building a Web API that supports gzip and deflate, and negotiating with the client, as described in the preceding table.

1. You can use the same project that you created with any of the previous exercises or you can create a new ASP.NET MVC 4 project using Web API template. I use the same project from the previous exercise.

2. Create a new class named EncodingSchema, as shown in Listing 4-12. The field supported is a dictionary with a key the same as the supported encoding scheme. Currently, there are only two of them: gzip and deflate. The value is a Func delegate that represents the method for creating and returning the stream object: GZipStream and DeflateStream respectively for gzip and deflate. The corresponding methods are GetGZipStream and GetDeflateStream.

Listing 4-12. EncodingSchema (Incomplete)

```
using System;
using System.Collections.Generic;
using System.IO;
```

```csharp
using System.IO.Compression;
using System.Linq;
using System.Net.Http.Headers;

public class EncodingSchema
{
    private const string IDENTITY = "identity";

    private IDictionary<string, Func<Stream, Stream>> supported =
                    new Dictionary<string, Func<Stream, Stream>>
                                    (StringComparer.OrdinalIgnoreCase);

    public EncodingSchema()
    {
        supported.Add("gzip", GetGZipStream);
        supported.Add("deflate", GetDeflateStream);
    }

    // rest of the class members go here
}
```

3. Add the two methods shown in Listing 4-13 to the class.

Listing 4-13. Methods to Get the Compression Streams

```csharp
public Stream GetGZipStream(Stream stream)
{
    return new GZipStream(stream, CompressionMode.Compress, true);
}

public Stream GetDeflateStream(Stream stream)
{
    return new DeflateStream(stream, CompressionMode.Compress, true);
}
```

4. Add another method, named GetStreamForSchema, for returning the Func delegate from the dictionary based on the schema passed in. For example, when the schema passed in is gzip, the Func<Stream, Stream> returned by this method corresponds to the GetGZipStream method that we defined in the previous step. See Listing 4-14.

Listing 4-14. GetStreamForSchema Method

```csharp
private Func<Stream, Stream> GetStreamForSchema(string schema)
{
    if (supported.ContainsKey(schema))
    {
        ContentEncoding = schema.ToLowerInvariant();
        return supported[schema];
    }

    throw new InvalidOperationException(String.Format("Unsupported encoding schema {0}",
                                                        schema));
}
```

5. Add a property named ContentEncoding and another method named GetEncoder, as shown in Listing 4-15. The ContentEncoding property is set by the GetEncoder method through the private setter. For the other classes, it is a read-only property. This property returns the value to be put into the Content-Encoding response header.

Listing 4-15. The ContentEncoding Property and the GetEncoder Method

```
public string ContentEncoding { get; private set; }

public Func<Stream, Stream> GetEncoder(
                        HttpHeaderValueCollection<StringWithQualityHeaderValue> list)
{
        // The following steps will walk you through
        // completing the implementation of this method
}
```

6. Add the code shown in Listing 4-16 to the GetEncoder method. If the incoming list is null or has a count of 0, no processing happens and a null is returned. The incoming list is of type HttpHeaderValueCollection<StringWithQualityHeaderValue>. Each element in this collection consists of the encoding scheme along with the quality value as requested by the client in the Accept-Encoding header. For example, Accept-Encoding: gzip;q=0.8, deflate will be represented by two elements in the collection: the first element with a Value of gzip and a Quality of 0.8 and the second element with a Value of deflate and a Quality of null. Quality is a nullable decimal.

Listing 4-16. The GetEncoder Method

```
if (list != null && list.Count > 0)
{
        // More code goes here
}

// Settle for the default, which is no transformation whatsoever
return null;
```

7. Add the code in Listing 4-17 to the if block for a list that is not null and has Count > 0. This is the part where negotiation happens, in the following steps. The end result of this process is that the encoding scheme to be used for encoding the response message is chosen.

   a. Order the incoming schemes in descending order of quality value. If quality value is absent, treat it as 1.0. Choose only the schemes that have either quality value absent or present and nonzero. Match these schemes against the list of supported schemes and get the first one. If this first scheme is not null, return the corresponding scheme's transformation function in the form of the Func delegate by calling the GetStreamForSchema method that we saw earlier. This method just returns a new Stream object corresponding to the chosen schema. Since we support only gzip and deflate, this Stream object could be either GZipStream or DeflateStream.

   b. If there is no match so far, see if there is a scheme of value * and quality factor of nonzero. If so, the client is willing to accept what the Web API supports. However, a client could specify a few exceptions through q=0 for specific schemes. Leave out those from the supported schemes and choose one as the scheme to use.

c. If there is still no match, try to use identity. For this, check whether the client has specifically refused to accept identity, by using q=0 against it. If so, fail the negotiation by throwing NegotiationFailedException.

d. As the final step, see if the client has refused all schemes through *;q=0 and has not explicitly asked for identity. In that case also, fail the negotiation by throwing NegotiationFailedException. This will send back the response status code of 406 - Not Acceptable.

e. If there is no match and we do not have to throw the NegotiationFailedException so far, just skip content encoding.

Listing 4-17. The GetEncoder Method Continuation

```
var headerValue = list.OrderByDescending(e => e.Quality ?? 1.0D)
                      .Where(e => !e.Quality.HasValue ||
                                  e.Quality.Value > 0.0D)
                      .FirstOrDefault(e => supported.Keys
                          .Contains(e.Value, StringComparer.OrdinalIgnoreCase));

// Case 1: We can support what client has asked for
if (headerValue != null)
    return GetStreamForSchema(headerValue.Value);

// Case 2: Client will accept anything we support except
// the ones explicitly specified as not preferred by setting q=0
if (list.Any(e => e.Value == "*" &&
        (!e.Quality.HasValue || e.Quality.Value > 0.0D)))
{
    var encoding = supported.Keys.Where(se =>
                        !list.Any(e =>
                                    e.Value.Equals(se, StringComparison.OrdinalIgnoreCase) &&
                                    e.Quality.HasValue &&
                                    e.Quality.Value == 0.0D))
                            .FirstOrDefault();
    if (encoding != null)
        return GetStreamForSchema(encoding);
}

// Case 3: Client specifically refusing identity
if (list.Any(e => e.Value.Equals(IDENTITY, StringComparison.OrdinalIgnoreCase) &&
        e.Quality.HasValue && e.Quality.Value == 0.0D))
{

    throw new NegotiationFailedException();
}

// Case 4: Client is not willing to accept any of the encodings
// we support and is not willing to accept identity
if (list.Any(e => e.Value == "*" &&
        (e.Quality.HasValue || e.Quality.Value == 0.0D)))
```

```
{
    if (!list.Any(e => e.Value.Equals(IDENTITY, StringComparison.OrdinalIgnoreCase)))
        throw new NegotiationFailedException();
}
```

8. Create a new Exception class:

```
public class NegotiationFailedException : ApplicationException { }.
```

It does not carry any additional information and just derives from ApplicationException.

9. Create a new class EncodedContent that derives from HttpContent, as shown in Listing 4-18.

   a. Accept an object of type HttpContent and the Func delegate in the constructor and store them in class-level fields. In the constructor, loop through the headers of the passed-in HttpContent object and add them to this instance.

   b. Override the TryComputeLength method and return false, since the length will not be known at the time method is called.

   c. Override the SerializeToStreamAsync method. Invoke the Func delegate and pass the resulting Stream object into the CopyToAsync method of the class-level field of type HttpContent.

   d. Note the usage of the await keyword to wait for the execution to return after the previous async call.

Listing 4-18. The EncodedContent Class

```
using System;
using System.IO;
using System.Linq;
using System.Net;
using System.Net.Http;
using System.Threading.Tasks;

public class EncodedContent : HttpContent
{
    private HttpContent content;
    private Func<Stream, Stream> encoder;

    public EncodedContent(HttpContent content, Func<Stream, Stream> encoder)
    {
        if (content != null)
        {
            this.content = content;
            this.encoder = encoder;

            content.Headers.ToList().ForEach(x =>
                        this.Headers.TryAddWithoutValidation(x.Key, x.Value));
        }
    }
```

```
    protected override bool TryComputeLength(out long length)
    {
        // Length not known at this time
        length = -1;
        return false;
    }

    protected async override Task SerializeToStreamAsync(Stream stream,
                                                TransportContext context)
    {
        using (content)
        {
            using (Stream encodedStream = encoder(stream))
            {
                await content.CopyToAsync(encodedStream);
            }
        }
    }
}
```

10. Create a new message handler named EncodingHandler, as shown in Listing 4-19. The
    message handler brings together the other classes we created in this exercise so far. It
    encodes the response and sets that as the current response content. It also adds the
    Content-Encoding response header. If NegotiationFailedException is thrown, it stops
    the processing by sending back a 406 - Not Acceptable status code.

Listing 4-19. The EncodingHandler

```
using System.Net;
using System.Net.Http;
using System.Threading;
using System.Threading.Tasks;

public class EncodingHandler : DelegatingHandler
{
    protected override async Task<HttpResponseMessage> SendAsync(
                            HttpRequestMessage request,
                                    CancellationToken cancellationToken)
    {
        var response = await base.SendAsync(request, cancellationToken);

        try
        {
            var schema = new EncodingSchema();
            var encoder = schema.GetEncoder(response.RequestMessage
                                            .Headers.AcceptEncoding);
```

```
            if (encoder != null)
            {
                response.Content = new EncodedContent(response.Content, encoder);

                // Add Content-Encoding response header
                response.Content.Headers.ContentEncoding.Add(schema.ContentEncoding);
            }
        }
        catch (NegotiationFailedException)
        {
            return request.CreateResponse(HttpStatusCode.NotAcceptable);
        }

        return response;
    }
}
```

11. Since it is preferable to encode the content as the final step of the ASP.NET Web API pipeline, we use the message handler. Hence, it is important to configure this as the first handler so that the response processing part runs last. See Listing 4-20, where I have added the message handler to the handlers collection in WebApiConfig in the App_Start folder. Since we use the same project as the previous exercises, you see additional lines of code in WebApiConfig, but those lines do not have any bearing on the outcome of this exercise.

Listing 4-20. Configuring a Message Handler

```
public static class WebApiConfig
{
    public static void Register(HttpConfiguration config)
    {
        config.Routes.MapHttpRoute(
            name: "DefaultApi",
            routeTemplate: "api/{controller}/{id}",
            defaults: new { id = RouteParameter.Optional }
        );

        config.Formatters.JsonFormatter
                            .SupportedEncodings
                                .Add(Encoding.GetEncoding(932));

        foreach (var encoding in config.Formatters.JsonFormatter.SupportedEncodings)
        {
            System.Diagnostics.Trace.WriteLine(encoding.WebName);
        }

        config.MessageHandlers.Add(new EncodingHandler());
        // Other handlers go here
    }
}
```

12. Rebuild the solution.

13. Make a GET request from Fiddler for `http://localhost:55778/api/employees/12345`. Use different values in the `Accept-Encoding` header and see how Web API responds. For example, in Figure 4-1 I used `Accept-Encoding: gzip;q=0.8, deflate`. Since `deflate` has the quality factor of 1 (default), it is chosen for encoding, as shown by Fiddler.

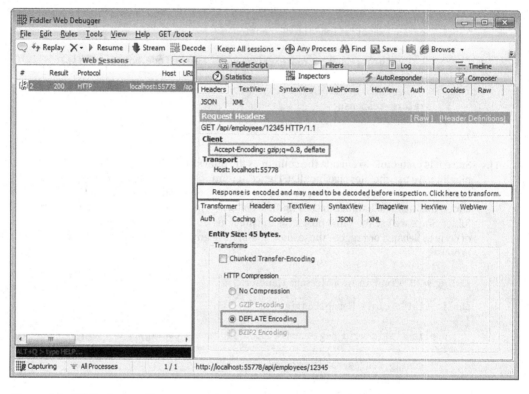

Figure 4-1. *Fiddler Responding to DEFLATE Encoding*

14. Now, make a GET request to `http://localhost:55778/api/employees`, keeping the `Accept-Encoding: gzip;q=0.8, deflate`. Note the `Content-Length`, which is 80. This could be different for you based on what you return from the action method.

15. Make the GET request one more time, the same as in the previous step but do not give the `Accept-Encoding` header. The `Content-Length` now is 155, since we have opted out of compression for this request. This is compression or content encoding in action.

16. Let us now see how `WebClient` handles content coding. Create a console application with a name of `TestConsoleApp`. The `Main` method is shown in Listing 4-21. Remember to replace the port 55778 with the actual port that your application runs on.

Listing 4-21. WebClient Requesting a Content Encoded Response

```
using System;
using System.Net;

class Program
{
    static void Main(string[] args)
    {
        string uri = "http://localhost:45379/api/employees/12345";

        using (WebClient client = new WebClient())
        {
            client.Headers.Add("Accept-Encoding", "gzip, deflate;q=0.8");
            var response = client.DownloadString(uri);

            Console.WriteLine(response);
        }
    }
}
```

17. The preceding code prints some gibberish, as expected. We ask for compressed response but download the response as string without decompressing the bytes.

    ¼   f «VòLQ²242610QrE,*.ñKIMU²RòEIESOQòI,<x"æ&æ)0; Jfàz2

18. To make WebClient work correctly, use the code shown in Listing 4-22. Instead of using WebClient directly, this code subclasses it and overrides the GetWebRequest method to set the AutomaticDecompression property of HttpWebRequest. That will ensure the response is automatically decompressed.

Listing 4-22. WebClient Decompressing the Response

```
class Program
{
    static void Main(string[] args)
    {
        string uri = "http://localhost.fiddler:55778/api/employees/12345";

        using (AutoDecompressionWebClient client = new AutoDecompressionWebClient())
        {
            client.Headers.Add("Accept-Encoding", "gzip, deflate;q=0.8");
            Console.WriteLine(client.DownloadString(uri));
        }
    }
}
```

```
class AutoDecompressionWebClient : WebClient
{
    protected override WebRequest GetWebRequest(Uri address)
    {
        HttpWebRequest request = base.GetWebRequest(address) as HttpWebRequest;
        request.AutomaticDecompression = DecompressionMethods.Deflate
                                      | DecompressionMethods.GZip;

        return request;
    }
}
```

4.4 Negotiating Language

The Accept-Language request header can be used by clients to indicate the set of preferred languages in the response. For example, Accept-Language: en-us, en-gb;q=0.8, en;q=0.7 indicates that the client prefers American English but when the server cannot support it, can accept British English. When that is also not supported, other types of English are also acceptable. The Accept-Language header is meant to specify the language preferences, but is commonly used to specify locale preferences as well.

4.4.1 Internationalizing the Messages to the User

In this exercise, you will internationalize the messages sent by Web API to the client. Based on the language preferences sent in the Accept-Language request header, CurrentUICulture of CurrentThread is set, and it will form the basis for language and local customization.

1. You can use the same project that you created with the previous exercise, as I do here, or you can create a new ASP.NET MVC 4 project using Web API template. If you create a new project, make sure you have the EmployeesController and the Employee classes copied into the project.

2. Create a new message handler, as shown in Listing 4-23. This message handler gets the language preferences from the Accept-Language request header and establishes the CurrentUICulture. As with the previous exercise, quality factor is taken into consideration while deciding on the language to be used. In this exercise, we support only two cultures: English, United States (en-us) and French, France (fr-fr).

Listing 4-23. CultureHandler

```
using System;
using System.Collections.Generic;
using System.Globalization;
using System.Linq;
using System.Net.Http;
using System.Threading;
using System.Threading.Tasks;
```

```
public class CultureHandler : DelegatingHandler
{
    private ISet<string> supportedCultures = new HashSet<string>() { "en-us", "en", "fr-fr", "fr" };

    protected override async Task<HttpResponseMessage> SendAsync(HttpRequestMessage request,
                                                    CancellationToken cancellationToken)
    {
        var list = request.Headers.AcceptLanguage;
        if (list != null && list.Count > 0)
        {
            var headerValue = list.OrderByDescending(e => e.Quality ?? 1.0D)
                                .Where(e => !e.Quality.HasValue ||
                                        e.Quality.Value > 0.0D)
                                .FirstOrDefault(e => supportedCultures
                                .Contains(e.Value, StringComparer.OrdinalIgnoreCase));

            // Case 1: We can support what client has asked for
            if (headerValue != null)
            {
                Thread.CurrentThread.CurrentUICulture =
                                CultureInfo.GetCultureInfo(headerValue.Value);
            }

            // Case 2: Client will accept anything we support except
            // the ones explicitly specified as not preferred by setting q=0
            if (list.Any(e => e.Value == "*" &&
                    (!e.Quality.HasValue || e.Quality.Value > 0.0D)))
            {
                var culture = supportedCultures.Where(sc =>
                                    !list.Any(e =>
                                            e.Value.Equals(sc, StringComparison.OrdinalIgnoreCase) &&
                                            e.Quality.HasValue &&
                                            e.Quality.Value == 0.0D))
                                        .FirstOrDefault();

                if (culture != null)
                    Thread.CurrentThread.CurrentUICulture =
                                CultureInfo.GetCultureInfo(culture);
            }
        }

        return await base.SendAsync(request, cancellationToken);
    }
}
```

3. Add the handler to the `Handlers` collection in `WebApiConfig` in the `App_Start` folder,
    as shown in Listing 4-24. Since we continue to use the same project from the previous
    exercises, you see additional lines of code in `WebApiConfig` but those lines do not have any
    bearing on the outcome of this exercise. Nonetheless, I have commented out those lines
    that are not necessary for this exercise in Listing 4-24.

Listing 4-24. Registration of CultureHandler

```
public static class WebApiConfig
{
    public static void Register(HttpConfiguration config)
    {
        config.Routes.MapHttpRoute(
            name: "DefaultApi",
            routeTemplate: "api/{controller}/{id}",
            defaults: new { id = RouteParameter.Optional }
        );

        //config.Formatters.JsonFormatter
        //                    .SupportedEncodings
        //                        .Add(Encoding.GetEncoding(932));

        //foreach (var encoding in config.Formatters.JsonFormatter.SupportedEncodings)
        //{
        //    System.Diagnostics.Trace.WriteLine(encoding.WebName);
        //}

        //config.MessageHandlers.Add(new EncodingHandler());

        config.MessageHandlers.Add(new CultureHandler());
    }
}
```

4. In the Visual Studio Solution Explorer, right-click the Web API project you are working on and select Add ➤ Add ASP.NET Folder ➤ App_GlobalResources.

5. Right click the App_GlobalResources folder created and select Add ➤ New Item. Select Resources File and give it a name of Messages.resx.

6. Add a new string with **Name** of NotFound and **Value** of Employee you are searching for does not exist. Save the resource file.

7. Duplicate the Message.resx by copying and pasting it into App_GlobalResourcesFolder. Rename the duplicate file Messages.fr-fr.resx.

8. Copy and paste the text **L'employé que vous recherchez n'existe pas** into **Value**. Save the file. Pardon my French, if it is not spot on. I just used a web translator for this!

9. Modify the Get method in EmployeesController, as shown in Listing 4-25.

Listing 4-25. Get Method Modified

```
public Employee Get(int id)
{
    var employee = list.FirstOrDefault(e => e.Id == id);
    if (employee == null)
    {
        var response = Request.CreateResponse(HttpStatusCode.NotFound,
                            new HttpError(Resources.Messages.NotFound));
```

```
            throw new HttpResponseException(response);
        }

        return employee;
    }
```

10. Rebuild the solution in Visual Studio.

11. Fire-up Fiddler and make a GET to an employee resource that does not exist, for example: http://localhost:55778/api/employees/**12399**.

12. Web API responds with a 404, as shown in Listing 4-26. Some headers are removed for brevity.

Listing 4-26. A 404 Response for English

```
HTTP/1.1 404 Not Found
Content-Type: application/json; charset=utf-8
Date: Mon, 01 Apr 2013 05:48:12 GMT
Content-Length: 59
```

{"Message":"**Employee you are searching for does not exist**"}

13. Now, make another GET request to the same URI, but this time include the request header Accept-Language: fr-fr. Web API once again responds with a 404, as shown in Listing 4-27. However, you can see that the message is in French now, in line with the language specified in the Accept-Language request header.

Listing 4-27. A 404 Response for French

```
HTTP/1.1 404 Not Found
Content-Type: application/json; charset=utf-8
Date: Mon, 01 Apr 2013 05:48:02 GMT
Content-Length: 57
```

{"Message":"**L'employé que vous recherchez n'existe pas**"}

INTERNATIONALIZING THE RESOURCE REPRESENTATION

It is possible to internationalize the resource representation as well. For example, take the case of a product. The product description, which is part of the response content, can be internationalized. When a GET request is made to /api/products/1234, as you return a Product object, you can retrieve the description of the product based on the Thread.CurrentThread.CurrentUICulture from your persistence store. In SQL terms, this means having an additional table with a primary key of the product ID and the culture and retrieving the description from this table through a join. If you use Entity Framework as the object-relational mapper, you can let it eager-load by using Include.

4.4.2 Internationalizing the Decimal Separators of Numbers

In this exercise, you will internationalize the numbers sent to the client, specifically the decimal separator. As with the previous exercise, we use the language preferences sent in the Accept-Language header. A number (whole and fractional) has different representations in different cultures. For example, one thousand two hundred thirty four and fifty six hundredths is 1,234.56 in the US (en-us), whereas it is 1.234,56 in some European countries like France (fr-fr).

When your application has to serialize an object into a persistence store and deserialize back, you can use the invariant culture to work around this inconsistency. However, as you serialize your objects to your clients through Web API, especially when the clients are distributed around the world, there is always a need to serialize respecting the locale preferred by the client. A client can explicitly ask Web API to send the response in a locale by sending the Accept-Language header.

1. You will use the same project that you worked with for Exercise 3.4.1. Open the project in Visual Studio.

2. Modify the CultureHandler so that Thread.CurrentThread.CurrentCulture is also set when you set Thread.CurrentThread.CurrentUICulture. You can add the line

```
Thread.CurrentThread.CurrentCulture = Thread.CurrentThread.CurrentUICulture;
```

immediately after the Thread.CurrentThread.CurrentUICulture is set (two places in the message handler). See Listing 4-28.

Listing 4-28. Setting CurrentCulture in the CultureHandler Class

```
public class CultureHandler : DelegatingHandler
{
    private ISet<string> supportedCultures = new HashSet<string>() { "en-us", "en", "fr-fr", "fr" };

    protected override async Task<HttpResponseMessage> SendAsync(HttpRequestMessage request,
                                               CancellationToken cancellationToken)
    {
        var list = request.Headers.AcceptLanguage;
        if (list != null && list.Count > 0)
        {
            var headerValue = list.OrderByDescending(e => e.Quality ?? 1.0D)
                            .Where(e => !e.Quality.HasValue ||
                                        e.Quality.Value > 0.0D)
                            .FirstOrDefault(e => supportedCultures
                            .Contains(e.Value, StringComparer.OrdinalIgnoreCase));

            // Case 1: We can support what client has asked for
            if (headerValue != null)
            {
                Thread.CurrentThread.CurrentUICulture =
                        CultureInfo.GetCultureInfo(headerValue.Value);

                Thread.CurrentThread.CurrentCulture =
                                        Thread.CurrentThread.CurrentUICulture;
            }
}
```

```
        // Case 2: Client will accept anything we support except
        // the ones explicitly specified as not preferred by setting q=0
        if (list.Any(e => e.Value == "*" &&
                (!e.Quality.HasValue || e.Quality.Value > 0.0D)))
        {
            var culture = supportedCultures.Where(sc =>
                                !list.Any(e =>
                                        e.Value.Equals(sc,
                                            StringComparison.OrdinalIgnoreCase) &&
                                        e.Quality.HasValue &&
                                            e.Quality.Value == 0.0D))
                                            .FirstOrDefault();

            if (culture != null)
            {
                Thread.CurrentThread.CurrentUICulture =
                                CultureInfo.GetCultureInfo(culture);

                Thread.CurrentThread.CurrentCulture =
                                        Thread.CurrentThread.CurrentUICulture;
            }
        }
    }

    return await base.SendAsync(request, cancellationToken);
    }
}
```

3. Add a property of type decimal with a name of Compensation to the Employee class, as
    shown in Listing 4-29, if this property does not exist in the model class in your project. If
    you have chosen to create a new project for this chapter, you will find the Compensation
    property missing in the Employee class.

Listing 4-29. New Decimal Property in the Employee Class

```
public class Employee
{
    public int Id { get; set; }
    public string FirstName { get; set; }
    public string LastName { get; set; }
    public decimal Compensation { get; set; }
}
```

4. Modify EmployeesController to populate a value for the new Compensation property, for
    employee with ID 12345, as shown in Listing 4-30.

Listing 4-30. Populating Compensation

```
public class EmployeesController : ApiController
{
    private static IList<Employee> list = new List<Employee>()
    {
        new Employee()
        {
            Id = 12345,
                FirstName = "John",
                    LastName = "Human",
                        Compensation = 45678.12M
        },

        new Employee()
        {
            Id = 12346, FirstName = "Jane", LastName = "Public"
        },

        new Employee()
        {
            Id = 12347, FirstName = "Joseph", LastName = "Law"
        }
    };

    // other members go here
}
```

5. Rebuild and issue a GET request to http://localhost:55778/api/employees/12345 from Fiddler, including the request header Accept-Language: fr-fr. Remember to replace the port 55778 with the actual port that your application runs on.

6. Web API responds with the following JSON:

    `{"Id":12345,"FirstName":"John","LastName":"Human","Compensation":45678.12}`

7. As you can see, the Compensation property is serialized without using the culture requested by the client. JSON serialization is done by ASP.NET Web API using the JsonMediaTypeFormatter class. By default, JsonMediaTypeFormatter uses the Json.NET library, which is a third-party open source library to perform serialization. Json.NET is flexible enough for us to change this behavior.

8. Create a new class NumberConverter that derives from JsonConverter, as shown in Listing 4-31.

    a. This convertor will support only decimal and nullable decimal (decimal?), as shown in the CanConvert method.

    b. The WriteJson method is overridden to write the value into JsonWriter, as returned by the ToString method. For this to work correctly, Thread.CurrentThread.CurrentCulture must be correctly set, which is done by our message handler that runs earlier in the ASP.NET Web API pipeline.

c. The ReadJson method does the reverse. It parses the value from the reader. Though this method is not related to what we set out to achieve in this exercise, we must override this method, as part of subclassing JsonConverter.

Listing 4-31. NumberConverter

```
using System;
using Newtonsoft.Json;

public class NumberConverter : JsonConverter
{
    public override bool CanConvert(Type objectType)
    {
        return (objectType == typeof(decimal) || objectType == typeof(decimal?));
    }

    public override object ReadJson(JsonReader reader, Type objectType,
                                    object existingValue, JsonSerializer serializer)
    {
        return Decimal.Parse(reader.Value.ToString());
    }

    public override void WriteJson(JsonWriter writer, object value, JsonSerializer serializer)
    {
        writer.WriteValue(((decimal)value).ToString());
    }
}
```

9. Add NumberConverter to the list of converters used by JsonMediaTypeFormatter in WebApiConfig in the App_Start folder, as shown in Listing 4-32.

Listing 4-32. Adding NumberConverter to the List of Converters

```
public static class WebApiConfig
{
    public static void Register(HttpConfiguration config)
    {
        config.Routes.MapHttpRoute(
            name: "DefaultApi",
            routeTemplate: "api/{controller}/{id}",
            defaults: new { id = RouteParameter.Optional }
        );

        config.Formatters.JsonFormatter
                .SerializerSettings
                    .Converters.Add(new NumberConverter());

        //config.Formatters.JsonFormatter
        //                    .SupportedEncodings
        //                        .Add(Encoding.GetEncoding(932));
```

```
//foreach (var encoding in config.Formatters.JsonFormatter.SupportedEncodings)
//{
//    System.Diagnostics.Trace.WriteLine(encoding.WebName);
//}

//config.MessageHandlers.Add(new EncodingHandler());

config.MessageHandlers.Add(new CultureHandler());

        }
    }
```

10. Rebuild the solution and make a GET request to http://localhost:55778/api/employees/12345 from Fiddler. Include the request header Accept-Language: fr-fr. Once again, remember to replace the port 55778 with the actual port that your application runs on.

11. Web API now responds with this JSON:

```
{"Id":12345,"FirstName":"John","LastName":"Human","Compensation":"45678,12"}.
```

12. We stop here with the changes we made to let Web API use the correct decimal separator. We do not proceed to format the number further on thousands separator and so on, as those aspects lean toward the formatting of the data rather than the data itself. From a Web API perspective, formatting is not relevant and is a concern of the application that presents the data to the end user.

13. JsonMediaTypeFormatter is extended to use the NumberConverter. However, if XML resource representation is preferred by the client, the preceding steps will not be sufficient. Let us now go through the steps to handle the case of the XML formatter.

14. Add a reference to the assembly System.Runtime.Serialization into your ASP.NET Web API project.

15. Modify the Employee class as shown in Listing 4-33. The code uses the OnSerializing serialization callback to format the number the way we wanted. Only the fields decorated with the DataMember attribute will be serialized. We ensure that the Compensation property is not marked for serialization. Instead, we introduce a new private property and mark it for serialization under the name of Compensation. In the method marked with the OnSerializing attribute, we call ToString and set the result in the private property to be serialized into the output resource representation.

Listing 4-33. Using the OnSerializing Callback

```
using System.Runtime.Serialization;

[DataContract]
public class Employee
{
    [DataMember]
    public int Id { get; set; }

    [DataMember]
    public string FirstName { get; set; }
```

```
    [DataMember]
    public string LastName { get; set; }

    public decimal Compensation { get; set; }

    [DataMember(Name = "Compensation")]
    private string CompensationSerialized { get; set; }

    [OnSerializing]
    void OnSerializing(StreamingContext context)
    {
        this.CompensationSerialized = this.Compensation.ToString();
    }
}
```

16. With this change, rebuild the solution in Visual Studio.

17. Make a GET request to http://localhost:55778/api/employees/12345 from Fiddler. Include the request header Accept-Language: fr-fr. Also, include another request header, Accept: application/xml.

18. The Web API response is shown in Listing 4-34. Some headers are removed for brevity.

Listing 4-34. The Web API XML Response

```
<Employee xmlns:i="http://www.w3.org/2001/XMLSchema-instance"
                        xmlns="http://schemas.datacontract.org/2004/07/HelloWebApi.Models">
        <Compensation>45678,12</Compensation>
        <FirstName>John</FirstName>
        <Id>12345</Id>
        <LastName>Human</LastName>
</Employee>
```

■ **Note** The serialization callback changes we made to the Employee class will get the JSON formatter working as well without the NumberConverter. You can remove the line in WebApiConfig where we add it to the converters list and test through a GET to http://localhost:55778/api/employees/12345.

19. Finally, restore the Employee class to its original state without the DataContract or DataMember attributes, as shown in Listing 4-35.

Listing 4-35. The Employee Class with the OnSerializing Callback Removed

```
public class Employee
{
    public int Id { get; set; }
    public string FirstName { get; set; }
    public string LastName { get; set; }

    public decimal Compensation { get; set; }
}
```

4.4.3 Internationalizing the Dates

In this exercise, you will internationalize the dates sent to the client. As with the previous exercises, we use the language preferences sent in the Accept-Language header. Unlike numbers, the date format can get really confusing to a client or an end user. For example, 06/02 could be June 02 or it could be February 06, depending on the locale.

1. You will use the same project that you worked with for Exercise 3.4.2.

2. Add a property to represent the employee's date of joining, of type DateTime to Employee, as shown in Listing 4-36.

    Listing 4-36. The Employee Class with the New Doj Property

    ```
    public class Employee
    {
        public int Id { get; set; }
        public string FirstName { get; set; }
        public string LastName { get; set; }

        public decimal Compensation { get; set; }

        public DateTime Doj { get; set; }
    }
    ```

3. Modify EmployeesController to populate some value for the new Doj property, for the employee with ID 12345, as shown in Listing 4-37.

    Listing 4-37. Populating Compensation

    ```
    public class EmployeesController : ApiController
    {
        private static IList<Employee> list = new List<Employee>()
        {
            new Employee()
            {
                Id = 12345,
                    FirstName = "John",
                        LastName = "Human",
                            Compensation = 45678.12M,
                                Doj = new DateTime(1990, 06, 02)
            },
            // other members of the list go here
        };

        // other class members go here
    }
    ```

4. Rebuild and issue a GET to http://localhost:55778/api/employees/12345 from Fiddler. Include the request header Accept-Language: fr-fr. Try it with the header Accept: application/xml, as well as without it.

5. In both cases, by default, the date is returned in the ISO 8601 format: 1990-06-02T00:00:00.

6. To extend the JSON Media formatter, create a new class DateTimeConverter that derives from DateTimeConverterBase, as shown in Listing 4-38, in your ASP.NET Web API project.

Listing 4-38. DateTimeConverter

```
using System;
using Newtonsoft.Json;
using Newtonsoft.Json.Converters;

public class DateTimeConverter : DateTimeConverterBase
{
    public override object ReadJson(JsonReader reader, Type objectType,
                                    object existingValue, JsonSerializer serializer)
    {
        return DateTime.Parse(reader.Value.ToString());
    }

    public override void WriteJson(JsonWriter writer, object value, JsonSerializer serializer)
    {
        writer.WriteValue(((DateTime)value).ToString());
    }
}
```

7. Add the converter to the list of converters in WebApiConfig, in the App_Start folder. For the converter to work correctly, Thread.CurrentThread.CurrentCulture must be correctly set, which is done by the CultureHandler message handler that runs earlier in the ASP.NET Web API pipeline. Ensure that the handler is registered. Listing 4-39 shows the changes.

Listing 4-39. Addition of DateTimeConverter to the List of Converters

```
public static class WebApiConfig
{
    public static void Register(HttpConfiguration config)
    {
        config.Routes.MapHttpRoute(
            name: "DefaultApi",
            routeTemplate: "api/{controller}/{id}",
            defaults: new { id = RouteParameter.Optional }
        );

        config.Formatters.JsonFormatter
                .SerializerSettings
                    .Converters.Add(new NumberConverter());

        config.Formatters.JsonFormatter
                .SerializerSettings
                    .Converters.Add(new DateTimeConverter());

        //config.Formatters.JsonFormatter
        //                    .SupportedEncodings
        //                        .Add(Encoding.GetEncoding(932));
```

```
//foreach (var encoding in config.Formatters.JsonFormatter.SupportedEncodings)
//{
//    System.Diagnostics.Trace.WriteLine(encoding.WebName);
//}

//config.MessageHandlers.Add(new EncodingHandler());

config.MessageHandlers.Add(new CultureHandler());

    }
}
```

8. Rebuild the solution in Visual Studio and issue a GET request to
    http://localhost:55778/api/employees/12345 from Fiddler. Include the request header
    Accept-Language: fr-fr. Web API returns the date as **02/06**/1990 00:00:00.

9. Issue a GET request to http://localhost:55778/api/employees/12345 from Fiddler.
    Include the request header Accept-Language: en-us. Web API returns the date as
    6/2/1990 12:00:00 AM.

10. Just as in the previous exercise, in order to get the formatting to work correctly with XML,
    we have to make changes to the Employee class. See Listing 4-40.

Listing 4-40. Using OnSerializing Callback for DateTime

```
[DataContract]
public class Employee
{
    [DataMember]
    public int Id { get; set; }

    [DataMember]
    public string FirstName { get; set; }

    [DataMember]
    public string LastName { get; set; }

    public DateTime Doj { get; set; }

    public decimal Compensation { get; set; }

    [DataMember(Name = "Compensation")]
    private string CompensationSerialized { get; set; }

    [DataMember(Name = "Doj")]
    private string DojSerialized { get; set; }

    [OnSerializing]
    void OnSerializing(StreamingContext context)
    {
        this.CompensationSerialized = this.Compensation.ToString();
        this.DojSerialized = this.Doj.ToString();
    }
}
```

Summary

Content negotiation is the process of selecting the best representation for a given response when there are multiple representations available. It is not called format negotiation, because the alternative representations may be of the same media type but use different capabilities of that type, they may be in different languages, and so on. The term *negotiation* is used because the client indicates its preferences. A client sends a list of options with a quality factor specified against each option, indicating the preference level. It is up to the service, which is Web API in our case, to fulfill the request in the way the client wants, respecting the client preferences. If Web API is not able to fulfill the request the way the client has requested, it can switch to a default or send a 406 - Not Acceptable status code in the response.

Character encoding denotes how the characters—letters, digits, and other symbols—are represented as bits and bytes for storage and communication. The HTTP request header Accept-Charset can be used by a client to indicate how the response message can be encoded. ASP.NET Web API supports UTF-8 and UTF-16 out of the box.

Content coding is the encoding transformation applied to an entity. It is primarily used to allow a response message to be compressed. An HTTP response message is compressed before it is sent from the server, and the clients indicate their preference for the compression schema to be used in the request header Accept-Encoding. A client that does not support compression can opt out of compression and receive an uncompressed response. The most common compression schemas are gzip and deflate. The .NET framework provides classes in the form of GZipStream and DeflateStream to compress and decompress streams.

The Accept-Language request header can be used by clients to indicate the set of preferred languages in the response. The same header can be used to specify locale preferences.

CHAPTER 5

Binding an HTTP Request into CLR Objects

The ASP.NET Web API framework reads each incoming HTTP request and creates the parameter objects for your action methods in the controller. This is one of the powerful features of the ASP.NET Web API framework that keeps the code in the controller classes free of the repetitive work related to HTTP infrastructure and helps you, the developer, focus on implementing the business requirements at hand. Table 5-1 shows the different types of bindings possible with ASP.NET Web API, the corresponding out-of-the-box class associated with the binding, the part of the request from which data is used for binding, the type of the parameter bound, and the extensibility options available.

Table 5-1. *Binding Requests to CLR Types*

Binding	Model Binding	Formatter Binding	Parameter Binding
Class	`ModelBinderParameterBinding`	`FormatterParameterBinding`	`HttpParameterBinding`
Class Category	Concrete	Concrete	Abstract
Request Part	URI (route and query string)	Request Body (Content)	Any part of the HTTP request as well as entities outside of the request
Parameter Type	Simple	Complex	Both simple and complex
Extensibility	(1) Create a custom model binder by implementing `IModelBinder`. (2) Create a custom value provider by implementing `IValueProvider`.	(1) Create a new media formatter by inheriting from `MediaTypeFormatter`. (2) Create a new media formatter by inheriting from one of the out-of-the-box media formatters.	Create a new parameter binder by inheriting from `HttpParameterBinding`.

The ASP.NET Web API framework reads the route data and the query string of the request URI and sets the parameters of the action methods that are simple types (primitives, `DateTime`, `Guid`, and so on) by a process called *model binding*. The parameters that are complex types are set based on the HTTP request body with the help of the media type formatters that we saw in Chapter 3. In Chapter 3, our focus was serialization: translation of CLR types into a format that can be transmitted over HTTP. In this chapter, we focus on deserialization: translation of an HTTP request message into CLR types. A media formatter can enlist itself in serialization and/or deserialization by returning true when the framework calls the `CanWriteType(Type)` and `CanReadType(Type)` methods respectively.

5.1 Reading the Raw HTTP Request

In this exercise, you will read the raw HTTP request without any help from the ASP.NET Web API framework. You will see that doing so is a lot of work and is error-prone. It is highly recommended to use the help that the ASP.NET Web API provides to read the requests so that you get nice, clean CLR objects to work with. This exercise is just to show you that it is possible to read the raw requests and help you appreciate the heavy lifting the framework does for you.

1. Create a new ASP.NET MVC 4 project with a name of RequestBinding, using the Web API template.

2. Create a new empty API controller with a name of EmployeesController.

3. Implement an action method to handle HTTP POST, as shown in Listing 5-1.

    Listing 5-1. An Action Method Reading a Raw HTTP Request

    ```
    using System;
    using System.Diagnostics;
    using System.Linq;
    using System.Net.Http;
    using System.Web.Http;

    public class EmployeesController : ApiController
    {
        public void Post(HttpRequestMessage req)
        {
            var content = req.Content.ReadAsStringAsync().Result;
            int id = Int32.Parse(req.RequestUri.Segments.Last());

            Trace.WriteLine(content);
            Trace.WriteLine(id);
        }
    }
    ```

4. Rebuild the solution and run the project in Visual Studio by pressing F5.

5. Fire-up Fiddler and issue a POST request to http://localhost:55778/api/employees/12345 from the Composer tab. Remember to replace the port 55778 with the actual port that your application runs on. Copy and paste Content-Type: application/json into the Request Headers text box and the JSON {"Id":12345,"FirstName":"John", "LastName":"Human"} into the Request Body text box. Click Execute.

6. This writes the following into the Output window of Visual Studio.

    ```
    {"Id":12345,"FirstName":"John","LastName":"Human"}
    12345
    ```

In Listing 5-1, we read the request message content as a string using the ReadAsStringAsync method and take the ID from the URI. The code is naïve. It does not handle any of the rainy-day scenarios such as the ID not being a number, ID absent, and so on. Also, we get the request message content as JSON. We will need to parse this into a CLR object. If a client sends XML, we need to handle that as well. Obviously, it is a lot of painful work.

PARTIAL UPDATES

There is one good thing with taking control from ASP.NET Web API. In Chapter 1, we saw that partial updates are possible with PATCH using Delta<T>.

The challenge we have with partial updates is that when a request comes in without a value, it will be the same as if the request had the field present but with a null value. We now have the visibility to determine whether a request has a specific field absent or present but containing null without using Delta<T>. This is especially useful for partial updates. If a request comes in with a content of {"FirstName":"Jon"}, it basically means we need to update only the first name of the employee with ID of 12345 to Jon without touching any other properties. By leaving out the rest of the properties, a client can indicate that only the property in the request content must be updated.

So the request {"FirstName":"Jon"} can be distinguished from {"FirstName":"Jon", "LastName":null}. The first request asks for only the first name to be updated, and the second one asks for the first name to be updated to a new value and the last name to be cleared out. If you have used an object of type Employee as the parameter, you will not be able to distinguish these two requests, since in both the cases the LastName property will be set to null.

5.2 Reading the HTTP Request into a CLR Type

In this exercise, you will read the HTTP request with the help of the ASP.NET Web API framework. It is one step in the right direction yet you will see how beneficial it is.

1. Change the action method from the previous exercise, as shown in Listing 5-2.

   Listing 5-2. An Action Method Reading a Raw HTTP Request into a CLR Type

   ```
   public void Post(HttpRequestMessage req)
   {
       //var content = req.Content.ReadAsStringAsync().Result;
       var content = req.Content.ReadAsAsync<Employee>().Result;
       int id = Int32.Parse(req.RequestUri.Segments.Last());

       Trace.WriteLine(content.Id);
       Trace.WriteLine(content.FirstName);
       Trace.WriteLine(content.LastName);
       Trace.WriteLine(id);
   }
   ```

2. Add the Employee class that we have been using all along in this book, into your project in the Models folder. Listing 5-3 shows the Employee class, for your easy reference.

   Listing 5-3. The Employee Model Class

   ```
   public class Employee
   {
       public int Id { get; set; }
       public string FirstName { get; set; }
       public string LastName { get; set; }
   }
   ```

3. In the EmployeesController class, right-click Employee, which is shown with a red wavy underline, and select Resolve ➤ using RequestBinding.Models;. That will add the necessary using directive.

4. Rebuild the solution and run the project in Visual Studio by pressing F5.

5. Make a POST to http://localhost:55778/api/employees/12345 from the Fiddler Composer tab. Remember to replace the port 55778 with the actual port that your application runs on. Copy and paste Content-Type: application/json into the Request Headers text box and the JSON {"Id":12345,"FirstName":"John","LastName":"Human"} into the Request Body text box. Click Execute.

6. This outputs the ID, first name, and last name of the employee from the request body.

7. Right click the Output window content and select Clear All.

8. Make another POST to http://localhost:55778/api/employees/12345. Copy and paste Content-Type: application/xml in the Request Headers text box and the XML shown in Listing 5-4 into the Request Body text box. Click Execute. The indentation of the XML is only for readability. If you have chosen a project name other than RequestBinding or created the Employee class with a namespace other than RequestBinding.Models, make sure you adjust the XML accordingly.

Listing 5-4. The Request XML

```
<Employee xmlns="http://schemas.datacontract.org/2004/07/RequestBinding.Models">
    <FirstName>John</FirstName>
    <Id>12345</Id>
    <LastName>Human</LastName>
</Employee>
```

9. Even with XML, the ID, first name, and last name of the employee from the request body are written out correctly. Now, we are able to handle requests with different media types without writing a single line of infrastructure code parsing JSON or XML!

10. However, the code we have in Listing 5-2 is still suboptimal. One obvious problem is the extraction of route data. Also, the action method is dependent on an HTTP request. Automated unit-testing of this action method will be difficult.

11. Change the action method from the previous exercise as shown in Listing 5-5.

Listing 5-5. Action Method Reading Raw HTTP Request into Parameters

```
public void Post(int id, Employee employee)
{
    Trace.WriteLine(employee.Id);
    Trace.WriteLine(employee.FirstName);
    Trace.WriteLine(employee.LastName);
    Trace.WriteLine(id);
}
```

12. Rebuild the solution and run the project in Visual Studio by pressing F5.

13. Make a POST to `http://localhost:55778/api/employees/12345` from the Fiddler Composer tab. Remember to replace the port 55778 with the actual port that your application runs on. Copy and paste `Content-Type: application/json` into the Request Headers text box and the JSON `{"Id":12345,"FirstName":"John","LastName":"Human"}` into the Request Body box. Click Execute.

This outputs the ID, first name, and last name of the employee from the request body, exactly the same as before. Regardless of the request media-type, XML or JSON, ASP.NET Web API correctly populates the parameter of type Employee as well as the `int` parameter. If a nonnumeric value is sent in the URI route, the framework catches it correctly, and you don't need to write code to handle any of those scenarios.

14. Since there is no dependency on the HTTP request, automated unit-testing is very easy. Of course, there is not much to unit-test in the current implementation but if there is, it will be easily unit-testable. You can vary the input, which consists of normal CLR types, and test all the conditions.

5.3 Binding the HTTP Request to Simple Types

In this exercise, you will see how ASP.NET Web API creates simple type parameters—the parameters of type such as primitives, `DateTime`, `Guid`, and so on—from the HTTP request message. By default, simple types are bound from the URI route data and query string.

1. Change the action method from the previous exercise, as shown in Listing 5-6. The parameters of the action method are all simple types.

   Listing 5-6. An Action Method with Simple Type Parameters

   ```
   public void Post(int id, string firstName, int locationId, Guid guid)
   {
       Trace.WriteLine(id);
       Trace.WriteLine(firstName);
       Trace.WriteLine(locationId);
       Trace.WriteLine(guid);
   }
   ```

2. Rebuild the solution and run the project in Visual Studio by pressing F5.

3. From the Fiddler Composer tab, make a POST request to the URI `http://localhost:55778/api/employees/12345?firstName=John&locationId=12&guid=31c9359d-d332-4703-a896-7e9655eff171`. Remember to replace the port 55778 with the actual port that your application runs on. Copy and paste `Content-Length: 0` in the Request Headers text box and leave Request Body empty. Click Execute.

4. The parameter ID is bound from the URI route data of 12345, and the rest of the parameters are bound from the query string. The corresponding values are written to the output as follows.

   ```
   12345
   John
   12
   31c9359d-d332-4703-a896-7e9655eff171
   ```

5. Make another POST to the same URI as you did in the previous step. This time leave out the `locationId` from the query string but include it in the request body. So, the URI will be `http://localhost:55778/api/employees/12345?firstName=John&guid=31c9359d-d332-4703-a896-7e9655eff171`. Copy and paste `Content-Type: application/json` into the Request Headers text box and `"locationId":12` into the Request Body text box. Click Execute.

You get a `404 - Not Found` with an error message that `No HTTP resource was found that matches the request URI`. The reason for the 404 is that ASP.NET Web API is unable to bind the `locationId` parameter. There is nothing in the URI path or the query string to match the parameter, and the framework is unable to find the right action method for the request, so it fails with a 404. Though `locationId` field is present in the request body JSON, ASP.NET Web API does not try to bind it, because the action method parameters are simple types. By default, the simple types are bound from the URI path and query string only.

6. To alter this default behavior, apply the `FromBody` attribute to the `locationId` parameter so that the action method signature is as follows:

    ```
    void Post(int id, string firstName, [FromBody]int locationId, Guid guid) { ... }
    ```

7. Rebuild the solution and press F5 to run the project in Visual Studio. Repeat Step 3. You will still get an error, but it is no longer a `404 - Not Found` but a `400 - Bad Request`, indicating that something is wrong with the request format.

8. We need to make one more adjustment to get the binding to work correctly. Repeat Step 3 but have just 12 in the Request Body text box. The request body must have only the number, like so:

    ```
    POST http://localhost:55778/api/employees/12345?firstName=John&guid=31c9359d-d332-4703-
    a896-7e9655eff171 HTTP/1.1
    Content-Type: application/json
    Host: localhost:55778
    Content-Length: 2

    12
    ```

The framework starts binding the values correctly.

THE WHOLE BODY BINDING

In the preceding exercise, we had to pass the integer 12 in the request body because of the way ASP.NET Web API binding is designed. The whole request body, not a piece of the body, is bound to a parameter. For this reason, you cannot have multiple parameters with the `FromBody` attribute in an action method. If that is the need, use a complex type such as a class with properties equivalent to the parameters. For example, instead of using `[FromBody]int locationId, [FromBody]string locationName`, use a class, as follows.

```
public class LocationDto
{
        public int LocationId {get; set;}
        public string LocationName {get; set;}
}
```

5.4 Binding the HTTP Request to Complex Types

By default, complex types are bound from the request message body and simple types are bound from the URI path and the query string. In Exercise 5.3, you saw how ASP.NET Web API binds a simple type from the URI and query string. Then we changed this default behavior by applying the FromBody attribute on a simple type parameter to let the framework bind the message body to a simple type.

In this exercise, you will see how a complex type parameter is bound from the HTTP request message. It is the default behavior of ASP.NET Web API to bind the request body to a complex type but just as we used the FromBody attribute to change that behavior, in this exercise, we will use the FromUri attribute to bind a complex type from the URI and query string.

ASP.NET Web API uses media formatters to bind the request body to complex types. Chapter 3 covered media type formatters from the perspective of the response message being mapped to a CLR object. In this chapter, we again see the media formatters in action but for mapping the request to a CLR object.

1. Change the Post action method from the previous exercise and place a breakpoint in the starting curly brace of the method, as shown in Figure 5-1.

Figure 5-1. The POST method of EmployeesController

2. Rebuild the solution and run the project in Visual Studio by pressing F5.

3. Make a POST to http://localhost:55778/api/employees/12345 from the Fiddler Composer tab, after changing the port number in the preceding URI to reflect the port used by your application. Copy and paste Content-Type: application/json into the Request Headers text box and the JSON {"Id":12345,"FirstName":"John","LastName":"Human"} into the Request Body text box. Click Execute.

4. When the breakpoint is hit, put the mouse cursor over the action method's parameters and inspect the values, as shown in Figure 5-2. You will see that the request body JSON is bound to the complex type Employee, with the properties showing the correct values.

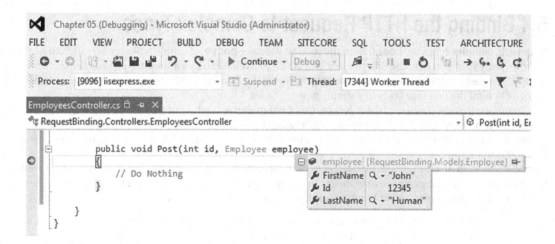

Figure 5-2. *POST method parameters when the breakpoint is hit*

5. Make another POST to http://localhost:55778/api/employees/12345. Copy and paste
    Content-Type: application/xml into the Request Headers text box and the XML shown
    in Listing 5-4 into the Request Body text box. The following XML repeats Listing 5-4, for
    your easy reference. Click Execute. Inspect the action method's parameters when the
    execution hits the breakpoint. It works this time, too, with the Employee parameter being
    bound correctly from the request body XML.

```
<Employee xmlns="http://schemas.datacontract.org/2004/07/RequestBinding.Models">
        <FirstName>John</FirstName>
        <Id>12345</Id>
        <LastName>Human</LastName>
</Employee>
```

6. Based on the Content-Type request header, conneg is able to find the correct
    formatter to deserialize the request body. It uses JsonMediaTypeFormatter and
    XmlMediaTypeFormatter, respectively, for JSON and XML.

Everything works fine so far because the action method parameter Employee is a complex type and ASP.NET Web
API binds the parameter from the request body with the help of formatters based on the content type. Let us now
change the request data coming in the body to a query string and see how it works.

7. Ensure that the project is running in Visual Studio. If it is not running, run the project by
    pressing F5.

8. Make a POST to http://localhost:55778/api/employees/12345?firstname=John&la
    stname=Human. Copy and paste Content-Length: 0 in the Request Headers text box and
    leave the Request Body text box empty. Click Execute.

9. When the execution breaks, inspect the Employee parameter. It is null. That is because the
    ASP.NET Web API framework, by default, tries to populate the Employee parameter, which
    is a complex type, from the request body, and in our case the request body is empty.

10. We can override the default behavior by applying the FromUri attribute to the Employee parameter so that the action method signature is as follows:

```
void Post(int id, [FromUri]Employee employee) { ... }
```

11. Rebuild the solution and run the application by pressing F5.

12. Repeat the previous POST request from Step 8. When the execution breaks, inspect the Employee parameter.

It works now with the Employee parameter being populated from the query string.

THE BODY CAN BE READ ONLY ONCE

The request body is a non-rewindable stream; it can be read only once. Modify the POST action method, as shown in the following code. It now takes two parameters: the first is the raw HTTP request and the second is Employee type.

```
public void Post(int id, HttpRequestMessage req, Employee employee)
{
    var content = req.Content.ReadAsStringAsync().Result;
    var employeeContent = req.Content.ReadAsAsync<Employee>().Result;

} // Place the break point here
```

Place a breakpoint on the ending curly brace. Rebuild the solution and run the project. Make a POST to http://localhost:<port>/api/employees/12345 from Fiddler with Content-Type: application/json in the Request Headers text box of the Composer tab and the JSON {"Id":12345,"FirstName":"John","LastName":"Human"} in the Request Body text box.

When the breakpoint is hit, inspect the variables content and employeeContent. The values are an empty string and null, respectively. Inspect the Employee type parameter. You will see that it is deserialized correctly with all the data from the request body. The reason we cannot read the HTTP request content inside the action method is that the stream can be read only once. The formatter has already read the stream and populated the Employee parameter object. So we are not able to read the stream again. This is an important point to understand.

5.5 Binding the HTTP Request to a Collection

In this exercise, you will see how a collection parameter such as List<T> is bound from the HTTP request message. List<T> is a complex type and by default, complex types are bound from the request message body.

1. Change the action method from the previous exercise as shown in Listing 5-7.

   Listing 5-7. The Action Method with a Collection Parameter

   ```
   public void Post(int id, List<string> nickNames)
   {
       Trace.WriteLine(String.Join(", ", nickNames));
   }
   ```

2. Rebuild the solution and run the project in Visual Studio by pressing F5.

3. Make a POST to `http://localhost:55778/api/employees/12345` from the Fiddler Composer tab. Copy and paste `Content-Type: application/json` into the Request Headers text box and the JSON `["Liz","Beth","Lisa"]` into the Request Body text box. Click Execute.

4. The nicknames from the message body are bound correctly to the `List<string>` parameter, and the action method writes `Liz, Beth, Lisa` to the Output window.

5. With the project running in Visual Studio, make another POST request but this time to `http://localhost:55778/api/employees/12345?nicknames=Liz&nicknames=Beth` from the Fiddler Composer tab. Copy and paste `Content-Length: 0` into the Request Headers text box and leave the Request Body text box empty. Click Execute.

This throws an exception, since the `nickNames` parameter is null this time around. Since `List<string>` is a complex type, ASP.NET Web API tries to bind the request body to this parameter. Since the request body is empty, the `nickNames` parameter is null.

6. Apply the `FromUri` attribute to the `nickNames` parameter so that the action method signature is as follows: `void Post(int id, [FromUri]List<string> nickNames)`.

7. Rebuild the solution and run the project in Visual Studio by pressing F5. Repeat Step 5. This time around, ASP.NET Web API populates the `nickNames` parameter correctly.

5.6 Binding the Form Data

An HTML form is a section of a document containing normal content, markup, special elements called controls (text boxes, checkboxes, radio buttons and so on), and labels on those controls. A form is submitted to a server-side program that processes the user-entered data.

When a web browser sends an HTTP POST of an HTML form, it specifies a media type of `application/x-www-form-urlencoded`. The data in the HTML form is sent as name-value pairs. For example, take the case of the HTML form shown in Listing 5-8.

Listing 5-8. An HTML Form

```
<form action=" http://localhost:55778/api/employees" method="post">
    <div>
        <label for="firstname">First Name:</label>
        <input type="text" name="firstname"/>
    </div>
    <div>
        <label for="lastname">Last Name:</label>
        <input type="text" name="lastname"/>
    </div>
    <input type="submit" value="Submit"/>
</form>
```

When I enter **John** in the First Name text box and **Human Being** in the Last Name text box and click Submit, the browser I use, Internet Explorer, posts the form data to the URI that I have specified in the action attribute of the form element. Listing 5-9 shows the HTTP request message (with some of the headers removed for brevity). The data I entered are encoded and sent in the form of name-value pairs.

Listing 5-9. Form Data

```
POST http://localhost:55778/api/employees HTTP/1.1
Content-Type: application/x-www-form-urlencoded
Host: localhost:55778
Content-Length: 35

firstname=John&lastname=Human+Being
```

Form-URL-encoded data is a widely used media type for submitting data from a browser to a server-side program. ASP.NET Web API is capable of handling requests with form-URL-encoded data. However, it is important to note that a browser posting a form directly to an ASP.NET Web API endpoint as in Listing 5-9 is not a likely scenario, for the simple reason that ASP.NET Web API does not typically produce HTML that can be rendered by the browser directly. The most likely use case for the form-URL-encoded data will be a JavaScript library such as jQuery posting a form through an AJAX call, or a client-side library used by a native application formatting user-entered data as name-value pairs and posting them to ASP.NET Web API as form-URL-encoded data.

ASP.NET Web API can bind form-URL-encoded data to a special class FormDataCollection in the System.Net. Http.Formatting namespace. It can also bind the form-URL-encoded data to custom classes like our Employee class. In the former case, the out-of-the-box media formatter FormUrlEncodedMediaTypeFormatter is used and in the latter case, JQueryMvcFormUrlEncodedFormatter is used.

5.6.1 Binding to FormDataCollection

In this exercise, you will see how ASP.NET Web API binds form-URL-encoded data to FormDataCollection. I start by showing you the media type formatters that handle the form-URL-encoded data (application/x-www-form-urlencoded).

1. Use the same project from Exercise 5.5. Modify the Register method of WebApiConfig in the App_Start folder, as shown in Listing 5-10.

   Listing 5-10. Listing Media Formatters

   ```
   using System.Diagnostics;
   using System.Linq;
   using System.Net.Http.Formatting;
   using System.Web.Http;
   using RequestBinding.Models;

   public static class WebApiConfig
   {
       public static void Register(HttpConfiguration config)
       {
           config.Routes.MapHttpRoute(
               name: "DefaultApi",
               routeTemplate: "api/{controller}/{id}",
               defaults: new { id = RouteParameter.Optional }
           );

           foreach (var formatter in config.Formatters.Where(f => f.SupportedMediaTypes
                                          .Any(m => m.MediaType.Equals(
                                             "application/x-www-form-urlencoded"))))
   ```

```
        {
            Trace.WriteLine(formatter.GetType().Name);
            Trace.WriteLine("\tCanReadType Employee: " + formatter
                                            .CanReadType(typeof(Employee)));
            Trace.WriteLine("\tCanWriteType Employee: " + formatter
                                            .CanWriteType(typeof(Employee)));
            Trace.WriteLine("\tCanReadType FormDataCollection: " +
                                        formatter
                                        .CanReadType(
                                            typeof(FormDataCollection)));
            Trace.WriteLine("\tCanWriteType FormDataCollection: " +
                                    formatter
                                    .CanWriteType(
                                        typeof(FormDataCollection)));
            Trace.WriteLine("\tBase: " + formatter.GetType().BaseType.Name);
            Trace.WriteLine("\tMedia Types: " +
                                string.Join(", ", formatter.SupportedMediaTypes));
        }

    }
}
```

2. The preceding code lists the media type formatters that support the media type
    application/x-www-form-urlencoded. Listing 5-11 shows the content of the Output
    window of Visual Studio, as you run the project by pressing F5.

    Listing 5-11. Media Type Formatters Supporting Form Data

```
FormUrlEncodedMediaTypeFormatter
      CanReadType Employee: False
      CanWriteType Employee: False
      CanReadType FormDataCollection: True
      CanWriteType FormDataCollection: False
      Base: MediaTypeFormatter
      Media Types: application/x-www-form-urlencoded
JQueryMvcFormUrlEncodedFormatter
      CanReadType Employee: True
      CanWriteType Employee: False
      CanReadType FormDataCollection: True
      CanWriteType FormDataCollection: False
      Base: FormUrlEncodedMediaTypeFormatter
      Media Types: application/x-www-form-urlencoded
```

There are two out-of-the-box formatters that support the media type application/x-www-form-urlencoded:

   FormUrlEncodedMediaTypeFormatter: Supports reading the data into FormDataCollection.

   JQueryMvcFormUrlEncodedFormatter: Supports reading the data into
   both FormDataCollection and custom types such as our Employee class.
   JQueryMvcFormUrlEncodedFormatter derives from FormUrlEncodedMediaTypeFormatter.

Neither of these two formatters serializes CLR types into the media type of application/x-www-form-urlencoded, as you can infer from the false returned by the CanWriteType method.

3. Modify EmployeesController as shown in Listing 5-12. Note the parameter of the Post action method, which is FormDataCollection.

Listing 5-12. The Revised POST Action Method

```
using System.Diagnostics;
using System.Net.Http.Formatting;
using System.Web.Http;

public class EmployeesController : ApiController
{
    public void Post(FormDataCollection data)
    {
        Trace.WriteLine(data.Get("firstName"));
        Trace.WriteLine(data.Get("lastName"));
    }
}
```

4. Add a breakpoint in the starting brace of the preceding action method.

5. Copy and paste the code in Listing 5-13 into the /Home/Index view of the same project where you have the web API. The file corresponding to this view will be Index.cshtml in the Views\Home folder. It is not mandatory to use an ASP.NET MVC controller and a view. You can even have this as a static HTML file.

Listing 5-13. Home/IndexView

```
<form action="/api/employees" method="post">
    <div>
        <label for="firstname">First Name:</label>
        <input type="text" name="firstname"/>
    </div>
    <div>
        <label for="lastname">Last Name:</label>
        <input type="text" name="lastname"/>
    </div>
    <input type="submit" value="Submit"/>
</form>
```

6. Rebuild the solution and run the project in Visual Studio. The home page is displayed.

7. Enter your first and last name and click Submit.

8. The breakpoint will be hit. Inspect the FormDataCollection parameter. It will have the data you entered in the form. Press F10 twice to verify that the two Trace statements inside the action method write the first and the last names.

9. To bind the form data to the FormDataCollection, ASP.NET Web API uses FormUrlEncodedMediaTypeFormatter. You can verify this by turning on tracing using System.Diagnostics. Go to Tools ➤ Library Package Manager ➤ Package Manager Console. At the prompt PM>, type the command shown in Listing 5-14 and press Enter.

Listing 5-14. Installing the NuGet Package

```
Install-Package Microsoft.AspNet.WebApi.Tracing
```

10. In the Register method of WebApiConfig in the App_Start folder, add the line shown in Listing 5-15.

Listing 5-15. Enabling Tracing

```
config.EnableSystemDiagnosticsTracing();
```

11. With this change, post the form again. Review the lines that are written into the Output window of Visual Studio. Listing 5-16 shows the output. All the lines are trimmed and some of the lines are removed for brevity. You can see that ASP.NET Web API uses FormUrlEncodedMediaTypeFormatter to read the request into FormDataCollection.

Listing 5-16. Trace Output

```
Message='Employees', Operation=DefaultHttpControllerSelector.SelectController
Message='HelloWebApi.Controllers.EmployeesController',
Operation=DefaultHttpControllerActivator.Create
Message='HelloWebApi.Controllers.EmployeesController',
Operation=HttpControllerDescriptor.CreateController
Message='Selected action 'Post(FormDataCollection data)'',
Operation=ApiControllerActionSelector.SelectAction
Message='Value read='System.Net.Http.Formatting.FormDataCollection'',
Operation=FormUrlEncodedMediaTypeFormatter.ReadFromStreamAsync
Message='Parameter 'data' bound to the value 'System.Net.Http.Formatting.FormDataCollection'',
Operation=FormatterParameterBinding.ExecuteBindingAsync
Message='Model state is valid. Values: data=System.Net.Http.Formatting.FormDataCollection',
Operation=HttpActionBinding.ExecuteBindingAsync
Message='Action returned 'null'',
Operation=ReflectedHttpActionDescriptor.ExecuteAsync
Operation=ApiControllerActionInvoker.InvokeActionAsync, Status=204 (NoContent)
Operation=EmployeesController.ExecuteAsync, Status=204 (NoContent)
Response, Status=204 (NoContent), Method=POST, Url=http://localhost:55778/api/employees,
Message='Content-type='none', content-length=unknown'
Operation=CultureHandler.SendAsync, Status=204 (NoContent)
Operation=EmployeesController.Dispose
```

5.6.2 Binding to Custom Class

This exercise is similar to Exercise 5.6.1, but instead of using the FormDataCollection parameter, it uses a custom model class Employee that we have been using all along in this book as the action method parameter.

1. Modify the POST action method of EmployeesController, as shown in Listing 5-17. Also, add a breakpoint in the starting brace of the Post action method.

   Listing 5-17. POST Action Method Using a Complex Type Parameter

   ```
   public int Post(Employee employee)
   {
       return new Random().Next();
   }
   ```

2. Rebuild the solution and run the project in Visual Studio. The home page is displayed.

3. Enter the first and last names and click Submit.

4. Inspect the action parameter when the breakpoint is hit. You will see that the form data is used to populate the corresponding properties of the Employee parameter correctly.

5. From the trace written to the Output window, you can see that ASP.NET Web API uses JQueryMvcFormUrlEncodedFormatter this time to read the request body into the Employee type parameter.

```
FormatterParameterBinding      ExecuteBindingAsync      Binding parameter 'employee'
JQueryMvcFormUrlEncodedFormatter      ReadFromStreamAsync      Type='Employee',
content-type='application/x-www-form-urlencoded'      JQueryMvcFormUrlEncodedFormatter
ReadFromStreamAsync      Value      read='HelloWebApi.Models.Employee'
```

In the previous steps we posted an HTML form from the browser by clicking the Submit button and making a web API call. This was only for illustration. In practice, you will never be posting by submitting a page. Instead, you will use a client-side script library like jQuery. Let us now modify our page to submit the form using jQuery AJAX.

6. Replace the existing markup in /Home/View by copying and pasting the code from Listing 5-18.

   Listing 5-18. /Home/Index View Making an Ajax Call

   ```
   @section scripts{
       <script type="text/javascript">
           $.support.cors = true; // Needed for IE

           $(document).ready(function () {
               $('#btnPost').click(function () {
                   $.post("http://localhost:55778/api/employees",
                               $('#employeeForm').serialize())
                       .done(function (data) { alert("New employee created. ID is " + data); })
                           .fail(function () { alert("Error creating employee"); });
               });
           });
       </script>
   }

   <form id="employeeForm" action=" http://localhost:37276/api/employees" method="post">
       <div>
           <label for="firstname">First Name:</label>
           <input type="text" name="firstname" />
       </div>
   ```

```
        <div>
            <label for="lastname">Last Name:</label>
            <input type="text" name="lastname" />
        </div>
    <input type="submit" value="Submit" />
    <input id="btnPost" type="button" value="jQuery POST" />
</form>
```

7. Rebuild the solution and run the project in Visual Studio. The home page is displayed. Enter a first and last name and click jQuery POST.

8. The breakpoint in the action method is hit. Inspect the `Employee` parameter and press F5 to continue.

9. The alert box is displayed with the ID of the newly added employee. Of course, it is just a random number that we generate inside the action method for illustration.

10. jQuery serializes the form and makes a POST with `Content-Type:` `application/x-www-form-urlencoded`. Because `Accept:` `*/*` is sent, the response comes back as JSON, which jQuery is able to parse and get the new ID.

Request	POST http://localhost:55778/api/employees HTTP/1.1 Accept: */* **Content-Type: application/x-www-form-urlencoded** **X-Requested-With: XMLHttpRequest** Content-Length: 35 firstname=John&lastname=Human+Being
Response	HTTP/1.1 200 OK **Content-Type: application/json; charset=utf-8** Content-Length: 9 544421176

5.6.3 Binding to a Simple Type

ASP.NET Web API can bind the form-URL-encoded data into a simple type parameter as well. We have seen in the previous exercises that the [FromBody] attribute will need to be applied to an action method parameter to let ASP.NET Web API bind the request body to a simple type. In Exercise 5.6.2, to bind to a complex type (our `Employee` type), we sent two name-value pairs: `firstname=John&lastname=Human+Being`. In the case of binding to a simple type, only one value can be sent, since the body must be used as a whole for binding. Also, a name-value pair cannot be sent; the value prefixed with an equal sign is all that can be sent.

1. Modify the POST action method of `EmployeesController` as shown in Listing 5-19. The action method has a parameter of type `string`.

Listing 5-19. POST Action Method Accepting a Simple Type

```
public void Post([FromBody]string lastName)
{
    Trace.WriteLine(lastName);
}
```

2. Rebuild the solution and press F5 to run the project in Visual Studio.

3. From Fiddler's Composer tab, make a POST to http://localhost:55778/api/employees.
   Remember to replace the port 55778 with the actual port that your application runs on.
   Copy and paste Content-Type: application/x-www-form-urlencoded into the Request
   Headers text box and =Human+Being into the Request Body box. Click Execute. The request
   message will be as follows:

```
POST http://localhost:55778/api/employees HTTP/1.1
Host: localhost:55778
Content-Type: application/x-www-form-urlencoded
Content-Length: 12

=Human+Being
```

4. When the execution breaks, inspect the lastName parameter. ASP.NET Web API should
   have set it to Human Being.

You can also use jQuery to submit a single value, as shown in Listing 5-20.

Listing 5-20. jQuery Posting a Single Value (/Home/Index View)

```
@section scripts{
    <script type="text/javascript">
        $.support.cors = true; // Needed for IE

        $(document).ready(function () {
            $('#btnPost').click(function () {
                $.post("http://localhost:55778/api/employees",
                            $('#employeeForm').serialize())
                    .done(function (data) { alert("New employee created. ID is " + data); })
                        .fail(function () { alert("Error creating employee"); });
            });

            $('#btnPostPartial').click(function () {
                $.post("http://localhost:55778/api/employees",
                            { "": $('#lastname').val() })
                    .done(function (data) { alert("Success"); })
                        .fail(function () { alert("Error creating employee"); });
            });
        });
    </script>
}

<form id="employeeForm" action=" http://localhost:55778/api/employees" method="post">
    <div>
        <label for="firstname">First Name:</label>
        <input type="text" id="firstname" name="firstname" />
    </div>
    <div>
        <label for="lastname">Last Name:</label>
        <input type="text" id="lastname" name="lastname" />
    </div>
```

```
        <input type="submit" value="Submit" />
        <input id="btnPost" type="button" value="jQuery POST" />
        <input id="btnPostPartial" type="button" value="jQuery POST Partial" />
</form>
```

■ **Note** ASP.NET Web API can bind form-URL-encoded data to a collection such as List<int>, which is a complex type. By default, ASP.NET Web API binds the request body to a complex type and hence there is no need for the [FromBody] attribute. For example, if you have an action method public void Post(List<int> numbers) {}, by making an HTTP POST with the request body of =1&=2&=3&=4, you can make ASP.NET Web API set the numbers parameter to a list of four integers: 1, 2, 3, and 4.

5.7 Binding dd/MM/yyyy Dates

In this exercise, you will see how to make ASP.NET Web API bind the message content to a DateTime parameter. By default, ASP.NET Web API returns the date in ISO 8601 format; for example 2nd June 1998 is 1998-06-02T00:00:00. If the incoming request payload contains the date in the same format, the Web API will have no trouble correctly binding the parameter. When the client sends a date in some other format, say dd/MM/yyyy, a bit more work is required. This exercise is related to Exercise 3.4.3, Internationalizing the Dates, which demonstrated the formatting of the date into the response content This exercise covers deserialization; that is, binding the date from the request message to a DateTime parameter.

1. Continue to use the same project from the previous exercise.

2. Add a property to the Employee class representing the date the employee joined the organization, with a name of Doj of type DateTime, as shown in Listing 5-21.

    Listing 5-21. Employee Class with Date of Joining

    ```
    using System;

    namespace RequestBinding.Models
    {
        public class Employee
        {
            public int Id { get; set; }
            public string FirstName { get; set; }
            public string LastName { get; set; }

            public DateTime Doj { get; set; }
        }
    }
    ```

3. Modify the Post action method of EmployeesController as shown in Listing 5-22. Put a breakpoint on the opening brace of the action method.

Listing 5-22. Action Method Handling POST

```
public void Post(Employee employee)
{
    // Do Nothing
}
```

4. Rebuild the solution and run the project in Visual Studio.

5. From Fiddler's Composer tab, make a POST to http://localhost:55778/api/employees.
   Remember to replace the port 55778 with the actual port that your application runs
   on. Copy and paste Content-Type: application/json into the Request Headers text
   box and {"Id":12345,"FirstName":"John","LastName":"Human","Doj":"1998-06-
   02T00:00:00"} into the Request Body box. Click Execute.

6. When the execution breaks, inspect the Employee parameter. You will notice that ASP.NET
   Web API has correctly bound the request to the Doj property, which is set to June 02, 1998.

7. Repeat the POST, changing only the Doj:

   {"Id":12345,"FirstName":"John","LastName":"Human","Doj":**"06/02/1998"**}

ASP.NET Web API has again correctly bound the request to the Doj property, which is set to June 02, 1998. Of
course, the correctness depends on which side of the Atlantic you are on! I have regional settings of English (United
States) in my computer, so this interpretation is not surprising. But if you are used to dd/MM/yyyy format, it is not
correct and you will be expecting February 06, 1998 instead.

8. To let ASP.NET Web API use the dd/MM/yyyy format while binding, change the
   SerializerSettings of JsonFormatter in the Register method of WebApiConfig in the
   App_Start folder, as shown in Listing 5-23. You might have a few more lines of code from
   the previous exercises in this class, but those lines will have no bearing on the outcome of
   this exercise. You can leave them as they are or comment them out.

Listing 5-23. Registering the Value Provider

```
public static class WebApiConfig
{
    public static void Register(HttpConfiguration config)
    {
        config.Routes.MapHttpRoute(
            name: "DefaultApi",
            routeTemplate: "api/{controller}/{id}",
            defaults: new { id = RouteParameter.Optional }
        );

        config.Formatters.JsonFormatter.SerializerSettings.Culture =
                                    new System.Globalization.CultureInfo("en-GB");
    }
}
```

9. Rebuild the solution and run the project in Visual Studio. Reissue the same POST. When the execution breaks in the action method, inspect the Doj property of the Employee parameter. Now, the Doj property is February 06, 1998.

This is great as long as your application can work with only one culture. It is not a scalable solution if you must handle multiple cultures at the same time on a per-request basis. As an alternative, we saw the request header Accept-Language being used for localization in the exercises in Chapter 4. We can use the same header to decide on the fly how the model should be bound.

10. Create a new class DateTimeConverter deriving from DateTimeConverterBase, as shown in Listing 5-24.

Listing 5-24. The DateTimeConverter Class

```
using System;
using Newtonsoft.Json;
using Newtonsoft.Json.Converters;

public class DateTimeConverter : DateTimeConverterBase
{
    public override object ReadJson(JsonReader reader, Type objectType,
                                    object existingValue, JsonSerializer serializer)
    {
        return DateTime.Parse(reader.Value.ToString());
    }

    public override void WriteJson(JsonWriter writer, object value, JsonSerializer serializer)
    {
        writer.WriteValue(((DateTime)value).ToString());
    }
}
```

11. For the converter to work correctly, Thread.CurrentCulture must be set correctly and based on Accept-Language. We will use the same message handler created in Chapter 3 for this purpose. Create a new class with a name of CultureHandler and copy and paste the code from Listing 5-25, which shows the earlier code here for your easy reference.

Listing 5-25. A Culture Message Handler

```
using System;
using System.Collections.Generic;
using System.Globalization;
using System.Linq;
using System.Net.Http;
using System.Threading;
using System.Threading.Tasks;

public class CultureHandler : DelegatingHandler
{
    private ISet<string> supportedCultures = new HashSet<string>() { "en-us", "en", "fr-fr", "fr" };
```

```csharp
        protected override async Task<HttpResponseMessage> SendAsync(HttpRequestMessage request,
                                                            CancellationToken cancellationToken)
    {
        var list = request.Headers.AcceptLanguage;
        if (list != null && list.Count > 0)
        {
            var headerValue = list.OrderByDescending(e => e.Quality ?? 1.0D)
                                .Where(e => !e.Quality.HasValue ||
                                        e.Quality.Value > 0.0D)
                                .FirstOrDefault(e => supportedCultures
                                    .Contains(e.Value, StringComparer.OrdinalIgnoreCase));

            // Case 1: We can support what client has asked for
            if (headerValue != null)
            {
                Thread.CurrentThread.CurrentUICulture =
                            CultureInfo.GetCultureInfo(headerValue.Value);

                Thread.CurrentThread.CurrentCulture = Thread.CurrentThread.CurrentUICulture;
            }


            // Case 2: Client is okay to accept anything we support except
            // the ones explicitly specified as not preferred by setting q=0
            if (list.Any(e => e.Value == "*" &&
                    (!e.Quality.HasValue || e.Quality.Value > 0.0D)))
            {
                var culture = supportedCultures.Where(sc =>
                                    !list.Any(e =>
                                        e.Value.Equals(sc,
                                            StringComparison.OrdinalIgnoreCase) &&
                                        e.Quality.HasValue &&
                                        e.Quality.Value == 0.0D))
                                            .FirstOrDefault();
                if (culture != null)
                {
                    Thread.CurrentThread.CurrentUICulture =
                                CultureInfo.GetCultureInfo(culture);

                    Thread.CurrentThread.CurrentCulture = Thread.CurrentThread.CurrentUICulture;
                }
            }
        }

        return await base.SendAsync(request, cancellationToken);
    }
}
```

12. Add the converter to the list of converters and the handler to the handlers collection in WebApiConfig in the App_Start folder, as shown in Listing 5-26. Also, comment out the line of code that hard-coded the culture to en-GB.

Listing 5-26. WebApiConfig with Converter and Handler Added

```
public static class WebApiConfig
{
    public static void Register(HttpConfiguration config)
    {
        config.Routes.MapHttpRoute(
            name: "DefaultApi",
            routeTemplate: "api/{controller}/{id}",
            defaults: new { id = RouteParameter.Optional }
        );

        //config.Formatters.JsonFormatter
        //    .SerializerSettings.Culture = new System.Globalization.CultureInfo("en-GB");

        config.Formatters.JsonFormatter
            .SerializerSettings
                .Converters.Add(new DateTimeConverter());

        config.MessageHandlers.Add(new CultureHandler());
    }
}
```

13. Rebuild the solution and run the project in Visual Studio.

14. From Fiddler's Composer tab, make a POST to `http://localhost:55778/api/employees`. Remember to replace the port 55778 with the actual port that your application runs on. Copy and paste the two headers `Content-Type: application/json` and `Accept-Language: fr-fr` into the Request Headers text box and `{"Id":12345,"FirstName":"John","LastName":"Human","Doj":"06/02/1998"}` into Request Body. Click Execute.

15. When the execution breaks in the action method, inspect the `Doj` property of the `Employee` parameter. Now, the property is February 06, 1998.

16. Repeat the request with `Accept-Language: en-us`, the `Doj` property becomes June 02, 1998. As you can see, our solution is flexible now. ASP.NET Web API binds the value in the request to `Doj` based on the `Accept-Language` header.

5.8 Using TypeConverter

In this exercise, you will use a custom `TypeConverter` to convert a single query string parameter to a complex type, which is a custom class named `Shift`. The `Shift` class has a `DateTime` property, which needs to be bound correctly from the query string parameter. Since the data is read from the query string, the binding type is model binding. In the previous exercise, the data was read from the request body and hence it was parameter binding.

For this exercise, our use case is to get a list of employees based on a shift on a given day. A shift starts and ends the same day. So the search criteria model, which is the `Shift` class, has a `DateTime` component which stores the day and two `TimeSpan` components representing the start and end times. You can model this in multiple ways, but that is not the point of this exercise. Assume this will be the model to which the query string data must be bound.

The query string value is in the form of a date, followed by a T, followed by hours and minutes of the start time, followed by a T and then the hours and minutes of the end time. For example, a request with `Accept-Language: en-us` with query string of `shift=06/02/2012T0800T1700` needs to be bound to a `Shift` object with a `Date` of June the 2nd and `Start` and `End` properties of 8 hours and 17 hours respectively. When the `Accept-Language` header is `fr-fr`, the date will be February the 6th.

1.   Continue to use the project from the previous exercise.

2.   Add the model class Shift to the Models folder, as shown in Listing 5-27.

   Listing 5-27. The Shift Model

```
public class Shift
{
    public DateTime Date { get; set; }

    public TimeSpan Start { get; set; }

    public TimeSpan End { get; set; }
}
```

3.   Add an action method to EmployeesController to handle GET, as shown in Listing 5-28.

   Listing 5-28. The GET Action Method

```
public HttpResponseMessage Get(Shift shift)
{
    // Do something with shift

    var response = new HttpResponseMessage(HttpStatusCode.OK)
    {
        Content = new StringContent("")
    };

    return response;
}
```

4.   Rebuild the solution. Set a breakpoint in the starting brace of the Get action method. Run the project in Visual Studio.

5.   From Fiddler's Composer tab, make a GET to http://localhost:55778/api/employees?shift=06/02/2012T0800T1700. Copy and paste the header Accept-Language: en-us into the Request Headers box and click Execute.

6.   As expected, the Shift parameter is null, since ASP.NET Web API will not be able to create the complex type out of the query string parameter.

7.   Now, create a new class ShiftTypeConverter that derives from TypeConverter, as shown in Listing 5-29. Notice two things about this code:

   a.   The overridden CanConvertFrom method accepts a Type. We check whether this is string and return true. The framework calls this to see if our converter can be used.

   b.   The overridden ConvertFrom method does the actual conversion: parse the data from the query string, which is of type value, and return a new Shift object.

   Listing 5-29. The ShiftTypeConverter Class

```
using System;
using System.ComponentModel;
using System.Globalization;
using RequestBinding.Models;
```

```
public class ShiftTypeConverter : TypeConverter
{
    public override bool CanConvertFrom(ITypeDescriptorContext context, Type sourceType)
    {
        if (sourceType == typeof(string))
            return true;

        return base.CanConvertFrom(context, sourceType);
    }

    public override object ConvertFrom(ITypeDescriptorContext context,
                                                CultureInfo culture, object value)
    {
        if (value is string)
        {
            var parts = ((string)value).Split('T');

            DateTime date;
            if (DateTime.TryParse((string)parts[0], out date))
            {
                return new Shift()
                    {
                        Date = date,
                        Start = parts[1].ToTimeSpan(),
                        End = parts[2].ToTimeSpan()
                    };
            }
        }

        return base.ConvertFrom(context, culture, value);
    }
}
```

8. ToTimeSpan is an extension method I have written for parsing the time part; it is shown in Listing 5-30.

Listing 5-30. The ToTimeSpan Extension Method

```
public static class TimeHelper
{
    public static TimeSpan ToTimeSpan(this string time)
    {
        int hour = Int32.Parse(time.Substring(0, 2));
        int min = Int32.Parse(time.Substring(2, 2));

        return new TimeSpan(hour, min, 0);
    }
}
```

9. To plug the converter in, apply the TypeConverter attribute to the Shift class, at the class level, as shown in Listing 5-31.

Listing 5-31. The Shift Class with TypeConverter

```
using System;
using System.ComponentModel;

[TypeConverter(typeof(ShiftTypeConverter))]
public class Shift
{
        public DateTime Date { get; set; }

        public TimeSpan Start { get; set; }

        public TimeSpan End { get; set; }
}
```

We are all set. For the converter to read and parse the date correctly, we need Thread.CurrentThread.CurrentCulture to be set correctly to the locale sent in the Accept-Language header. The CultureHandler method we saw earlier takes care of this for you when plugged into the pipeline.

10. Rebuild the solution. Set a breakpoint in the starting brace of the Get action method, if it is not already set. Run the project in Visual Studio.

11. From Fiddler's Composer tab, make a GET to http://localhost:55778/api/employees?shift=06/02/2012T0800T1700. Copy and paste the header Accept-Language: en-us into the Request Headers text box and click Execute.

Now, the Shift parameter is correctly set, with the Date property set to June the 2nd.

12. Issue another GET to the same URI with Accept-Language changed to fr-fr. The Shift parameter is correctly set this time as well, with Date property set to February the 6th.

We saw in Exercise 5.4 earlier that a complex type can be bound from a query string. What is the difference here? In Exercise 5.4, the complex type was mapped from multiple query string parameters, with property names matching exactly the query string parameter field name. But in this exercise, we converted the value from one query string parameter into a complex Shift type, hence the use of TypeConverter.

5.9 Creating a Custom Value Provider

In the preceding exercises of this chapter, I showed how the ASP.NET Web API framework binds the incoming HTTP request message, specifically the route data and the query string part of the URI. This is called model binding, the same concept you will be familiar with if you have ASP.NET MVC experience. There are two entities in action here: the *model binder* and the *value provider*. The job of a value provider is to get data from the HTTP request message and feed the values into a model binder to build the model. The value provider abstraction ensures that a model binder is decoupled from the details of the request message. There are two extensibility options associated with model binding:

- A custom Value Provider, implementing IValueProvider
- A custom Model Binder, implementing IModelBinder

The value provider reads a value and maps that to a simple type, typically without any conversion. The model binder builds a model, typically a complex type, based on the values provided by the value providers. Though it is possible to build a model based on entities outside of the request message URI, it is typical for a model binder to limit the scope to the request URI. After all, model binding is limited to the request URI. For binding a model based on entities outside the URI and even outside the request itself, you can use parameter binding.

■ **Note**   A custom value provider or a model binder is applicable only for model binding. If you have experience with ASP.NET MVC, where there is only model binding, it might be difficult at times to realize that model binding is for the URI path and query string only and not for the message body, which is bound by formatter binding.

In this exercise, you will create a custom value provider that gets the value from an HTTP header. To create a new custom value provider, you need to implement the IValueProvider interface and subclass the abstract class ValueProviderFactory.

By default, the model binding acts on the URI path and query, while the formatter binding acts on the request message body. There is no binder out of the box for reading headers. So this exercise shows the steps to create a value provider that does the same thing. A value provider does nothing fancy. As the name indicates, it just provides a value based on some part of the HTTP request message, for the out-of-the-box binders or your own custom binder to bind the values to a model, which could very well be a complex type. A value provider, however, just provides value for simple types.

Before we start writing code, it is important to understand that a request can contain multiple headers of same name but with different values. Not all, but some of them can. The multiple values can also be put into one header with a comma separating them. For example, the following two requests are the same and are valid.

Request 1
```
GET http://localhost:55778/api/employees HTTP/1.1
Host: localhost:55778
Accept: application/xml; q=0.2
Accept: application/json; q = 0.3
```

Request 2
```
GET http://localhost:55778/api/employees HTTP/1.1
Host: localhost:55778
Accept: application/xml; q=0.2, application/json; q = 0.3
```

Our custom value provider must handle these cases. If there are multiple values, they will be bound to a list, as in IEnumerable<T>. If one value, it will be bound to just a simple type. Another point for consideration is the naming convention. HTTP headers typically contain hyphens, while C# variables do not. The value provider must be able to ignore the hyphens and retrieve the value from the header.

1. Continue to use the same project from the previous exercise.

2. Comment out the `public HttpResponseMessage Get(Shift shift) { ... }` action method in EmployeesController from the previous exercise.

3. Add an action method to EmployeesController to handle HTTP GET, as shown in Listing 5-32. The ModelBinder attribute is applied to the ifmatch parameter. By doing this, we are telling Web API that this parameter must be populated using model binding. Web API will figure out the correct value provider, which is HeaderValueProvider, our custom provider, since we will register the corresponding factory. Or we can tell Web API explicitly to use our value provider, like so:

```
Get([ValueProvider(typeof(HeaderValueProviderFactory))]IEnumerable<string> ifmatch)
```

Listing 5-32. The GET Action Method with ModelBinder Applied to the Parameter

```
public HttpResponseMessage Get(
                     [System.Web.Http.ModelBinding.ModelBinder]IEnumerable<string> ifmatch)
{
    var response = new HttpResponseMessage(HttpStatusCode.OK)
    {
        Content = new StringContent(ifmatch.First().ToString())
    };

    return response;
}
```

4. Place a breakpoint in the starting curly brace of the Get action method.

5. Create a class HeaderValueProvider implementing IValueProvider, as shown in Listing 5-33.

    a. The ContainsPrefix method will be called by the model binder to see if our value
        provider can provide a value. If this method returns true, our value provider will be
        chosen by the model binder to provide the value through the GetValue method.

    b. The GetValue method gets the value from the headers based on the key passed in and
        returns it as a new ValueProviderResult object. The basic objective of the method
        is to map the incoming key, which is the name of the parameter, to a request header.
        There are three possible scenarios: (1) if the GetValues method of HttpHeaders
        returns a list with more than one item, it returns that list as IEnumerable. (2) If the list
        contains only one item but the value is a comma separated list of values, it splits the
        individual values and returns them as IEnumerable. (3) If the value is just a normal
        and a single value, GetValue returns it as-is.

Listing 5-33. A Custom Value Provider Class

```
using System;
using System.Collections.Generic;
using System.Globalization;
using System.Linq;
using System.Net.Http.Headers;
using System.Web.Http.ValueProviders;

public class HeaderValueProvider : IValueProvider
{
    private readonly HttpRequestHeaders headers;

    // The function to test each element of the header, which is a KeyValuePair
    // for matching key ignoring the dashes. For example, the If-Match header
    // will be chosen if the parameter is defined with a name ifmatch, ifMatch, etc.
    private Func<KeyValuePair<string, IEnumerable<string>>, string, bool> predicate =
        (header, key) =>
        {
            return header.Key.Replace("-", String.Empty)
                            .Equals(key, StringComparison.OrdinalIgnoreCase);
        };
```

```
        public HeaderValueProvider(HttpRequestHeaders headers)
        {
            this.headers = headers;
        }

        public bool ContainsPrefix(string prefix)
        {
            return headers.Any(h => predicate(h, prefix));
        }

        public ValueProviderResult GetValue(string key)
        {
            var header = headers.FirstOrDefault(h => predicate(h, key));

            if (!String.IsNullOrEmpty(header.Key))
            {
                key = header.Key; // Replace the passed-in key with the header name

                var values = headers.GetValues(key);

                if (values.Count() > 1) // We got a list of values
                    return new ValueProviderResult(values, null, CultureInfo.CurrentCulture);
                else
                {
                    // We could have received multiple values (comma separated) or just one value
                    string value = values.First();
                    values = value.Split(',').Select(x => x.Trim()).ToArray();
                    if (values.Count() > 1)
                        return new ValueProviderResult(values, null, CultureInfo.CurrentCulture);
                    else
                        return new ValueProviderResult(value, value, CultureInfo.CurrentCulture);
                }
            }

            return null;
        }
    }
```

6. Create a class HeaderValueProviderFactory inheriting from ValueProviderFactory, as shown in Listing 5-34. Override the GetValueProvider method to return an instance of our custom value provider.

Listing 5-34. A Value Provider Factory

```
using System.Web.Http.Controllers;
using System.Web.Http.ValueProviders;

public class HeaderValueProviderFactory : ValueProviderFactory
{
    public override IValueProvider GetValueProvider(HttpActionContext actionContext)
    {
```

```
        var request = actionContext.ControllerContext.Request;

        return new HeaderValueProvider(request.Headers);
    }
}
```

7. Register the value provider factory in the `Register` method of `WebApiConfig` in the App_Start folder, as shown in Listing 5-35. You might have few more lines of code from the previous exercises in this class but those lines have no bearing on the outcome of this exercise. You can leave them as they are or comment them out.

Listing 5-35. Registering the Value Provider

```
public static class WebApiConfig
{
    public static void Register(HttpConfiguration config)
    {
        config.Routes.MapHttpRoute(
            name: "DefaultApi",
            routeTemplate: "api/{controller}/{id}",
            defaults: new { id = RouteParameter.Optional }
        );

        //config.Formatters.JsonFormatter
        //     .SerializerSettings.Culture = new System.Globalization.CultureInfo("en-GB");

        config.Services.Add(typeof(
                        System.Web.Http.ValueProviders.ValueProviderFactory),
                                            new HeaderValueProviderFactory());

        config.Formatters.JsonFormatter
            .SerializerSettings
                .Converters.Add(new DateTimeConverter());

        config.EnableSystemDiagnosticsTracing();

        config.MessageHandlers.Add(new CultureHandler());

    }
}
```

8. Rebuild the solution and run the project in Visual Studio.

9. Issue a GET request using Fiddler for `http://localhost:55778/api/employees`, specifying the request header: `If-Match:hello` in the Request Headers text box.

10. Inspect the action method's `ifmatch` parameter when the execution breaks. It is now a list of one value, which is `hello`.

11. Issue another GET request to the same URI. Have two headers, as follows:

    ```
    If-Match:hello
    If-Match:world
    ```

12. The action method `ifmatch` parameter is now a list of two values, which are `hello` and `world`.

13. Issue another GET request using Fiddler for `http://localhost:55778/api/employees`, specifying the request header `If-Match:hello, world` in the Request Headers text box.

14. The action method's `ifmatch` parameter continues to be a list of two values, which are `hello` and `world`.

15. You can change the parameter type from `IEnumerable<string>` to `string` and pass a single header for the value to be mapped correctly. If you pass multiple values, the first one will be mapped to the parameter.

■ **Note** At this point, you might wonder why we bother creating a value provider, when the headers can be directly read from the request in the action method. First of all, the value provider encapsulates the logic of getting the value from the header. We can reuse it in all the places we need the data from the headers. Second, the action method has no dependency on the request object, and unit-testing the action method will be easier.

5.10 Creating a Custom Model Binder

In this exercise, you will create a custom model binder. We saw in the preceding exercises that a type converter reads a value and performs some conversion steps before creating a complex type, whereas a value provider reads a value and maps that to a simple type, typically without any conversion. A model binder, on the other hand, builds a model, typically a complex type, based on the values provided by one or more value providers.

To understand the custom model binder, consider an analogy. If a chef is making the Italian dessert tiramisu, she needs ladyfingers (Savoiardi). She need not make the ladyfingers herself. The chef can have someone else provide it, and she can concentrate on the core business of making tiramisu using the ladyfingers and other ingredients. Now, the chef is the model binder. Whoever provides the ladyfingers is the value provider, and the value is the ladyfinger. The model binder creates the model, which is tiramisu! (This is just an analogy though, so don't read too much into it!)

Let us get on with creating the custom model binder. The URI from which our custom model binder will extract data is `http://localhost:55778/api/employees?dept=eng&dept=rch&doj=06/02/2012`. The request message has a custom header X-CTC-Based, which will need to be bound to the model as well. We will create a custom model binder that will cook up a nice single model based on the URI as well as the header.

1. Continue to use the same project from the previous exercise.

2. Comment out the `public HttpResponseMessage Get([ModelBinder] IEnumerable<string> ifmatch) { ... }` action method in `EmployeesController` from the previous exercise.

3. Add an action method to handle HTTP GET, as shown in Listing 5-36. Since the parameter is a complex type, we apply the `ModelBinder` attribute to the parameter and also let the framework know that the custom binder provided by `TalentScoutModelBinderProvider` must be used.

Listing 5-36. The GET Action Method with Custom Model Binder

```
using System.Net;
using System.Net.Http;
using System.Web.Http;
using System.Web.Http.ModelBinding;
using RequestBinding.Models;

public class EmployeesController : ApiController
{
    public HttpResponseMessage Get(
                        [ModelBinder(typeof(TalentScoutModelBinderProvider))]
                            TalentScout scout)
    {
        // Do your logic with scout model
        var response = new HttpResponseMessage(HttpStatusCode.OK)
        {
            Content = new StringContent("")
        };

        return response;
    }
}
```

4. Place a breakpoint in the starting curly brace of the Get action method.

5. Create a model class named TalentScout in the Models folder, as shown in Listing 5-37.
    The Departments list and Doj will be bound from the query string, whereas IsCtcBased
    will be based on the header. As in the other exercises, the date will be parsed according to
    the thread culture.

Listing 5-37. The TalentScout Model

```
public class TalentScout
{
        public IList<string> Departments { get; set; }
        public bool IsCtcBased { get; set; }
        public DateTime Doj { get; set; }
}
```

6. Create the provider class TalentScoutModelBinderProvider deriving from
    ModelBinderProvider, as shown in Listing 5-38.

Listing 5-38. A Binder Provider

```
using System;
using System.Web.Http;
using System.Web.Http.ModelBinding;

public class TalentScoutModelBinderProvider : ModelBinderProvider
{
    public override IModelBinder GetBinder(HttpConfiguration configuration, Type modelType)
```

```
    {
        return new TalentScoutModelBinder();
    }
}
```

7. Create the custom model binder class that implements IModelBinder, as shown in
    Listing 5-39. The BindModel method is the heart of the model binder. This code takes the
    following steps:

    a. We get the value using context.ValueProvider. If you add a breakpoint and check
        out its type, it will be CompositeValueProvider. It routes the call to all the registered
        value providers, including the one we registered as part of Exercise 5.9. This is how we
        can get the value from different parts of the request message using just one call.

    b. When the call context.ValueProvider.GetValue("dept") is made, the value will be
        provided by QueryStringValueProvider. We split the values by comma and create a
        list out of the values.

    c. When the call context.ValueProvider.GetValue("xctcbased") is made, the value
        will be provided by HeaderValueProvider, the custom value provider we created in
        Exercise 5.9.

    d. When the call context.ValueProvider.GetValue("doj") is made, the value will
        be provided once again by QueryStringValueProvider. We parse the value using
        DateTime.TryParse method. The culture in the thread will be used for this. Since
        the message handler CultureHandler we created in the previous exercise runs in the
        ASP.NET Web API pipeline, it will make sure the culture is set in the thread, before
        execution comes here.

    e. We did not use any value bound from the route. If necessary, we can simply call, for
        example, context.ValueProvider.GetValue("id"), and change the URI to send the
        ID in. That value will be returned to us by RouteDataValueProvider.

Listing 5-39. A Custom Model Binder

```
using System;
using System.Linq;
using System.Web.Http.Controllers;
using System.Web.Http.ModelBinding;
using RequestBinding.Models;

public class TalentScoutModelBinder : IModelBinder
{
    public bool BindModel(HttpActionContext actionContext, ModelBindingContext context)
    {
        var scoutCriteria = (TalentScout)context.Model ?? new TalentScout();

        var result = context.ValueProvider.GetValue("dept");
        if (result != null)
            scoutCriteria.Departments = result.AttemptedValue
                                              .Split(',')
                                                  .Select(d => d.Trim()).ToList();
```

```
        result = context.ValueProvider.GetValue("xctcbased");
        if (result != null)
        {
            int basedOn;
            if (Int32.TryParse(result.AttemptedValue, out basedOn))
            {
                scoutCriteria.IsCtcBased = (basedOn > 0);
            }
        }

        result = context.ValueProvider.GetValue("doj");
        if (result != null)
        {
            DateTime doj;
            if (DateTime.TryParse(result.AttemptedValue, out doj))
            {
                scoutCriteria.Doj = doj;
            }
        }

        context.Model = scoutCriteria;

        return true;
    }
}
```

8. Rebuild the solution and run the project in Visual Studio.

9. Issue a GET request from the Fiddler Composer tab for `http://localhost:55778/api/em ployees?dept=eng&dept=rch&doj=06/02/2012`, specifying two request headers, `Accept-Language: fr-fr` and `X-CTC-Based: 1`, in the Request Headers text box.

10. When the execution breaks, inspect the `TalentScout` parameter. The values are bound, as follows:

    a. `Departments` will be a list of values: `eng` and `rch`. The values are taken directly from the query string for the parameter `dept`.

    b. `IsCtcBased` will be `true`. The value is set based on the numeric value in the header `X-CTC-Based`. Any value greater than zero is considered `true`.

    c. `Doj` will be February 06, since we specify `fr-fr` in the `Accept-Language` header. The value is taken from the query string parameter `doj` but parsed based on the culture in the thread. This is done automatically by the .NET framework.

11. Reissue the previous request with `Accept-Language` as `en-us` and leaving out the `X-CTC-Based` header. `IsCtcBased` will be `false` now. Also, `Doj` will be June 02.

5.11 Creating a Custom Parameter Binder

The two major types of parameter binding in ASP.NET Web API are model binding and formatter binding, respectively represented by the classes `ModelBinderParameterBinding` and `FormatterParameterBinding`. You've seen that model binding binds request URI parts to the action method parameter (simple types, by default) whereas formatter binding binds the request body to the action method parameter (complex types, by default) using media type formatters. Both `ModelBinderParameterBinding` and `FormatterParameterBinding` derive from the abstract class `HttpParameterBinding`.

It is possible to create your own parameter binder by subclassing this abstract class. Typically, a custom parameter binder is created only when the out-of-the-box binding (even after customizing using the extensibility points) is not able to meet your requirements. One good example use case for a custom parameter binder is binding a value that is totally unrelated to the request message. Another example is building your model from multiple request parts: URI, request body, and headers. Out of the box, you can bind from either URI or the request message body but not both. In this exercise, You'll see how to create a custom parameter binder that builds a model from all the three parts: URI, request body, and headers.

For the purpose of this exercise, the incoming request is a PUT request, shown in Listing 5-40.

Listing 5-40. A Request Message

```
PUT http://localhost:55778/api/employees/12345?doj=6/2/1998 HTTP/1.1
Host: localhost:55778
Content-Length: 41
Content-Type: application/json
X-Affiliation: Green Planet

{"FirstName":"John", "LastName":"Human" }
```

The model we will bind this request to is the `Employee` class. The mapping of the request parts to the model will happen as follows:

- The route data `12345` will be mapped to `Employee.Id`.

- The value `6/2/1998` for the parameter `doj` in the query string will be mapped to `Employee.Doj`.

- The value `Green Planet` in the custom header `X-Affiliation` will be mapped to `Employee.Xaffiliation`.

- The values `John` and `Human` in the request body will be mapped to `Employee.FirstName` and `LastName` respectively.

Take the following steps to create and use a custom parameter binder:

1. Continue to use the same project from the previous exercise.

2. Implement an action method in `EmployeesController` to handle HTTP PUT, as shown in Listing 5-41. The method does nothing, but our focus here is to see how the employee parameter is populated from different request parts. Set a breakpoint in the starting brace of the action method and when the execution breaks here, inspect the employee parameter.

   Listing 5-41. A PUT Action Method

   ```
   public void Put(int id, Employee employee)
   {
       // Does nothing!
   }
   ```

3. Modify the `Employee` model class to add a new property, as shown in Listing 5-42. I've used the slightly odd name `Xaffiliation` for the property to match the custom header. This can be fixed by improving the `HeaderValueProvider` that we created in Exercise 5.9. I'll skip that part, since it is not the focus of this exercise.

Listing 5-42. The Employee Class

```
public class Employee
{
        public int Id { get; set; }

        public string FirstName { get; set; }

        public string LastName { get; set; }

        public DateTime Doj { get; set; }

        public string Xaffiliation { get; set; }
}
```

4.   Create a class `AllRequestParameterBinding` deriving from `HttpParameterBinding`, as
     shown in Listing 5-43. There are two private fields, `modelBinding` and `formatterBinding`,
     respectively for model binding and formatter binding. In the constructor, we receive the
     `HttpParameterDescriptor`, which we use to get the corresponding binding by calling the
     `GetBinding` method on new instances of `ModelBinderAttribute` and `FromBodyAttribute`.
     The first `GetBinding` method call on the `ModelBinderAttribute` object returns us
     an object of type `ModelBinderParameterBinding`, and the second call returns an
     object of type `FormatterParameterBinding`. Of course, for both types, the base type is
     `HttpParameterBinding`.

Listing 5-43. The AllRequestParameterBinding Class (Incomplete)

```
using System.Threading;
using System.Threading.Tasks;
using System.Web.Http;
using System.Web.Http.Controllers;
using System.Web.Http.Metadata;
using System.Web.Http.ModelBinding;
using RequestBinding.Models;

public class AllRequestParameterBinding : HttpParameterBinding
{
    private HttpParameterBinding modelBinding = null;
    private HttpParameterBinding formatterBinding = null;

    public AllRequestParameterBinding(HttpParameterDescriptor descriptor)
                                                          : base(descriptor)
    {
        // GetBinding returns ModelBinderParameterBinding
        modelBinding = new ModelBinderAttribute().GetBinding(descriptor);

        // GetBinding returns FormatterParameterBinding
        formatterBinding = new FromBodyAttribute().GetBinding(descriptor);
    }

    // other methods go here
}
```

5. Override the ExecuteBindingAsync method, as shown in Listing 5-44. The step-wise comments are in the listing.

   a. First, we call the ExecuteBindingAsync method of the formatter binder and retrieve the Employee object that was created based on the request body from the context.

   b. Then we call the ExecuteBindingAsync method of the model binder and retrieve the Employee object that was created based on the URI from the context.

   c. Finally, we merge them both and set the merged object that contains the properties from all the request parts back in the context.

   d. Set a breakpoint anywhere inside the method.

Listing 5-44. The ExecuteBindingAsync Method

```
public override async Task ExecuteBindingAsync(ModelMetadataProvider metadataProvider,
                                               HttpActionContext context,
                                               CancellationToken cancellationToken)
{

    // Perform formatter binding
    await formatterBinding.ExecuteBindingAsync(metadataProvider, context,
                                                        cancellationToken);

    // and store the resulting model
    var employee = GetValue(context) as Employee;

    // Perform model binding
    await modelBinding.ExecuteBindingAsync(metadataProvider, context, cancellationToken);

    // and store the resulting model
    var employeeFromUri = GetValue(context) as Employee;

    // Apply the delta on top of the employee object resulting from formatter binding
    employee = Merge(employee, employeeFromUri);

    // Set the merged model in the context
    SetValue(context, employee);
}
```

6. Listing 5-45 shows the Merge method. It uses reflection to compare the properties and sets the changes to the base model and return that as the merged model. Since we use the C# keywords as variable names, we use the @ symbol to make the compiler happy. There is no other special meaning or importance for the use of @.

Listing 5-45. The Merge Method

```
private Employee Merge(Employee @base, Employee @new)
{
    Type employeeType = typeof(Employee);

    foreach (var property in employeeType.GetProperties(
                            BindingFlags.Instance | BindingFlags.Public))
    {
        object baseValue = property.GetValue(@base, null);
        object newValue = property.GetValue(@new, null);

        object defaultValue = property.PropertyType.IsValueType ?
                            Activator.CreateInstance(property.PropertyType) :
                                null;

        if(baseValue == null || baseValue.Equals(defaultValue))
            property.SetValue(@base, newValue);
    }

    return @base;
}
```

7. Modify the Register method of WebApiConfig in the App_Start folder, as shown in Listing 5-46. Ensure that the line that we added to this method as part of the preceding exercise, to add the HeaderValueProviderFactory, still remains in the method. This is needed by the model binder to bind the value from the header.

Listing 5-46. Registering the Binder

```
public static class WebApiConfig
{
    public static void Register(HttpConfiguration config)
    {
        config.Routes.MapHttpRoute(
            name: "DefaultApi",
            routeTemplate: "api/{controller}/{id}",
            defaults: new { id = RouteParameter.Optional }
        );

        config.Services.Add(typeof(System.Web.Http.ValueProviders.ValueProviderFactory),
                            new HeaderValueProviderFactory());

        config.Formatters.JsonFormatter
            .SerializerSettings
                .Converters.Add(new DateTimeConverter());

        config.EnableSystemDiagnosticsTracing();

        config.MessageHandlers.Add(new CultureHandler());

        var rules = config.ParameterBindingRules;
        rules.Insert(0, p =>
        {
```

```
            if (p.ParameterType == typeof(Employee))
            {
                return new AllRequestParameterBinding(p);
            }

            return null;
        });
    }
}
```

8.   Rebuild the solution and run the project in Visual Studio.

9.   Issue a PUT request from the Fiddler Composer tab for http://localhost:55778/
     api/employees/12345?doj=6/2/1998, specifying two request headers, Content-Type:
     application/json and X-Affiliation: Green Planet, in the Request Headers text box.
     Copy and paste the JSON {"FirstName":"John", "LastName":"Human"} in the Request
     Body text box. Click Execute.

10. Execution must break at the breakpoint you have set in the ExecuteBindingAsync
     method. Hover the mouse pointer over the modelBinding field. Keep expanding to
     ModelBinderParameterBinding to ValueProviderFactories. You will see that there are
     three, and the third one is HeaderValueProviderFactory. Only with the help of this is the
     model binder able to bind the X-Affiliation header to the Xaffiliation property.

11. Press F5 and let execution continue until it breaks again in the action method.

12. Inspect the employee parameter. All the properties will be correctly populated from the
     various parts of the request.

5.12 Creating a Custom Media Formatter

In Chapter 3, we created a custom media formatter for serialization. In this exercise, you will extend the same
formatter to bind the request body, which is the fixed-width text, to the action method's Employee type parameter.

   The incoming fixed-width text request will take this format: Employee ID will be 6 digits and zero-prefixed,
followed by the first name and the last name. Both the names will have a length of 20 characters padded with
trailing spaces to ensure the length. Thus, a record for an employee John Human with ID of 12345 will be
012345John<followed by 16 spaces>Human<followed by 15 spaces>.

1.   Continue to use the same project from the previous exercise.

2.   Make sure the EmployeesController class has the action method to handle PUT, which we
     added in Exercise 5.11. Also make sure the breakpoint is still there in the starting brace of
     the action method.

3.   Add a new FixedWidthTextMediaFormatter class to the project, as shown in Listing 5-47.
     This class is taken from Chapter 3. The CanReadType method is modified to return true if
     the type is Employee.

     Listing 5-47. The FixedWidthTextMediaFormatter Class

```
public class FixedWidthTextMediaFormatter : MediaTypeFormatter
{
    public FixedWidthTextMediaFormatter()
```

```csharp
{
    SupportedEncodings.Add(Encoding.UTF8);
    SupportedEncodings.Add(Encoding.Unicode);

    SupportedMediaTypes.Add(new MediaTypeHeaderValue("text/plain"));
}

public override bool CanReadType(Type type)
{
    //return false;
    return typeof(Employee) == type;
}

public override bool CanWriteType(Type type)
{
    return typeof(IEnumerable<Employee>)
                        .IsAssignableFrom(type);
}

public override async Task WriteToStreamAsync(
                            Type type,
                                object value,
                                    Stream stream,
                                        HttpContent content,
                                            TransportContext transportContext)
{
    using (stream)
    {
        Encoding encoding = SelectCharacterEncoding(content.Headers);

        using (var writer = new StreamWriter(stream, encoding))
        {
            var employees = value as IEnumerable<Employee>;
            if (employees != null)
            {
                foreach (var employee in employees)
                {
                    await writer.WriteLineAsync(
                                String.Format("{0:000000}{1,-20}{2,-20}",
                                                employee.Id,
                                                    employee.FirstName,
                                                        employee.LastName));
                }

                await writer.FlushAsync();
            }
        }
    }
}

// ReadFromStreamAsync method goes here
}
```

4. Override the ReadFromStreamAsync method to read the request message body, parse and create an Employee object out of it, as shown in Listing 5-48. We call the SelectCharacterEncoding method from the MediaTypeFormatter base class to get the most appropriate encoding (either the one the client has specifically asked for or the default) and use it to create the StreamReader. Place a breakpoint on the line that creates the new StreamReader.

Listing 5-48. The ReadFromStreamAsync Method

```
public async override Task<object> ReadFromStreamAsync(
                        Type type,
                            Stream readStream,
                                HttpContent content,
                                    IFormatterLogger formatterLogger)
{
    using (readStream)
    {
        Encoding encoding = SelectCharacterEncoding(content.Headers);

        using (var reader = new StreamReader(readStream, encoding))
        {
            string messageBody = await reader.ReadToEndAsync();

            var employee = new Employee();

            employee.Id = Int32.Parse(messageBody.Substring(0, 6));
            employee.FirstName = messageBody.Substring(6, 20).Trim();
            employee.LastName = messageBody.Substring(26, 20).Trim();

            return employee;
        }
    }
}
```

5. Register the formatter in the Register method of WebApiConfig in the App_Start folder, as shown in Listing 5-49.

Listing 5-49. Adding the Formatter to the Collection

```
config.Formatters.Add(
                new FixedWidthTextMediaFormatter());
```

6. Rebuild the solution and run the project from Visual Studio.

7. Make a PUT request to http://localhost:55778/api/employees/12345 from the Composer tab of Fiddler. Remember to include Content-Type: text/plain;charset=utf-16, to indicate to the Web API that you are sending fixed-width format text encoded in UTF-16. Copy and paste the following string without quotes into the Request Body text box and click Execute: "012345John Human".

Request	PUT http://localhost:55778/api/employees/12345 HTTP/1.1 Host: localhost:55778 Content-Type: text/plain;charset=utf-16 Content-Length: 92 012345John Human
Response	HTTP/1.1 204 No Content

8. When the execution breaks in the ReadFromStreamAsync method of the media formatter class, inspect the encoding variable. It will be System.Text.UnicodeEncoding, which is UTF-16. So, the MediaTypeFormatter base class is giving us the encoding coming in the request so we can construct the StreamReader object correctly and read the stream.

9. Press F5 to let the execution continue. When the execution breaks in the action method, inspect the parameter. It will be set in accordance with what we have sent in the request body.

■ **Note** If you leave out charset=utf-16 from the Content-Type header, you will not see any difference other than the encoding returned by the SelectCharacterEncoding method changing to UTF-8. Since we use all English characters and numbers (ASCII characters), it makes no difference, but it is always the best practice to respect the charset in Content-Type header of the request and read the request body accordingly. When you start dealing with charsets corresponding to other languages, this does make a difference.

Summary

One of the powerful features of the ASP.NET Web API framework is *binding*, the process that creates the parameter objects for your action methods in the controller classes. Binding allows a developer to leave the repetitive work related to HTTP infrastructure to the framework and focus on implementing the business requirements at hand.

The ASP.NET Web API framework reads the route data and the query string of the request URI and sets the parameters of the action methods that are simple types (primitives, DateTime, Guid and so on) by the process called *model binding*. The out-of-the-box class that performs model binding is ModelBinderParameterBinding. The parameters that are complex types are set based on the HTTP request message body with the help of media type formatters by the process called *formatter binding*. The out-of-the-box class that performs formatter binding is FormatterParameterBinding. Both classes derive from an abstract class called HttpParameterBinding. By deriving our own custom class from HttpParameterBinding, we can create both simple and complex type parameters from any part of the HTTP request as well as entities outside of the request.

Media formatters have a role to play in both serialization and deserialization. A media formatter can enlist itself in serialization and/or deserialization by returning true when the framework calls the CanWriteType(Type) and CanReadType(Type) methods respectively.

There are various extensibility points available for us to hook our custom code into the binding process, such as creating a custom model binder by implementing IModelBinder, creating a custom value provider by implementing IValueProvider, creating a new media formatter by inheriting from MediaTypeFormatter, extending the capabilities of the out-of-the-box media formatters, creating a new parameter binder by inheriting from HttpParameterBinding, and so on.

CHAPTER 6

Validating Requests

Chapter 5 covered binding, the process by which the ASP.NET Web API framework maps the incoming HTTP request to the parameters of your action methods. As part of the binding process, ASP.NET Web API runs the validation rules you set against the properties of your model classes—a feature called *model validation*. The greatest benefit to using model validation instead of having your validation logic in other classes like controllers, helpers, or domain classes is that the validation logic is isolated in one place instead of duplicated in multiple places where it is difficult to maintain. Model validation helps you follow the Don't Repeat Yourself (DRY) principle.

6.1 Validation Using Data Annotations

In the .NET framework, you can use data annotation attributes to declaratively specify the validation rules. In this exercise, you will use the out-of-the-box attribute classes that are part of the `System.ComponentModel.DataAnnotations` namespace to enforce the validity of the incoming request.

1. Create a new ASP.NET MVC 4 project named `RequestValidation`, using the Web API template.

2. Create a new empty API controller named `EmployeesController`.

3. Create a new model class named `Employee`, as shown in Listing 6-1. Create this class in the `Models` folder. The properties of the `Employee` class have data annotations applied to enforce the following requirements:

    a. For the `Id` property, the input must be between 10000 and 99999.

    b. The `LastName` property must contain a value, and the value cannot exceed a length of 20.

    c. The `Department` property must match the regular expression [0-1][0-9]. In other words, values 00 through 19 are allowed.

Listing 6-1. The Employee Model

```
using System.ComponentModel.DataAnnotations;

public class Employee
{
        [Range(10000, 99999)]
        public int Id { get; set; }
```

```
        public string FirstName { get; set; }

        [Required]
        [MaxLength(20)]
        public string LastName { get; set; }

        [RegularExpression("[0-1][0-9]")]
        public string Department { get; set; }
    }
```

4. Implement an action method to handle HTTP POST in EmployeesController, as shown in
    Listing 6-2. Place a breakpoint on the starting brace of the action method.

    Listing 6-2. The POST Action Method

```
using System.Linq;
using System.Web.Http;
using RequestValidation.Models;

public class EmployeesController : ApiController
{
    public void Post(Employee employee)
    {
        if (ModelState.IsValid)
        {
            // Just be happy and do nothing
        }
        else
        {
            var errors = ModelState.Where(e => e.Value.Errors.Count > 0)
                            .Select(e => new
                            {
                                Name = e.Key,
                                Message = e.Value.Errors.First().ErrorMessage
                            }).ToList();
        }
    }
}
```

5. Rebuild the solution and press F5 to run the project in Visual Studio.

6. Run Fiddler, go to the Composer tab, and issue a POST to the URI
    http://localhost:55778/api/employees. Remember to replace the
    port 55778 with the actual port that your application runs on. Copy the JSON
    {"Id":12345, "FirstName":"John", "LastName":"Human", "Department":"19"}
    into the Request Body text box. Copy Content-Type: application/json into the
    Request Headers text box. Click Execute.

7. When the breakpoint is hit, inspect the IsValid property of ModelState. For this request,
    it will be true, indicating that all is well in terms of the rules you have specified through
    data annotations.

8. Issue another POST to the same URI, keeping `Content-Type: application/json` in the Request Headers text box and putting the JSON `{"Id":12345, "FirstName":"John", "LastName":"Human", "Department":"190"}` in the Request Body text box. Notice the invalid department number that we are supplying in this request.

9. When the breakpoint is hit, inspect `ModelState.IsValid`. For this request, it will be `false`. Step over by pressing F10 until the line that sets `errors` is executed. Inspect `errors`. See Figure 6-1.

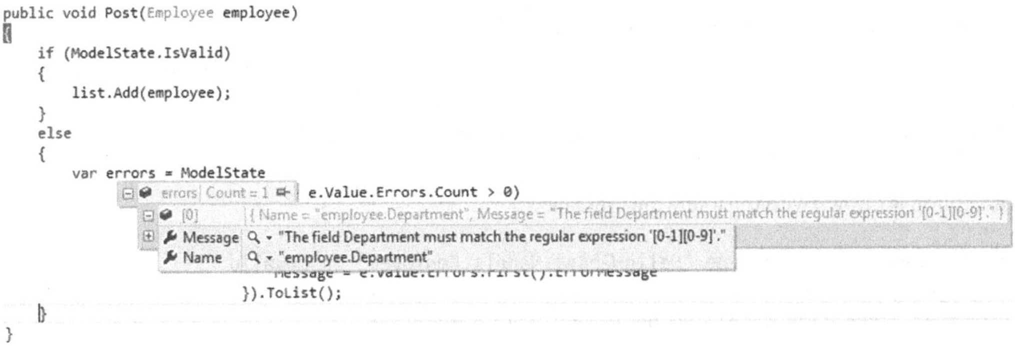

```
public void Post(Employee employee)
{
    if (ModelState.IsValid)
    {
        list.Add(employee);
    }
    else
    {
        var errors = ModelState
```

errors | Count = 1 | e.Value.Errors.Count > 0)
  [0] | { Name = "employee.Department", Message = "The field Department must match the regular expression '[0-1][0-9]'." }
    Message | "The field Department must match the regular expression '[0-1][0-9]'."
    Name | "employee.Department"

```
                message = e.value.errors.rirst().errormessage
                }).ToList();
    }
}
```

Figure 6-1. Model state errors

10. Repeat the request with different JSON payloads like the following, and inspect the resulting errors collection:

  a. `{"Id":123455, "FirstName":"John", "LastName":"Human", "Department":"190"}`

  b. `{"Id":12345, "FirstName":"John", "LastName":"Humannnnnnnnnnnnnnnnnn", "Department":"19"}`

  c. `{"Id":12345, "FirstName":"John", "Department":"19"}`

  d. `{"Id":123455, "FirstName":"John", "LastName":" Humannnnnnnnnnnnnnnnnnn ", "Department":"190"}`

11. By simply checking `ModelState.IsValid` in the action method, you are able to perform the input validation, with the help of data annotation attributes. Generally, in an application these rules are universally applicable and there is no need to replicate the rule in multiple places. Because we've placed the rule in the model class and used model validation, you can simply check `ModelState.IsValid` to determine if all is well in terms of the request validity.

Now, let us examine the unique case of the `Required` attribute being used with a value type such as `int`.

12. Modify the `Employee` class as shown in Listing 6-3. The `Department` property type is changed to `int` and the `Required` attribute has been applied.

Listing 6-3. The Modified Employee Class

```
public class Employee
{
        [Range(10000, 99999)]
        public int Id { get; set; }

        public string FirstName { get; set; }
```

```
        [Required]
        [MaxLength(20)]
        public string LastName { get; set; }

        [Required]
        public int Department { get; set; }
    }
```

13. Rebuild the solution and press F5 to run the project in Visual Studio.

14. From Fiddler's Composer tab, issue a POST to the URI http://localhost:55778/api/employees
    with Content-Type: application/json in the Request Headers text box and the JSON
    {"Id":12345, "FirstName":"John", "LastName":"Human"} in the Request Body box.
    Notice the missing Department field in JSON.

15. An exception is thrown with the following message:

```
Property 'Department' on type 'HelloWebApi.Models.Employee' is invalid.
Value-typed properties marked as [Required] must also be marked with
[DataMember(IsRequired=true)] to be recognized as required.
```

16. A class that is part of the ASP.NET Web API framework, System.Web.Http.Validation.
    Providers.InvalidModelValidatorProvider, is responsible for throwing this exception.
    Depending on when you work through these steps and the version of the ASP.NET Web
    API framework you use at that time, you might not get the exception in the previous
    step. According to the commit f60aadf2b44b (http://aspnetwebstack.codeplex.
    com/SourceControl/changeset/f60aadf2b44ba8d8aee5fd7d09c73d27f9ef7a82),
    InvalidModelValidatorProvider has been removed from the list of default providers,
    but that change has not been released at the time of writing this chapter. If this commit
    is part of the framework version that you use, as you read and work through this chapter,
    you will not get the exception.

17. Put a breakpoint anywhere inside the Register method of WebApiConfig in the App_Start
    folder. Press F5 to run the project. When the execution breaks on this breakpoint, type the
    following line (including the question mark) in the Immediate window of Visual Studio
    and press Enter:

```
?config.Services.GetModelValidatorProviders().ToList()
```

18. Three model validator providers will be displayed.

```
Count = 3
    [0]: {System.Web.Http.Validation.Providers.DataAnnotationsModelValidatorProvider}
    [1]: {System.Web.Http.Validation.Providers.DataMemberModelValidatorProvider}
    [2]: {System.Web.Http.Validation.Providers.InvalidModelValidatorProvider}
```

19. If the version of the ASP.NET Web API framework that you use includes the changes
    from commit f60aadf2b44b to remove InvalidModelValidatorProvider, you will not
    see the provider in the preceding list. However, if you do see the provider, you can easily
    remove it yourself by adding a line of code to the Register method of WebApiConfig in the
    App_Start folder, as shown in Listing 6-4.

Listing 6-4. Removal of InvalidModelValidatorProvider

```
using System.Web.Http;
using System.Web.Http.Validation;
using System.Web.Http.Validation.Providers;

public static class WebApiConfig
{
    public static void Register(HttpConfiguration config)
    {
        config.Routes.MapHttpRoute(
            name: "DefaultApi",
            routeTemplate: "api/{controller}/{id}",
            defaults: new { id = RouteParameter.Optional }
        );

        config.Services.RemoveAll(typeof(ModelValidatorProvider),
                                  v => v is InvalidModelValidatorProvider);
    }
}
```

20. Now, make a slight modification to the Post action method, as shown in Listing 6-5. This modification and the following steps are required, regardless of the version of ASP.NET Web API you are working with.

Listing 6-5. Changes to the Post Action Method

```
public void Post(Employee employee)
{
    if (ModelState.IsValid)
    {
        list.Add(employee);
    }
    else
    {
        var errors = ModelState
                        .Where(e => e.Value.Errors.Count > 0)
                            .Select(e => new
                            {
                                Name = e.Key,
                                Message = e.Value.Errors.First().ErrorMessage,
                                Exception = e.Value.Errors.First().Exception
                            }).ToList();
    }
}
```

21. Rebuild the solution and press F5 to run the project in Visual Studio.

22. From Fiddler's Composer tab, issue a POST to the URI http://localhost:55778/api/employees. Remember to replace the port 55778 with the actual port that your application runs on. Copy the JSON {"Id":12345, "FirstName":"John", "LastName":"Human"} into the Request Body text box. Note the missing Department in the JSON. Copy Content-Type: application/json into the Request Headers box. Click Execute.

23. There is no exception this time. When the execution breaks inside the action method of the controller, inspect `ModelState.IsValid`. It is `false`. Keep stepping by pressing F10 a few times, until the errors variable is populated. Inspect `errors`. You will see that Exception has a clear message: `Required property 'Department' not found in JSON. Path '', line 1, position 52.`

24. Press F5 to continue.

25. With the project still running in Visual Studio, issue another POST request from Fiddler with `Content-Type: application/xml` in the Request Headers text box and the following XML in the Request Body text box. This XML is very similar to the JSON we used earlier in that Department is missing here as well.

```
<Employee xmlns="http://schemas.datacontract.org/2004/07/RequestValidation.Models">
    <FirstName>John</FirstName>
    <Id>12345</Id>
    <LastName>Human</LastName>
</Employee>
```

26. There is no exception this time as well, as expected. When the execution breaks, inspect `ModelState.IsValid`. It is true, and that is unexpected!

27. The major reason for having the `InvalidModelValidatorProvider` is to prevent the situation we are in right now. When the value is missing, the property, being a value type, cannot be null and is assigned the default value (0 in the case of `int`). Some formatters will not raise a model error, making the developer think all is well, when it is actually not. `XmlMediaTypeFormatter` does exactly this and will only raise a model error when the `DataMember(IsRequired=true)` attribute is applied.

28. `InvalidModelValidatorProvider` will be removed in a future release (unless it has already been removed by the time you read this), but it is worth noting the challenge of using the `Required` attribute on value types. It is important to note that `XmlMediaTypeFormatter` will not work correctly with the `Required` attribute against value types. It will need the `DataMember(IsRequired=true)` attribute to be applied to create model errors correctly, when a value type is missing in the request.

6.2 Handling Validation Errors

In this exercise, you will handle the errors raised by model validation as part of the binding process. Model validation runs the checks and sets the `ModelState` accordingly. It does not fail the request by sending back the errors. You must check the `ModelState` and take actions that are appropriate for the requirement at hand.

In the ASP.NET Web API pipeline, after the request processing part of the message handlers runs, the authorization filters are run (if you have used the `Authorize` attribute). Following this, model binding and the model validation occur. Then the action filters are run. More specifically, the `OnActionExecuting` method of each action filter is run, and then the action method of the controller runs. Hence, we can check for `ModelState` and send the error back in the `OnActionExecuting` method of an action filter. This is ideal because the model validation is finished by the time execution comes to the action filter, but the action method of the controller is yet to run. See Figure 6-2.

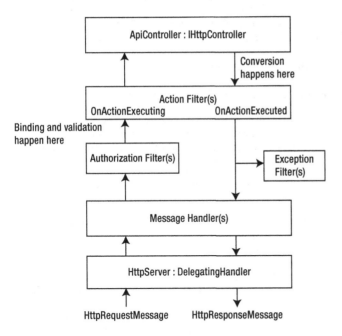

Figure 6-2. Action filters in the ASP.NET Web API pipeline

1. Add a new class named ValidationErrorHandlerFilterAttribute that derives from ActionFilterAttribute, as shown in Listing 6-6.

Listing 6-6. The ValidationErrorHandlerFilterAttribute Class

```
using System.Net;
using System.Net.Http;
using System.Web.Http.Controllers;
using System.Web.Http.Filters;

public class ValidationErrorHandlerFilterAttribute : ActionFilterAttribute
{
    public override void OnActionExecuting(HttpActionContext actionContext)
    {
        if (!actionContext.ModelState.IsValid)
        {
            actionContext.Response = actionContext.Request
                                                .CreateErrorResponse(
                                                    HttpStatusCode.BadRequest,
                                                    actionContext.ModelState);
        }
    }
}
```

163

2. You can apply this selectively on your controller classes or configure it as a global filter in the `Register` method of `WebApiConfig` in the `App_Start` folder, like so:

    ```
    config.Filters.Add(new ValidationErrorHandlerFilterAttribute());
    ```

3. Rebuild the solution and press F5 to run the project in Visual Studio.

4. From Fiddler's Composer tab, issue a POST to the URI `http://localhost:55778/api/employees` with the JSON `{"Id":12345, "FirstName":"John", "LastName":"Humansssssssssssssss ssssssssssssssssssss"}` in the Request Body text box and `Content-Type: application/json` in the Request Headers box.

5. Review the response message in the Inspectors tab in Fiddler. You will get a response with a 400 status code and a response body containing JSON:

    ```
    {
        "Message":"The request is invalid.",
        "ModelState":{
            "employee":[
                "Required property 'Department' not found in JSON. Path '', line 1, position 85."
            ],
            "employee.LastName":[
                "The field LastName must be a string or array type with a maximum length of '20'."
            ]
        }
    }
    ```

6. Issue a POST to the URI `http://localhost:55778/api/employees` with the following XML in the Request Body text box and `Content-Type: application/xml` in the Request Headers box:

    ```
    <Employee xmlns="http://schemas.datacontract.org/2004/07/RequestValidation.Models">
            <FirstName>John</FirstName>
            <Id>12345</Id>
            <LastName>Humansssssssssssssssssssssssssssssssssssssss</LastName>
    </Employee>
    ```

7. You will now get an XML response:

    ```
    <Error>
            <Message>The request is invalid.</Message>
            <ModelState>
                    <employee.LastName>
                     The field LastName must be a string or array type with a maximum length of '20'.
                    </employee.LastName>
            </ModelState>
    </Error>
    ```

You can see that ASP.NET Web API is serializing even the errors into the appropriate media type based on the results of content negotiation.

It's also important to notice that although we did not supply a value for department in the XML request, there is no error, unlike in the JSON behavior. Recall that in an earlier exercise we removed InvalidModelValidatorProvider. XmlMediaTypeFormatter will not work with the Required attribute against value types. It will need the DataMember(IsRequired=true) attribute to be applied to create model errors correctly.

8. Change the Employee class as shown in Listing 6-7. This time we specify the error message that needs to be sent back when the validation fails.

   Listing 6-7. The Employee Class with a Custom Error Message

```
public class Employee
{
    [Range(10000, 99999)]
    public int Id { get; set; }

    public string FirstName { get; set; }

    [Required]
    [MaxLength(20,
        ErrorMessage="You can enter only 20 characters.
                                    No disrespect it is only a system constraint")]
    public string LastName { get; set; }

    [Required]
    public int Department { get; set; }
}
```

9. Rebuild the solution and from Fiddler issue a POST to the URI http://localhost:55778/api/employees with the JSON {"Id":12345, "FirstName":"John", "LastName":"Human ssssssssssssssssssssssssssssssssss"} in the Request Body text box and Content-Type: application/json in the Request Headers box. The response is as follows:

```
{
    "Message":"The request is invalid.",
    "ModelState":{
        "employee.LastName":[
            "You can enter only 20 characters. No disrespect it is only a system constraint"
        ]
    }
}
```

10. Change the Employee class as shown in Listing 6-8. Here we don't specify the error message directly but point to the resource file from which the message is to be picked up.

    Listing 6-8. The Employee Class with a Custom Error Message From the Resource File

```
using System.ComponentModel.DataAnnotations;
using Resources;

public class Employee
{
    [Range(10000, 99999)]
    public int Id { get; set; }
```

```
        public string FirstName { get; set; }

        [Required]
        [MaxLength(20,
            ErrorMessageResourceName = "InvalidLastNameLength",
            ErrorMessageResourceType = typeof(Messages))]

        public string LastName { get; set; }

        [Required]
        public int Department { get; set; }
    }
```

11. Let us create the resource files now. Right-click on the project in Solution Explorer from Visual Studio and select Add ➤ Add ASP.NET Folder ➤ App_GlobalResources.

12. Right-click the App_GlobalResources folder created and select Add ➤ New Item... Select Resources File and give it a name of Messages.resx.

13. Add a new string with a Name of InvalidLastNameLength and a Value of You can enter only 20 characters. No disrespect it is only a system constraint. Save.

14. Duplicate the Message.resx by pasting the file into the same folder. Rename the duplicate file as Messages.fr-fr.resx.

15. Copy and paste **Vous pouvez entrer que 20 caractères. Sans manquer de respect, il est seulement une contrainte de système** into Value. Save.

16. We need the CultureHandler message handler that we created in Chapter 4. This message handler gets the language preferences from the Accept-Language request header and establishes the CurrentUICulture. For simplicity, this exercise supports only two cultures, English, United States (en-us) and French, France (fr-fr). Create a new class named CultureHandler and copy and paste the code from Listing 6-9.

Listing 6-9. The CultureHandler Class

```
using System;
using System.Collections.Generic;
using System.Globalization;
using System.Linq;
using System.Net.Http;
using System.Threading;
using System.Threading.Tasks;

public class CultureHandler : DelegatingHandler
{
    private ISet<string> supportedCultures = new HashSet<string>() { "en-us", "en", "fr-fr", "fr" };

    protected override async Task<HttpResponseMessage> SendAsync(HttpRequestMessage request,
                                                    CancellationToken cancellationToken)
    {
        var list = request.Headers.AcceptLanguage;
        if (list != null && list.Count > 0)
```

```
    {
        var headerValue = list.OrderByDescending(e => e.Quality ?? 1.0D)
                              .Where(e => !e.Quality.HasValue ||
                                          e.Quality.Value > 0.0D)
                              .FirstOrDefault(e => supportedCultures
                                      .Contains(e.Value, StringComparer.OrdinalIgnoreCase));

        // Case 1: We can support what client has asked for
        if (headerValue != null)
        {
            Thread.CurrentThread.CurrentUICulture =
                        CultureInfo.GetCultureInfo(headerValue.Value);

            Thread.CurrentThread.CurrentCulture =
                                        Thread.CurrentThread.CurrentUICulture;
        }

        // Case 2: Client is okay to accept anything we support except
        // the ones explicitly specified as not preferred by setting q=0
        if (list.Any(e => e.Value == "*" &&
                (!e.Quality.HasValue || e.Quality.Value > 0.0D)))
        {
            var culture = supportedCultures.Where(sc =>
                                !list.Any(e =>
                                        e.Value.Equals(sc, StringComparison.OrdinalIgnoreCase) &&
                                        e.Quality.HasValue &&
                                        e.Quality.Value == 0.0D))
                                    .FirstOrDefault();
            if (culture != null)
            {
                Thread.CurrentThread.CurrentUICulture =
                                CultureInfo.GetCultureInfo(culture);

                Thread.CurrentThread.CurrentCulture =
                                        Thread.CurrentThread.CurrentUICulture;
            }
        }
    }

    return await base.SendAsync(request, cancellationToken);
    }
}
```

17. Add the handler to the handlers collection in WebApiConfig in the App_Start folder:

    ```
    config.MessageHandlers.Add(new CultureHandler());
    ```

18. Rebuild the solution and issue a POST from Fiddler to the URI http://localhost:55778/
    api/employees with the JSON {"Id":12345, "FirstName":"John", "LastName":"Human
    sssssssssssssssssssssssssssssssssssss", "Department": 5} in the Request Body text box
    and Content-Type: application/json in the Request Headers box.

19. The response is in English and is as follows.

```
{
    "Message":"The request is invalid.",
    "ModelState":{
       "employee.LastName":[
          "You can enter only 20 characters. No disrespect it is only a system constraint"
       ]
    }
}
```

20. Repeat the previous POST request with an additional request header of Accept-Language: fr-fr.

21. The response is now in French and the JSON is as follows:

```
{
    "Message":"The request is invalid.",
    "ModelState":{
       "employee.LastName":[
          "Vous pouvez entrer que 20 caractères. Sans manquer de respect, il est seulement une
          contrainte de système"
       ]
    }
}
```

6.3 Extending an Out-of-the-Box Validation Attribute

When an out-of-the-box validation attribute does not meet all your requirements, you can extend it with additional functionality. To illustrate this point, in this exercise, you will extend the out-of-the-box validation attribute Range to make the range validation applicable for all the members of a collection.

1. Modify the Employee class, as shown in Listing 6-10. The Department property type is changed to List<int>, and the MemberRange attribute, which we create based on the Range attribute, has been applied.

   Listing 6-10. The Modified Employee Class with the MemberRange Attribute

```
public class Employee
{
        [Range(10000, 99999)]
        public int Id { get; set; }

        public string FirstName { get; set; }

        [Required]
        [MaxLength(20)]
        public string LastName { get; set; }

        [MemberRange(0, 9)]
        public List<int> Department { get; set; }
}
```

2. Create the `MemberRangeAttribute` class, which derives from `RangeAttribute`, as shown in
    Listing 6-11. This code overrides the `IsValid` method to validate every individual member
    of the collection that calls the `IsValid` method of the base class.

    Listing 6-11. The MemberRangeAttribute Class

    ```
    using System.Collections;
    using System.ComponentModel.DataAnnotations;
    using System.Linq;

    public class MemberRangeAttribute : RangeAttribute
    {
        public MemberRangeAttribute(int minimum, int maximum) : base(minimum, maximum) { }

        public override bool IsValid(object value)
        {
            if (value is ICollection)
            {
                var items = (ICollection)value;
                return items.Cast<int>().All(i => IsValid(i));
            }
            else
                return base.IsValid(value);
        }
    }
    ```

3. Rebuild the solution and issue a POST from Fiddler to the URI
    `http://localhost:55778/api/employees` with the JSON
    `{"Id":12345, "FirstName":"John", "LastName":"Human", "Department":[0,9]}`
    in the Request Body text box and `Content-Type: application/json` in the Request
    Headers box.

This request goes through without any validation failures and an HTTP status code of `204 - No Content`
is returned.

4. Issue another POST to the URI `http://localhost:55778/api/employees` with the JSON
    `{"Id":12345, "FirstName":"John", "LastName":"Human", "Department":[90,9]}`
    in the Request Body text box and `Content-Type: application/json` in the Request
    Headers box.

The response is

```
{"Message":"The request is invalid.","ModelState":{"employee.Department":["The field Department must
be between 0 and 9."]}}
```

As you can see, we have extended the out-of-the-box `RangeAttribute` and created a new attribute that applies
the range validation logic on each of the members of the collection.

6.4 Creating Your Own Validation Attribute

In this exercise, you will create your own validation attribute that enforces validation based on the value of some other property. In the examples we have seen so far, the validation is limited to the value of a property in isolation. In reality, the rules to be checked against a property can be dependent on some other property of the same model. Say, you want to implement an internal policy related to the employee contribution to 401K, which is that an employee can contribute a maximum of 75 percent of their annual income. Here the validation rule for the contribution amount depends on a static value of 75 percent and the value of the other property that stores the annual income.

1. Modify the Employee class as shown in Listing 6-12. Two new properties are introduced: AnnualIncome and Contribution401K. The LimitChecker custom attribute is applied to the Contribution401K property.

   Listing 6-12. The Employee Class with a Custom Validation Attribute

   ```
   public class Employee
       {
           [Range(10000, 99999)]
           public int Id { get; set; }

           public string FirstName { get; set; }

           [Required]
           [MaxLength(20,
               ErrorMessageResourceName = "InvalidLastNameLength",
               ErrorMessageResourceType = typeof(Messages))]

           public string LastName { get; set; }

           [MemberRange(0, 9)]
           public List<int> Department { get; set; }

           public decimal AnnualIncome { get; set; }

           [LimitChecker("AnnualIncome", 75)]
           public decimal Contribution401K { get; set; }
       }
   ```

2. Create the new LimitCheckerAttribute class, deriving from ValidationAttribute, as shown in Listing 6-13. This code works as follows:

   a. The BaseProperty and Percentage properties store the values passed in, respectively the name of the property that is the basis for the property to which this attribute is applied, and the percentage value. In our example, BaseProperty will be the string "AnnualIncome", which is the name of the property that Contribution401K will be based on.

   b. In the IsValid method, we just get the base amount, which is the value in the AnnualIncome property from the ValidationContext object. Then it is simple math to check whether the value passed in, which is the value of Contribution401K, is less than or equal to 75 percent of AnnualIncome.

c.   In the FormatErrorMessage method, we just plug in the property names and the percentage value so that the resulting error message is easy to understand.

Listing 6-13. The LimitCheckerAttribute Class

```
using System.ComponentModel.DataAnnotations;

public class LimitCheckerAttribute : ValidationAttribute
{
    public LimitCheckerAttribute(string baseProperty, double percentage)
    {
        this.BaseProperty = baseProperty;
        this.Percentage = percentage;
        this.ErrorMessage = "{0} cannot exceed {1}% of {2}";
    }

    public string BaseProperty { get; set; }
    public double Percentage { get; set; }

    public override string FormatErrorMessage(string name)
    {
        return string.Format(ErrorMessageString, name, this.Percentage, BaseProperty);
    }

    protected override ValidationResult IsValid(object value,
                                                ValidationContext validationContext)
    {
        decimal amount = (decimal)value;

        var propertyInfo = validationContext
                                    .ObjectType
                                        .GetProperty(this.BaseProperty);

        if (propertyInfo != null)
        {
            decimal baseAmount = (decimal)propertyInfo.GetValue(
                                            validationContext.ObjectInstance, null);

            decimal maxLimit = baseAmount * (decimal)this.Percentage / 100;

            if(amount <= maxLimit)
                return ValidationResult.Success;
        }

        return new ValidationResult(
                    FormatErrorMessage(validationContext.DisplayName));
    }
}
```

3. Rebuild the solution and issue a POST from Fiddler to the URI
   http://localhost:55778/api/employees with the JSON {"Id":12345,
   "FirstName":"John", "LastName":"Human", "Department": [1],
   "AnnualIncome": 100, "Contribution401K":75.01} in the Request Body text box
   and Content-Type: application/json in the Request Headers box

4. The response is as follows.

```
{
    "Message":"The request is invalid.",
    "ModelState":{
        "employee.Contribution401K":[
            "Contribution401K cannot exceed 75% of AnnualIncome"
        ]
    }
}
```

6.5 Implementing the IValidatableObject Interface

In this exercise, you will implement the System.ComponentModel.DataAnnotations.IValidatableObject interface in the Employee class. So far in this chapter, we have been focusing on the validity of a property in isolation. Even in the case of the custom validation attribute, our focus is on a specific property, which is Contribution401K. Although we compared it to the value of another property (AnnualIncome) in the process of validating the original property, our basic objective is validating the Contribution401K property.

By implementing the IValidatableObject interface, however, you can examine the object as a whole with all the properties to determine if the object state is valid or not. Though validation attributes help you keep the validation logic in one place, implementing IValidatableObject lets you keep all the business and the validation rules of a model class in one place, which is the class itself. Using validation attributes lets you specify the rules in a declarative way, whereas implementing IValidatableObject lets you specify the rules in an imperative way.

1. Modify the Employee class by commenting out the existing class and pasting the code from Listing 6-14. Here we implement the IValidatableObject interface and as part of that, implement the Validate method. We just make all the validations in this method imperatively and yield the return ValidationResult.

Listing 6-14. The Employee Class Implementing IValidatableObject

```
using System;
using System.Collections.Generic;
using System.ComponentModel.DataAnnotations;

public class Employee : IValidatableObject
{
    private const decimal PERCENTAGE = 0.75M;

    public int Id { get; set; }

    public string FirstName { get; set; }

    public string LastName { get; set; }
```

```
public decimal AnnualIncome { get; set; }

public decimal Contribution401K { get; set; }

public IEnumerable<ValidationResult> Validate(ValidationContext validationContext)
{
    if(this.Id < 10000 || this.Id > 99999)
        yield return new ValidationResult("ID must be in the range 10000 - 99999");

    if (String.IsNullOrEmpty(this.LastName))
        yield return new ValidationResult("Last Name is mandatory");
    else if(this.LastName.Length > 20)
        yield return new ValidationResult(
                    "You can enter only 20 characters. No disrespect it is only a system constraint");

    if (this.Contribution401K > Decimal.Zero &&
            this.Contribution401K > this.AnnualIncome * PERCENTAGE)
        yield return new ValidationResult(
                            "You can contribute a maximum of 75% of your annual income to 401K");
    }
}
```

2. Rebuild the solution and issue a POST to the URI http://localhost:55778/api/ employees with the JSON {"Id":123455, "FirstName":"Johnny", "LastName":" Humanssssssssssssssssssssssssssssssssssssssssssss", "AnnualIncome": 100, "Contribution401K":75.01} in the Request Body box.

3. The response is as follows.

```
{
    "Message":"The request is invalid.",
    "ModelState":{
        "employee":[
            "ID must be in the range 10000 - 99999",
            "You can enter only 20 characters. No disrespect it is only a system constraint",
            "You can contribute a maximum of 75% of your annual income to 401K"
        ]
    }
}
```

Summary

Binding is the process by which the ASP.NET Web API framework maps the incoming HTTP request to the parameters of your action methods. As part of the binding process, ASP.NET Web API runs the validation rules you set against the properties of your model classes; this feature is called model validation. The greatest benefit of using model validation is that your validation code is all in one place, following the Don't Repeat Yourself (DRY) principle.

In the .NET framework, you can use data annotation attributes to specify the validation rules declaratively. You can use the out-of-the-box attribute classes that are part of the System.ComponentModel.DataAnnotations namespace to enforce the validity of the incoming request with ASP.NET Web API.

Model validation runs the checks and sets the ModelState based on the result of these checks. However, model binding does not fail the request by sending back the errors. A developer must check the ModelState and take actions that are appropriate for the requirement at hand. You can check for ModelState and send the error back in the OnActionExecuting method of an action filter. This is ideal for most cases because the model validation is complete by the time execution comes to the action filter, but the action method of the controller is yet to run.

In addition to using the out-of-the-box validation attributes from the System.ComponentModel.DataAnnotations namespace, you can also subclass an existing attribute and extend its out-of-the-box functionality. Another option is to create your own custom validation attribute by deriving from the System.ComponentModel.DataAnnotations. ValidationAttribute abstract class.

Finally, by creating a validatable object by implementing the System.ComponentModel.DataAnnotations. IValidatableObject interface, you can look at the model object as a whole with all the properties to determine if the object state is valid or not. Though validation attributes help you keep the validation logic in one place, implementing IValidatableObject lets you keep all the business and the validation rules of a model class in one place, which is the model class itself. Using validation attributes lets you specify the rules in a declarative way, whereas implementing IValidatableObject lets you specify the rules in an imperative way.

■ ■ ■

CHAPTER 7

Managing Controller Dependencies

The term *dependency* or *coupling* is used to denote the degree to which a software component depends on another. The controller class that you create is one of the important components in ASP.NET Web API, since it is the business end where all the application-specific action happens.

ASP.NET Web API uses the same convention-over-configuration programming model as ASP.NET MVC. One of the great things—maybe the greatest thing—about ASP.NET MVC compared to ASP.NET Web Forms is the ease with which controller classes can be unit-tested without spinning the wheels of ASP.NET infrastructure. In that aspect, ASP.NET Web API is as testable as ASP.NET MVC. However, you need to pay attention to the dependencies your controller classes take, as you design and construct your service to ensure testability.

A very common dependency that an ASP.NET Web API controller takes is the dependency on the classes related to persistence infrastructure such as a database. If your controller classes are tightly coupled to the database, unit tests you write will start exercising the database, and they will no longer be unit tests but become integration tests. In this chapter, I'll show you how to use the Entity Framework, which is the Microsoft-recommended technology for data access with ASP.NET Web API in a loosely coupled way. The Entity Framework is an object-relational mapper (ORM) that enables .NET developers to work with a relational database such as Microsoft SQL Server using normal CLR objects.

7.1 Taking Dependency on the Entity Framework

In this exercise, you will use Microsoft SQL Server 2012 as the persistence store for your web API. You will use Entity Framework as the ORM and adopt the simplest approach, which is to use the Entity Framework classes directly inside your controller class and thereby take a *hard dependency* on EF. For this exercise, I've used Microsoft SQL Server 2012 Developer Edition but you can also use Express Edition.

It is quite possible for you to work with the existing tables and the data using the Entity Framework's Code First approach. Code First allows you to define your classes and map the classes and properties to tables and columns using a nice fluent API. You will follow this approach in this exercise and create two entities: Employee and Department.

1. Run Visual Studio 2012. Select File ➤ New ➤ Project and create a blank solution named TalentManager, as shown in Figure 7-1.

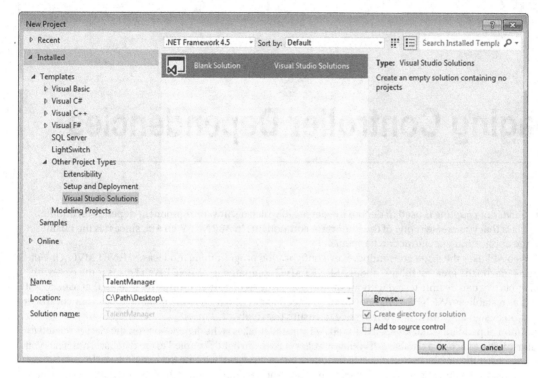

Figure 7-1. *A blank solution*

2. In the Solution Explorer, right-click Solution 'TalentManager' and choose Add ➤ New Project. Under Visual C# templates, select Web and choose ASP.NET MVC 4 Web Application. Give it a name of `TalentManager.Web`.

3. Select the Web API template and leave the View engine as Razor. Click OK.

4. In the Solution Explorer, right-click Solution 'Talent Manager' and choose Add ➤ New Project. Under Visual C# templates, select Windows and choose Class Library. Give it a name of `TalentManager.Data`. Click OK. Delete `Class1`.

5. Repeat the previous step and create one more Class Library project named `TalentManager.Domain`. Delete `Class1`.

6. Right-click References under TalentManager.Data. Select Manage NuGet Packages ➤ EntityFramework and click Install. My example uses EntityFramework 5.0.0.

7. Right-click References under TalentManager.Data and select Add Reference. If it is not already checked, check `System.Data.Entity` and `System.ComponentModel.DataAnnotations` under Framework. Also, check `TalentManager.Domain` under Projects. Click OK.

8. Right-click References under `TalentManager.Web`. Select Add Reference. Check `TalentManager.Domain` and `TalentManager.Data` under Projects. Click OK.

9. Rebuild the solution to make sure all is well.

10. In the TalentManager.Domain project, create new classes Employee and Department, as shown in Listing 7-1. An employee must always be part of a department, and the association reflects this rule. The Employee class has Department property and the navigation is one way only. The RowVersion property is for concurrency handling, which we will see in Chapter 8.

Listing 7-1. Domain Classes

```
public class Employee
{
    public int Id { get; set; }

    public string FirstName { get; set; }

    public string LastName { get; set; }

    // Foreign key association
    public int DepartmentId { get; set; }

    // Independent association
    public virtual Department Department { get; set; }

    public byte[] RowVersion { get; set; }
}

public class Department
{
    public int Id { get; set; }

    public string Name { get; set; }

    public byte[] RowVersion { get; set; }
}
```

11. In the TalentManager.Data project, create a new folder named Configuration. Create two classes: EmployeeConfiguration and DepartmentConfiguration, as shown in Listing 7-2.

Listing 7-2. Configuration Classes

```
using System.ComponentModel.DataAnnotations.Schema;
using System.Data.Entity.ModelConfiguration;
using TalentManager.Domain;

public class EmployeeConfiguration : EntityTypeConfiguration<Employee>
{
    public EmployeeConfiguration()
    {
        HasKey(k => k.Id);

        Property(p => p.Id)
            .HasColumnName("employee_id")
                .HasDatabaseGeneratedOption(DatabaseGeneratedOption.Identity);
```

```
        Property(p => p.FirstName).HasColumnName("first_name");
        Property(p => p.LastName).HasColumnName("last_name");
        Property(p => p.DepartmentId).HasColumnName("department_id");

        HasRequired(x => x.Department);

        Property(p => p.RowVersion).HasColumnName("row_version").IsRowVersion();
    }
}


using System.ComponentModel.DataAnnotations.Schema;
using System.Data.Entity.ModelConfiguration;
using TalentManager.Domain;

public class DepartmentConfiguration : EntityTypeConfiguration<Department>
{
    public DepartmentConfiguration()
    {
        HasKey(k => k.Id);

        Property(p => p.Id)
            .HasColumnName("department_id")
                .HasDatabaseGeneratedOption(DatabaseGeneratedOption.Identity);

        Property(p => p.Name).HasColumnName("name");

        Property(p => p.RowVersion).HasColumnName("row_version")
            .IsRowVersion();
    }
}
```

12. In the TalentManager.Data project, create a class Context, as shown in Listing 7-3.

Listing 7-3. The Context Class

```
using System.Data.Entity;
using System.Data.Entity.ModelConfiguration.Conventions;
using TalentManager.Data.Configuration;
using TalentManager.Domain;

public class Context : DbContext
{
    public Context() : base("DefaultConnection") { }

    public DbSet<Employee> Employees { get; set; }
    public DbSet<Department> Departments { get; set; }

    protected override void OnModelCreating(DbModelBuilder modelBuilder)
    {
        modelBuilder.Conventions
                        .Remove<PluralizingTableNameConvention>();
```

```
        modelBuilder.Configurations
            .Add(new EmployeeConfiguration())
            .Add(new DepartmentConfiguration());


    }
}
```

13. Modify the Application_Start method of the Globax.asax.cs file under
    TalentManager.Web, as shown in Listing 7-4. We create the database and tables manually
    and so we tell the Entity Framework not to do any of those tasks.

    Listing 7-4. The Application_Start Method

```
using System.Data.Entity;
using System.Web.Http;
using System.Web.Mvc;
using System.Web.Optimization;
using System.Web.Routing;
using TalentManager.Data;

public class WebApiApplication : System.Web.HttpApplication
{
    protected void Application_Start()
    {
        AreaRegistration.RegisterAllAreas();

        WebApiConfig.Register(GlobalConfiguration.Configuration);
        FilterConfig.RegisterGlobalFilters(GlobalFilters.Filters);
        RouteConfig.RegisterRoutes(RouteTable.Routes);
        BundleConfig.RegisterBundles(BundleTable.Bundles);

        Database.SetInitializer<Context>(null);
    }
}
```

14. In the Web.config file of TalentManager.Web, change the connection string as shown in
    Listing 7-5. My example uses SQL Server 2012 Development Edition. If you use the Express
    Edition, your connection string will need to reflect that. Also, give the server name and
    credentials appropriate for your SQL Server installation.

    Listing 7-5. A Connection String in Web.Config

```
<connectionStrings>
        <add name="DefaultConnection" providerName="System.Data.SqlClient"
            connectionString="Server=MyServer;Database=talent_manager;
                                        User Id=appuser;Password=p@ssw0rd!;" />
    </connectionStrings>
```

15. In TalentManager.Web, delete ValuesController and add a new empty API controller named EmployeesController, as shown in Listing 7-6.

Listing 7-6. The EmployeesController Class

```
using System.Linq;
using System.Net;
using System.Net.Http;
using System.Web.Http;
using TalentManager.Data;
using TalentManager.Domain;

public class EmployeesController : ApiController
{
    private Context context = new Context();

    public HttpResponseMessage Get(int id)
    {
        var employee = context.Employees.FirstOrDefault(e => e.Id == id);
        if (employee == null)
        {
            var response = Request.CreateResponse(HttpStatusCode.NotFound,
                                                  "Employee not found");

            throw new HttpResponseException(response);
        }

        return Request.CreateResponse<Employee>(HttpStatusCode.OK, employee);
    }

    protected override void Dispose(bool disposing)
    {
        if(context != null)
                context.Dispose();

        base.Dispose(disposing);
    }
}
```

16. Run Microsoft SQL Server Management Studio and create a new database named talent_manager.

17. Create two tables, employee and department, with the structure shown in Figure 7-2. The table employee has a primary key of employee_id, which is an identity column. The table department has a primary key of department_id, which is an identity column as well.

Employee

Column Name	Data Type	Allow Nulls
⚷ employee_id	int	☐
first_name	varchar(20)	☐
last_name	varchar(20)	☐
department_id	int	☐
row_version	timestamp	☐

Department

Column Name	Data Type	Allow Nulls
⚷ department_id	int	☐
name	varchar(10)	☐
row_version	timestamp	☐

Figure 7-2. *The structure of our tabless*

18. Create the foreign key relationship shown in Figure 7-3. The field `department_id` in the employee table has an FK relationship with `department.department_id`.

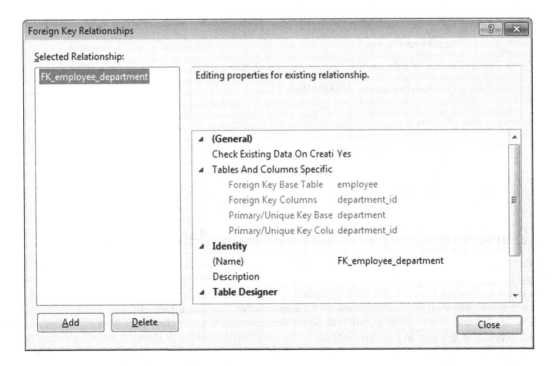

Figure 7-3. *The Relationship between our tables*

19. Run the SQL statements shown in Listing 7-7 from Microsoft SQL Server Management Studio to seed the tables.

Listing 7-7. SQL Statements

```
INSERT INTO dbo.department (name) VALUES('HR');
INSERT INTO dbo.department (name) VALUES('Finance');
INSERT INTO dbo.department (name) VALUES('Marketing');

INSERT INTO dbo.employee (first_name, last_name, department_id)
     VALUES('John', 'Human', 1);
INSERT INTO dbo.employee (first_name, last_name, department_id)
     VALUES('Joe', 'Border', 1);
INSERT INTO dbo.employee (first_name, last_name, department_id)
     VALUES('Pete', 'Callaghan', 1);
INSERT INTO dbo.employee (first_name, last_name, department_id)
     VALUES('Alan', 'Dime', 2);
INSERT INTO dbo.employee (first_name, last_name, department_id)
     VALUES('Rich', 'Nickel', 2);
INSERT INTO dbo.employee (first_name, last_name, department_id)
     VALUES('Nick', 'Greenback', 2);
```

20. Rebuild the solution. Fire up Fiddler and make a GET request to http://localhost:39188/api/employees/1. The port on which my application runs is 39188. You will need to adjust the URI based on the port where your application runs.

21. The response JSON is as follows:

```
{
    "Department": {
        "Id": 1,
        "Name": "HR",
        "RowVersion": "AAAAAAAAB+E="
    },
    "Id": 1,
    "FirstName": "Johnny",
    "LastName": "Human",
    "DepartmentId": 1,
    "RowVersion": "AAAAAAAAF3U="
}
```

7.2 Inverting Entity Framework Dependencies

In this exercise, you will invert the dependency EmployeesController has taken on the Entity framework. The dependency here is that the EmployeesController class has full knowledge of the Context class (which derives from the Entity Framework's DbContext). EmployeesController is tightly coupled with the Context class. Imagine you have to move away from the Entity Framework for some reason. With the implementation we have currently, you would need to rewrite the Get action method. So the EmployeesController class has a *hard dependency* on the Entity Framework. Also, as you start writing unit tests for the action method of the EmployeesController class, they will all exercise the database. As you unit-test the Get method, the data will be retrieved from the database. Not only is that unnecessary overhead in most cases, it also slows down things. The unit tests take more time to run, and if the database is down all the tests will fail. Effectively, such unit tests are not unit tests at all. They are integration tests.

In object-oriented programming, the dependency inversion principle is one of the SOLID[1] design principles. According to this principle, high-level modules should not depend on low-level modules, and both should depend on abstractions. In our case, the high-level module is the EmployeesController class. It depends on the low-level module, which is the Context class.

What we want is for the EmployeesController class not to depend on the Context class but to depend only on an abstraction. The abstraction will be an interface. Let's call it IContext. The EmployeesController class and the Context class will depend only on the IContext interface. Though the EmployeesController class depends on the Context class, what it really needs is DbSet<T>, which implements the IDbSet<T> interface. We will use this to invert the dependency the EmployeesController class has on the Context class.

1. Create a new interface in the TalentManager.Data project named IContext, as shown in Listing 7-8.

   Listing 7-8. The IContext Interface

   ```
   using System.Data.Entity;
   using TalentManager.Domain;

   public interface IContext
   {
       IDbSet<Employee> Employees { get; set; }
       IDbSet<Department> Departments { get; set; }
   }
   ```

2. Change the Context class, as shown in Listing 7-9. It implements the IContext interface that we created in the previous step.

   Listing 7-9. The Modified Context Class Implementing IContext

   ```
   public class Context : DbContext, IContext
   {
       public Context() : base("DefaultConnection") { }

       public IDbSet<Employee> Employees { get; set; }
       public IDbSet<Department> Departments { get; set; }

       protected override void OnModelCreating(DbModelBuilder modelBuilder)
       {
           modelBuilder.Conventions.Remove<PluralizingTableNameConvention>();

           modelBuilder.Configurations
               .Add(new EmployeeConfiguration())
               .Add(new DepartmentConfiguration());

       }
   }
   ```

---

[1]Single responsibility, Open-closed, Liskov substitution, Interface segregation and Dependency inversion.

3. Change the EmployeesController class, as shown in Listing 7-10. The improvement now is that except for one line of code inside the parameter-less constructor, the rest of the class has no idea about the Context class or DbSet<T>. The touch points are all through the interfaces IContext and IDbSet<T>. It is possible to remove the line that creates an instance of Context by using an Inversion of Control (IoC) container, but more on that later. The EmployeesController class is now programmed to the interfaces and not to the implementations, as recommended by the Gang of Four. The changes are shown in bold type.

Listing 7-10. The Dependency-Inverted EmployeesController Class

```
public class EmployeesController : ApiController
{
    // private Context context = new Context();

    private IContext context = null;

    public EmployeesController()
    {
        this.context = new Context();
    }

    public EmployeesController(IContext context)
    {
        this.context = context;
    }

    public HttpResponseMessage Get(int id)
    {
        var employee = context.Employees.FirstOrDefault(e => e.Id == id);
        if (employee == null)
        {
            var response = Request.CreateResponse(HttpStatusCode.NotFound, "Employee not found");

            throw new HttpResponseException(response);
        }

        return Request.CreateResponse<Employee>(HttpStatusCode.OK, employee);
    }

    protected override void Dispose(bool disposing)
    {
        //if (context != null)
        //    context.Dispose();

        if (context != null && context is IDisposable)
        {
            ((IDisposable)context).Dispose();
        }

        base.Dispose(disposing);
    }
}
```

4. Rebuild the solution and make a GET request to http://localhost:39188/api/employees/1. You get back the same JSON as the previous exercise. So we have successfully refactored the code to invert the dependency the EmployeesController class has on Context (implicitly DbContext and DbSet). It now depends only on the abstractions of IContext and IDbSet.

5. You will be able to unit-test this class by creating a fake object of type IContext and setting it in the constructor. The unit test will not hit the database but only call the fake object. However, it will become harder to unit-test as you start writing complex queries and using features like lazy loading.

LEAKY ABSTRACTION

A leaky abstraction is one that intends to hide the complexity of the underlying details but is not very successful in doing so; the underlying details are not completely hidden and leak through the abstraction. The IDbSet interface, specifically its parent IQueryable, is considered a leaky abstraction. For example, the query we use is FirstOrDefault(e => e.Id == id). In this case, id is an integer but assume it is a string. The query will return an employee based on the case-sensitivity of the database. A database can be created to be case-sensitive or not. So, if you query for an ID of johnh and the database stores the ID as JohnH, you will get the employee back if the database is case-insensitive. Your unit test has succeeded so far based on this assumption that an ID of johnh will not return any data, but it will be proved wrong once you hit the database. Leaky abstraction is an important consideration when you are designing to invert the controller dependencies using the technique covered in Exercise 7-2.

7.3 Using the Repository Pattern

In this exercise, you will use the repository pattern to invert the dependency that EmployeesController has on the Entity Framework. Here is the definition of the repository pattern, as defined in the *Catalog of Patterns of Enterprise Application Architecture* by Martin Fowler: it "mediates between the domain and data mapping layers using a collection-like interface for accessing domain objects" (source: http://martinfowler.com/eaaCatalog/repository.html).

The application of the repository pattern over an object-relational mapper (ORM) is a topic for debate and there are arguments for and against the usage of the repository pattern. The major argument against using this pattern with an ORM is that ORM itself is an abstraction from the database, and why do we need another abstraction over ORM? We will nonetheless apply the pattern to see how it helps us in our objective of inverting the dependency that EmployeesController has on the Entity Framework.

1. Create an interface with named IEmployeeRepository in the TalentManager.Data project, as shown in Listing 7-11.

Listing 7-11. The Repository Interface

```
using System;
using System.Collections.Generic;
using TalentManager.Domain;

public interface IEmployeeRepository : IDisposable
{
    IEnumerable<Employee> GetByDepartment(int departmentId);

    Employee Get(int id);
}
```

2. Create the concrete repository class EmployeeRepository, implementing
    IEmployeeRepository in the TalentManager.Data project, as shown in Listing 7-12.

    Listing 7-12. The Repository Implementation

```
using System;
using System.Collections.Generic;
using System.Linq;
using TalentManager.Domain;

public class EmployeeRepository : IEmployeeRepository
{
    private Context context = new Context();

    public IEnumerable<Employee> GetByDepartment(int departmentId)
    {
        return context.Employees.Where(e => e.DepartmentId == departmentId);
    }

    public Employee Get(int id)
    {
        return context.Employees.FirstOrDefault(e => e.Id == id);
    }

    private bool disposed = false;

    protected virtual void Dispose(bool disposing)
    {
        if (!this.disposed)
        {
            if (disposing)
            {
                if(context != null)
                    context.Dispose();
            }
        }
        this.disposed = true;
    }

    public void Dispose()
    {
        Dispose(true);
        GC.SuppressFinalize(this);
    }
}
```

3. Change EmployeesController by commenting out the entire code of the class and copying
    and pasting the code from Listing 7-13.

Listing 7-13. EmployeesController Using Repository

```
using System.Collections.Generic;
using System.Linq;
using System.Net;
using System.Net.Http;
using System.Web.Http;
using TalentManager.Data;
using TalentManager.Domain;

public class EmployeesController : ApiController
{
    private readonly IEmployeeRepository repository = null;

    public EmployeesController()
    {
        this.repository = new EmployeeRepository();
    }

    public EmployeesController(IEmployeeRepository repository)
    {
        this.repository = repository;
    }

    public HttpResponseMessage Get(int id)
    {
        var employee = repository.Get(id);
        if (employee == null)
        {
            var response = Request.CreateResponse(HttpStatusCode.NotFound, "Employee not found");

            throw new HttpResponseException(response);
        }

        return Request.CreateResponse<Employee>(HttpStatusCode.OK, employee);
    }

    public HttpResponseMessage GetByDepartment(int departmentId)
    {
        var employees = repository.GetByDepartment(departmentId);
        if (employees != null && employees.Any())
        {
            return Request.CreateResponse<IEnumerable<Employee>>(HttpStatusCode.OK, employees);
        }

        throw new HttpResponseException(HttpStatusCode.NotFound);
    }
```

```
        protected override void Dispose(bool disposing)
        {
            if(repository != null)
                    repository.Dispose();

            base.Dispose(disposing);
        }
    }
```

4. Rebuild the solution and make a GET request to http://localhost:39188/api/employees/1.
    You get back the same JSON as the previous exercise.

5. We have implemented an additional action method that returns a list of employees
    based on the department. Test this method by making a GET request to the URI
    http://localhost: 39188/api/employees?departmentid=1. It returns all the employees
    that belong to department 1.

Even with the refactoring we have done to implement the repository pattern, EmployeesController continues
to work perfectly, returning the list of employees from a department as well as individual employees based on ID.
Except for the parameterless constructor, the controller has no dependency on any database-related infrastructure.
Of course, the dependency the parameterless constructor has can be fixed by using an IoC, which we will look at later
in this chapter. By moving the code closely related to the database to repository classes, controllers can be fully unit-
tested. The repository classes can be integration-tested.

An important point to note is that this simplistic repository approach can result in a proliferation of classes with
one repository per entity. It might not be a concern for simple projects, though.

7.4 Using the Generic Repository Pattern

In this exercise, you will use the generic repository pattern to invert the dependency EmployeesController has on the
Entity Framework. A generic repository uses .NET generics and is generic enough to be used with any entity.

1. Create a new interface IIdentifiable, as shown in Listing 7-14, in the project
    TalentManager.Domain.

    Listing 7-14. The IIdentifiable Interface

```
public interface IIdentifiable
{
        int Id { get; }
}
```

2. Modify the classes Employee and Department in the project TalentManager.Domain so that
    they both implement the IIdentifiable interface, as shown in Listing 7-15.

    Listing 7-15. Modified Employee and Department Domain Classes

```
public class Employee : IIdentifiable
{
        // Existing properties remain unchanged
}


public class Department : IIdentifiable
{
        // Existing properties remain unchanged
}
```

3. Create a new interface, as shown in Listing 7-16, in the project `TalentManager.Data`. This generic repository interface will be the main contract or abstraction between the controller and the Entity framework classes. This interface defines methods for retrieving, creating, updating, and deleting entities.

Listing 7-16. The IRepository Interface

```
using System;
using System.Linq;
using System.Linq.Expressions;
using TalentManager.Domain;

public interface IRepository<T> : IDisposable where T : class, IIdentifiable
{
    IQueryable<T> All { get; }
    IQueryable<T> AllEager(params Expression<Func<T, object>>[] includes);
    T Find(int id);

    void Insert(T entity);

    void Update(T entity);

    void Delete(int id);
}
```

4. Create the two interfaces `IMyContext` and `IUnitOfWork`, as shown in Listing 7-17, in the project `TalentManager.Data`. `IRepository` does not have a method to save changes. If you implement one, you will be able to save the changes to the individual entities. But when you need to make changes to two different entities, this approach can potentially result in corrupt data when changes to one entity succeed and those to the other one fail. By using the unit of work, you can ensure that the same database context is used across all the repositories. The Save method in the class implementing `IUnitOfWork` will call the SaveChanges method of `IMyContext`.

Listing 7-17. IMyContext and IUnitOfWork Interfaces

```
public interface IMyContext : IDisposable
{
    int SaveChanges();
}

public interface IUnitOfWork : IDisposable
{
    int Save();
    IMyContext Context { get; }
}
```

5. Create the `MyContext` class in the project `TalentManager.Data`, as shown in Listing 7-18. This code calls the `SetInitializer` method in the static constructor instead of `Application_Start`. You can use `Application_Start` as well, but I do it this way to illustrate that there is more than one way to accomplish the task.

Listing 7-18. The Context Class

```
using System.Data.Entity;
using System.Data.Entity.ModelConfiguration.Conventions;
using TalentManager.Data.Configuration;

public class MyContext : DbContext, IMyContext
{
    static MyContext()
    {
        Database.SetInitializer<MyContext>(null);
    }

    public MyContext() : base("DefaultConnection") { }

    protected override void OnModelCreating(DbModelBuilder modelBuilder)
    {
        modelBuilder.Conventions.Remove<PluralizingTableNameConvention>();

        modelBuilder.Configurations
            .Add(new EmployeeConfiguration())
            .Add(new DepartmentConfiguration());
    }
}
```

6. Create the unit-of-work class `UnitOfWork` in the project `TalentManager.Data`, as shown
   in Listing 7-19. It takes in an object of type `IMyContext`, which it returns in the `Context`
   property. In this exercise, we will use the parameterless constructor but we will use the
   other one in the later parts of this chapter. The `Save` method simply calls the `SaveChanges`
   method of the context.

Listing 7-19. The UnitOfWork Class

```
public class UnitOfWork : IUnitOfWork
{
    private readonly IMyContext context;

    public UnitOfWork()
    {
        context = new MyContext();
    }

    public UnitOfWork(IMyContext context)
    {
        this.context = context;
    }
    public int Save()
    {
        return context.SaveChanges();
    }

    public IMyContext Context
    {
```

```
        get
        {
            return context;
        }
    }

    public void Dispose()
    {
        if (context != null)
            context.Dispose();
    }
}
```

7. Create the repository class in the project TalentManager.Data, as shown in Listing 7-20. Notice two things about this code:

    a. We specify two generic type constraints: T must be a reference type, and it must implement a simple interface of IIdentifiable. The IIdentifiable interface just has an Id property that enables an entity to be identified.

    b. The All method returns DbSet<T> by calling Set<T> on the context. The AllEager method is the eager-load version of the All method.

Listing 7-20. The Repository Class

```
using System;
using System.Data;
using System.Data.Entity;
using System.Linq;
using System.Linq.Expressions;
using TalentManager.Domain;

public class Repository<T> : IRepository<T> where T : class, IIdentifiable
{
    private readonly MyContext context;

    public Repository(IUnitOfWork uow)
    {
        context = uow.Context as MyContext;
    }

    public IQueryable<T> All
    {
        get
        {
            return context.Set<T>();
        }
    }

    public IQueryable<T> AllEager(params Expression<Func<T, object>>[] includes)
    {
        IQueryable<T> query = context.Set<T>();
```

```
        foreach (var include in includes)
        {
            query = query.Include(include);
        }

        return query;
    }

    public T Find(int id)
    {
        return context.Set<T>().Find(id);
    }

    public void Insert(T item)
    {
        context.Entry(item).State = EntityState.Added;
    }

    public void Update(T item)
    {
        context.Set<T>().Attach(item);
        context.Entry(item).State = EntityState.Modified;
    }

    public void Delete(int id)
    {
        var item = context.Set<T>().Find(id);
        context.Set<T>().Remove(item);
    }

    public void Dispose()
    {
        if(context != null)
                context.Dispose();
    }
}
```

8. In the project TalentManager.Web, open EmployeesController. Delete or comment the existing lines of code and copy and paste the code from Listing 7-21.

Listing 7-21. The Revised EmployeesController Class (Incomplete)

```
public class EmployeesController : ApiController
{
    private readonly IUnitOfWork uow = null;
    private readonly IRepository<Employee> repository = null;

    public EmployeesController()
    {
        uow = new UnitOfWork();
        repository = new Repository<Employee>(uow);
    }
```

```
    public EmployeesController(IUnitOfWork uow, IRepository<Employee> repository)
    {
        this.uow = uow;
        this.repository = repository;
    }

    // Action methods go here

    protected override void Dispose(bool disposing)
    {
        if(repository != null)
                repository.Dispose();

        if(uow != null)
                uow.Dispose();

        base.Dispose(disposing);
    }
}
```

9. Copy and paste the action methods for GET, POST, PUT, and DELETE, as shown in
   Listing 7-22. We have two GET methods: one for retrieving an employee by ID and a
   second one for retrieving all employees in a department.

Listing 7-22. The EmployeesController Class, Continued (Action Methods)

```
public HttpResponseMessage Get(int id)
{
    var employee = repository.Find(id);
    if (employee == null)
    {
        var response = Request.CreateResponse(HttpStatusCode.NotFound,
                                              "Employee not found");

        throw new HttpResponseException(response);
    }

    return Request.CreateResponse<Employee>(HttpStatusCode.OK, employee);
}

public HttpResponseMessage GetByDepartment(int departmentId)
{
    var employees = repository.All.Where(e => e.DepartmentId == departmentId);
    if (employees != null && employees.Any())
    {
        return Request.CreateResponse<IEnumerable<Employee>>(
                                        HttpStatusCode.OK, employees);
    }

    throw new HttpResponseException(HttpStatusCode.NotFound);
}
```

```
public HttpResponseMessage Post(Employee employee)
{
    repository.Insert(employee);
    uow.Save();

    var response = Request.CreateResponse<Employee>(HttpStatusCode.Created, employee);

    string uri = Url.Link("DefaultApi", new { id = employee.Id });
    response.Headers.Location = new Uri(uri);
    return response;
}

public void Put(int id, Employee employee)
{
    repository.Update(employee);
    uow.Save();
}

public void Delete(int id)
{
    repository.Delete(id);
    uow.Save();
}
```

10. Rebuild the solution. Run Fiddler and from the Composer tab make a GET request to http://localhost:39188/api/employees/1. Remember to replace port 39188 with the actual port that your application runs on in all the following steps. You'll get back the JSON representation of the employee with ID 1 as the response.

11. Make a POST request to http://localhost:39188/api/employees by pasting the JSON {"FirstName":"Brent","LastName":"Dodge","DepartmentId":1} into the Request Body text box and the header Content-Type: application/json into the Request Headers box. Right-click the dbo.employee table in the SQL Server Management Studio and choose Select Top 1000 Rows. You will see a record for Brent now.

12. Make a POST request to http://localhost:39188/api/employees by pasting the JSON {"Department":{"Name":"Training"},"FirstName":"Johnny","LastName":"Scholar", "DepartmentId":1} into the Request Body text box and the header Content-Type: application/json into the Request Headers box. If you query the employee table, you will see a record for Johnny, but the department will not be 1 but the new department named Training. Also, you will be able to see that a new record is inserted in the department table for Training.

13. Make a GET to http://localhost:39188/api/employees/2. Make a note of the RowVersion returned.

14. Make a PUT request by pasting the JSON {"Id":2,"FirstName":"Joseph","LastName" :"Border","DepartmentId":1,"RowVersion":"AAAAAAAB9U="} into the Request Body text box and the header Content-Type: application/json into Request Headers. You will need to use the exact row version, as returned by the previous GET. If you query the employee table, you will see that the name has been changed from Joe to Joseph.

15. Make a DELETE request to http://localhost:39188/api/employees/8. If you query the employee table, you will see that the record for Johnny Scholar has been deleted.

In this exercise we have implemented CRUD operations with SQL Server as the persistence store, with the help of the Entity Framework. Most importantly, if you review the EmployeesController code, you will see that it has no dependency on any of the classes related to the Entity Framework. All the operations are through the contracts of IUnitOfWork and IRepository<Employee>.

■ **Note** Since we expose IQueryable (a leaky abstraction) to the controller, you need to be careful about the queries that you write. A weakness of the generic repository is that it makes the IRepository contract so generic that it becomes possible to write any kind of queries. If you write complex queries or make use of lazy loading, as we implicitly do here, you need to be careful about what you do. While having tight APIs exposed through type-specific repositories, as we did in Exercise 7-3, prevents the abstraction from leaking, maintenance can be difficult with so many classes. On the other hand, having a generic repository minimizes the number of classes, but using IQueryable means that the abstraction is no longer tight. By adopting a hybrid approach of using a generic repository for simple operations (which is unit-tested) and using a type-specific repository that exposes a tight API (which is integration-tested with the database), you can achieve optimal effect.

7.5 Mapping a Domain to Data Transfer Object (DTO)

In this exercise, you will use AutoMapper (https://github.com/AutoMapper/AutoMapper) to map the domain to data-transfer object and vice versa. If you have a keen eye for detail, you should have felt uncomfortable in the previous exercise, where a POST request to EmployeesController results in a new department getting created.

You can try it one more time! Make a POST request by copying and pasting the JSON {"Department":{"Name": "Sales"},"FirstName":"Evelyn","LastName":"Evilicious","DepartmentId":1} into the Request Body text box and the header Content-Type: application/json into Request Headers. If you query the employee table, you will see a record for Evelyn but you will also be able to see that a new record is inserted in the department table for Sales. This is over-posting in action.

This approach makes sense for the use case at hand, where a user may be from the Human Resources team to create an employee. Allowing this user to create new departments, however, does not make sense. By over-posting, either intentionally or otherwise, we allow a user to create new departments.

The root cause of this problem is that we are using the domain objects as models for the request to be bound to. It is good practice to use data transfer objects as models for binding and copy the properties over to the domain or entity objects and persist them.

Similarly, for serialization, the controller serializes the department details for each employee. For example, if you do a GET for an employee, the department details are also sent back (see the following JSON). This is not desirable in most cases. Using a DTO will help ensure that you send back only the details you intend to.

```
{
    "Department": {
        "Id": 1,
        "Name": "HR",
        "RowVersion": "AAAAAAAAB+E="
    },
    "Id": 1,
    "FirstName": "John",
    "LastName": "Human",
    "DepartmentId": 1,
    "RowVersion": "AAAAAAAAF3U="
}
```

1. In the TalentManager.Web project, right-click References in the Solution Explorer of Visual
    Studio and select Manage NuGet Packages. Search for AutoMapper. Click Install, as
    shown in Figure 7-4.

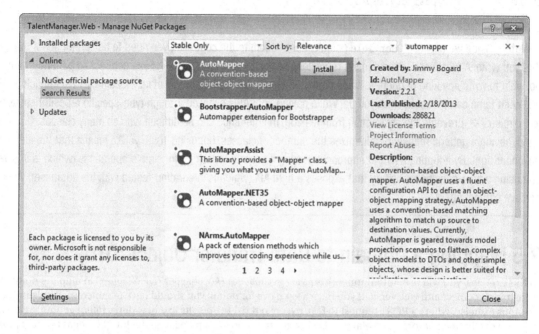

Figure 7-4. *The AutoMapper NuGet package*

2. In the TalentManager.Web project, create the EmployeeDto class, as shown in Listing 7-23.
    We use the Models folder for this. This class does not have a Department property but only
    the DepartmentId property.

Listing 7-23. The EmployeeDto Class

```
public class EmployeeDto
{
    public int Id { get; set; }

    public string FirstName { get; set; }

    public string LastName { get; set; }

    public int DepartmentId { get; set; }

    public byte[] RowVersion { get; set; }
}
```

3. In the TalentManager.Web project, create a class DtoMapperConfig in the App_Start folder,
    as shown in Listing 7-24. Use the namespace TalentManager.Web.

Listing 7-24. The DtoMapperConfig Class

```
using AutoMapper;
using TalentManager.Domain;
using TalentManager.Web.Models;

namespace TalentManager.Web
{
    public static class DtoMapperConfig
    {
        public static void CreateMaps()
        {
            Mapper.CreateMap<EmployeeDto, Employee>();
        }
    }
}
```

4. In Global.asax.cs, add the following line to the end of the Application_Start method:

```
DtoMapperConfig.CreateMaps();
```

5. Modify EmployeesController, as shown in Listing 7-25. The changes are shown in bold type.

Listing 7-25. EmployeesController Using AutoMapper

```
using System;
using System.Collections.Generic;
using System.Linq;
using System.Net;
using System.Net.Http;
using System.Web.Http;
using AutoMapper;
using TalentManager.Data;
using TalentManager.Domain;
using TalentManager.Web.Models;

public class EmployeesController : ApiController
{
    private readonly IUnitOfWork uow = null;
    private readonly IRepository<Employee> repository = null;
    private readonly IMappingEngine mapper = null;

    public EmployeesController()
    {
        uow = new UnitOfWork();
        repository = new Repository<Employee>(uow);
        mapper = Mapper.Engine;
    }
```

```
        public EmployeesController(IUnitOfWork uow, IRepository<Employee> repository,
                                IMappingEngine mapper)
        {
            this.uow = uow;
            this.repository = repository;
            this.mapper = mapper;
        }

        public HttpResponseMessage Post(EmployeeDto employeeDto)
        {
            var employee = mapper.Map<EmployeeDto, Employee>(employeeDto);

            repository.Insert(employee);
            uow.Save();

            var response = Request.CreateResponse<Employee>(HttpStatusCode.Created, employee);

            string uri = Url.Link("DefaultApi", new { id = employee.Id });
            response.Headers.Location = new Uri(uri);
            return response;
        }
    }
```

6. Rebuild the solution.

7. Make a POST request by pasting the JSON {"Department":{"Name":"ITSupport"},"Fir stName":"Alice","LastName":"Smith","DepartmentId":1} into the Request Body text box and the header Content-Type: application/json into the Request Headers box. If you query the employee table, you will see a record for Alice but you will not be able to see a new record in the department table, unlike last time.

8. Now, let us map Employee to EmployeeDto on the way out. Modify the DtoMapperConfig class as shown in Listing 7-26.

Listing 7-26. Changes to the DtoMapperConfig Class

```
public static class DtoMapperConfig
{
    public static void CreateMaps()
    {
        Mapper.CreateMap<EmployeeDto, Employee>();
        Mapper.CreateMap<Employee, EmployeeDto>();
    }
}
```

9. Modify the GET action method in EmployeesController as shown in Listing 7-27. Changes are shown in bold type.

Listing 7-27. The GET Action Method Using AutoMapper

```
public HttpResponseMessage Get(int id)
{
    var employee = repository.Find(id);
    if (employee == null)
```

```
    {
        var response = Request.CreateResponse(HttpStatusCode.NotFound, "Employee not found");

        throw new HttpResponseException(response);
    }

    return Request.CreateResponse<EmployeeDto>(
                    HttpStatusCode.OK,
                        mapper.Map<Employee, EmployeeDto>(employee));
}
```

10. Rebuild the solution and make a GET request to `http://localhost:39188/api/employees/1`. The response JSON will not contain any department information except for the department ID, as follows:

```
{
    "Id":1,
    "FirstName":"John",
    "LastName":"Human",
    "DepartmentId":1,
    "RowVersion":"AAAAAAAAF3U="
}
```

7.6 Injecting Dependencies Using StructureMap

In this exercise, you will constructor-inject the dependencies into a controller using StructureMap. Dependency Injection (DI) is a pattern that enables you to develop loosely coupled code. When we started using the Entity Framework in this chapter, our controller class had a hard dependency on the classes related to the framework. Then we managed to invert the dependency using one or more interfaces as the contract. Even in the case of Exercise 7-4, where we used the repository pattern, technically, the controller class still depends on a few classes, though not directly on the classes from the Entity Framework. In the constructor we will now create new instances of these dependencies and hence the controller will be dependent on the UnitOfWork and Repository<T> classes. By injecting these dependencies into the constructor, you will be able to achieve a clean separation. The ASP.NET Web API framework provides an entity called the dependency resolver, which creates the dependency objects for the framework, including ApiController. By creating a custom dependency resolver, you can configure the dependencies to be plugged in when the framework creates the controller instance.

1. In the TalentManager.Web project, right-click References in the Solution Explorer of Visual Studio and select Manage NuGet Packages. Search for StructureMap. Click Install.

2. Create a class StructureMapDependencyScope in the TalentManager.Web project, as shown in Listing 7-28. In the GetService method, we call the GetInstance method on the container, if the type to be resolved is not an abstract class or an interface. Otherwise, we call the TryGetInstance method. TryGetInstance can create instances of the types registered with StructureMap, and concrete classes like controllers are not registered. In that case, GetInstance is called.

Listing 7-28. The StructureMapDependencyScope Class

```
using System;
using System.Collections.Generic;
using System.Linq;
```

```
using System.Web.Http.Dependencies;
using StructureMap;

public class StructureMapDependencyScope : IDependencyScope
{
    private readonly IContainer container = null;

    public StructureMapDependencyScope(IContainer container)
    {
        this.container = container;
    }

    public object GetService(Type serviceType)
    {
        bool isConcrete = !serviceType.IsAbstract && !serviceType.IsInterface;

        return isConcrete ?
                    container.GetInstance(serviceType) :
                        container.TryGetInstance(serviceType);
    }

    public IEnumerable<object> GetServices(Type serviceType)
    {
        return container.GetAllInstances<object>()
                    .Where(s => s.GetType() == serviceType);
    }

    public void Dispose()
    {
        if (container != null)
            container.Dispose();
    }
}
```

3. Create a class StructureMapContainer in the TalentManager.Web project, as shown in Listing 7-29.

Listing 7-29. The StructureMapContainer Class

```
using System.Web.Http.Dependencies;
using StructureMap;

public class StructureMapContainer : StructureMapDependencyScope, IDependencyResolver
{
    private readonly IContainer container = null;

    public StructureMapContainer(IContainer container) : base(container)
    {
        this.container = container;
    }
```

```
        public IDependencyScope BeginScope()
        {
            return new StructureMapDependencyScope(container.GetNestedContainer());
        }
    }
}
```

4. In the App_Start folder, create a class IocConfig, as shown in Listing 7-30. Use the namespace TalentManager.Web. This code does the following:

a. We configure StructureMap to scan the assemblies with names starting "TalentManager", namely TalentManager.Web, TalentManager.Data, and TalentManager.Domain, to resolve types using the default convention. If a class Foo implements IFoo, StructureMap will be able to automatically instantiate Foo, when the type to be resolved is IFoo, with this configuration.

b. In addition, we manually set up the mapping for IMappingEngine of AutoMapper and IRepository<T>.

c. The DependencyResolver property of the configuration object is set to an instance of StructureMapContainer passing in the Container of the ObjectFactory initialized in the method.

Listing 7-30. The IocConfig Class

```
using System;
using System.Linq;
using System.Web.Http;
using AutoMapper;
using StructureMap;
using TalentManager.Data;

namespace TalentManager.Web
{
    public static class IocConfig
    {
        public static void RegisterDependencyResolver(HttpConfiguration config)
        {
            ObjectFactory.Initialize(x =>
            {
                x.Scan(scan =>
                {
                    scan.WithDefaultConventions();

                    AppDomain.CurrentDomain.GetAssemblies()
                        .Where(a => a.GetName().Name.StartsWith("TalentManager"))
                            .ToList()
                                .ForEach(a => scan.Assembly(a));
                });

                x.For<IMappingEngine>().Use(Mapper.Engine);
                x.For(typeof(IRepository<>)).Use(typeof(Repository<>));

            });
```

```
        config.DependencyResolver = new StructureMapContainer(ObjectFactory.
                                                                        Container);
    }
  }
}
```

5. In Global.asax.cs, add the following line to the Application_Start method:

    ```
    IocConfig.RegisterDependencyResolver(GlobalConfiguration.Configuration);
    ```

6. Remove the parameterless constructor from EmployeesController, as shown in Listing 7-31.

    Listing 7-31. EmployeesController with No Dependencies

    ```
    public class EmployeesController : ApiController
    {
        private readonly IUnitOfWork uow = null;
        private readonly IRepository<Employee> repository = null;
        private readonly IMappingEngine mapper = null;

        public EmployeesController(IUnitOfWork uow, IRepository<Employee> repository,
                                                            IMappingEngine mapper)
        {
            this.uow = uow;
            this.repository = repository;
            this.mapper = mapper;
        }

        // Action Methods go here
    }
    ```

7. Rebuild the solution and test the action methods. They will all work, as they did before the changes.

8. Make a GET request to http://localhost:39188/api/employees/1 from Fiddler. Remember to replace the port 39188 with the actual port that your application runs on. You will get the JSON back.

9. Make a POST request to http://localhost:39188/api/employees from Fiddler by copy-pasting the JSON {"FirstName":"Jane","LastName":"Bowen","DepartmentId":2} in the Request Body text box and the header Content-Type: application/json in Request Headers. If you query the employee table, you will see a record for Jane.

Thus, we managed to free the EmployeesController class from all low-level class dependencies. The controller now depends only on the abstractions: the three interfaces IUnitOfWork, IRepository<Employee>, and IMappingEngine.

7.7 Unit-Testing the Controller

In this exercise, you will unit-test the action methods in EmployeesController. The greatest benefit in isolating the controller dependencies is that you can perform automated unit-testing on all the action methods of the controllers by mocking the dependencies to simulate various scenarios that you will want to test. A mock object is a simulated object (generally proxies) that mimics the behavior of the real object in controlled ways. A programmer sets expectations on the mock object, that is, a certain method will be called with certain parameters and when that happens, an expected result will be returned. I use Rhino Mocks for mocking the dependency types and Visual Studio Unit Testing Framework for creating tests. You will need at a minimum the Professional Edition of Visual Studio, but the Ultimate Edition is recommended for this exercise.

1. In the Solution Explorer, right-click Solution 'Talent Manager' and select Add ➤ New Project. Under Visual C# templates, select Test and choose Unit Test Project. Give it a name of TalentManager.Test.

2. Rename the UnitTest1 class generated by Visual Studio to EmployeesControllerTest.

3. In the TalentManager.Test project, right-click References in the Solution Explorer of Visual Studio and select Manage NuGet Packages. Search for rhinomocks. Click Install.

4. Similarly, search for Automapper and Json.NET and install them as well.

5. In the TalentManager.Test project, right-click References in the Solution Explorer of Visual Studio and select Add Reference. Click Solution on the left and check TalentManager.Web, TalentManager.Data, and TalentManager.Domain. Click OK.

6. Also, add references to the System.Net.Http, System.Net.Http.Formatting, and System.Web.Http assemblies under Assemblies ➤ Extensions, similar to the previous step.

7. Add a test method MustReturnEmployeeForGetUsingAValidId to the EmployeesControllerTest, as shown in Listing 7-32. There are three parts to the unit test, namely Arrange, Act, and Assert.

Listing 7-32. The EmployeesControllerTest Class (Incomplete)

```
[TestClass]
public class EmployeesControllerTest
{
    [TestMethod]
    public void MustReturnEmployeeForGetUsingAValidId()
    {
        // Arrange
        // Act
        // Assert
    }
}
```

8. Arrange refers to setting the test target and the necessary mock objects in place. See Listing 7-33. In this test, we test the Get(int id) method of the controller. To create an instance of the controller, we need objects of type IUnitOfWork, IRepository<Employee>, and IMappingEngine.

   a. We let Rhino Mocks create a mock object for IRepository<Employee>. Here, by calling Stub, we tell the mock object to return the employee object that we just created in the previous step, when the Find method was called on the mock object.

   b. In this test, methods will not be called on IUnitOfWork. So, we just generate a mock.

   c. It is possible to create a mock for IMappingEngine but I choose to actually run AutoMapper as part of the test. AutoMapper just maps in-memory objects and there is only a very small overhead. So, I create a map by calling Mapper.CreateMap.

   d. Finally, create an instance of the controller passing in both the mock object and Mapper. Engine. We also call an extension method EnsureNotNull on the controller instance.

Listing 7-33. The MustReturnEmployeeForGetUsingAValidId Test Method (Arrange)

```
using System.Net;
using System.Net.Http;
using System.Web.Http;
using AutoMapper;
using Microsoft.VisualStudio.TestTools.UnitTesting;
using Rhino.Mocks;
using TalentManager.Data;
using TalentManager.Domain;
using TalentManager.Web.Controllers;
using TalentManager.Web.Models;

[TestClass]
public class EmployeesControllerTest
{
    [TestMethod]
    public void MustReturnEmployeeForGetUsingAValidId()
    {
        // Arrange
        int id = 12345;
        var employee = new Employee()
        {
            Id = id, FirstName = "John", LastName = "Human"
        };

        IRepository<Employee> repository = MockRepository
                                    .GenerateMock<IRepository<Employee>>();
        repository.Stub(x => x.Find(id)).Return(employee);

        IUnitOfWork uow = MockRepository.GenerateMock<IUnitOfWork>();

        Mapper.CreateMap<Employee, EmployeeDto>();

        var controller = new EmployeesController(uow, repository, Mapper.Engine);
        controller.EnsureNotNull();

        // Act

        // Assert
    }
}
```

9. Create a static class `ControllerHelper`, as shown in Listing 7-34. The `EnsureNotNull` extension method creates an instance of `HttpRequestMessage`, and sets that in the controller instance along with setting the configuration and a related request property. We need the `Request` property of the controller to be not null, since we call the `Request.CreateResponse` method in the action method.

Listing 7-34. The SetBlankRequest Extension Method

```
using System.Net.Http;
using System.Web.Http;
```

```
using System.Web.Http.Hosting;
using System.Web.Http.Routing;

public static class ControllerHelper
{
    public static void EnsureNotNull(this ApiController controller)
    {
        controller.Configuration = new HttpConfiguration();
        controller.Request = new HttpRequestMessage();
        controller.Request.Properties.Add(HttpPropertyKeys.HttpConfigurationKey,
                                          controller.Configuration);
    }
}
```

10. Complete the MustReturnEmployeeForGetUsingAValidId test method, as shown in
    Listing 7-35. Calling the Get method on the controller instance is the Act part of the unit
    test. Then, we inspect the HttpResponseMessage returned to check if all is well, which
    constitutes the Assert part. Since we return EmployeeDto from the controller, we assert that
    response.Content is of the type ObjectContent<EmployeeDto>. Also, we assert the status
    code to be 200 - OK and check for correct values in the response. If anything is not in line
    with the assertion, the unit test will fail and indicate that there is some difference between
    how we expect the code to work and how it actually works.

    Listing 7-35. The MustReturnEmployeeForGetUsingAValidId Test Method (Act and Assert)

```
public void MustReturnEmployeeForGetUsingAValidId()
{
    // Arrange
    // Code from the previous steps

    // Act
    HttpResponseMessage response = controller.Get(id);

    // Assert
    Assert.IsNotNull(response);
    Assert.IsNotNull(response.Content);
    Assert.IsInstanceOfType(response.Content, typeof(ObjectContent<EmployeeDto>));
    Assert.AreEqual(HttpStatusCode.OK, response.StatusCode);

    var content = (response.Content as ObjectContent<EmployeeDto>);
    var result = content.Value as EmployeeDto;

    Assert.AreEqual(employee.Id, result.Id);
    Assert.AreEqual(employee.FirstName, result.FirstName);
    Assert.AreEqual(employee.LastName, result.LastName);
}
```

11. Add one more test method MustReturn404WhenForGetUsingAnInvalidId to check that
    the action method returns a 404 - Not Found, if an invalid employee ID is passed in. See
    Listing 7-36. This test is almost the same as the previous one, but by configuring Stub in
    such a way that the mock returns null, we simulate the scenario of an invalid ID coming
    in. We catch HttpResponseException and check whether the status code is 404.

Listing 7-36. The MustReturn404WhenForGetUsingAnInvalidId Test Method

```
[TestMethod]
public void MustReturn404WhenForGetUsingAnInvalidId()
{
    // Arrange
    int invalidId = 12345;

    IRepository<Employee> repository = MockRepository
                                    .GenerateMock<IRepository<Employee>>();
    repository.Stub(x => x.Find(invalidId)).Return(null); // Simulate no match

    IUnitOfWork uow = MockRepository.GenerateMock<IUnitOfWork>();

    Mapper.CreateMap<Employee, EmployeeDto>();

    var controller = new EmployeesController(uow, repository, Mapper.Engine);
    controller.EnsureNotNull();

    // Act
    HttpResponseMessage response = null;
    try
    {
        response = controller.Get(invalidId);
        Assert.Fail();
    }
    catch (HttpResponseException ex)
    {
        // Assert
        Assert.AreEqual(HttpStatusCode.NotFound, ex.Response.StatusCode);
    }
}
```

12. Add another extension method to the class ControllerHelper, as shown in Listing 7-37. This is an upgraded version of the EnsureNotNull method. This method not only ensures that Request is not null but also configures the route.

Listing 7-37. The SetRequest Extension Method

```
public static void SetRequest(this ApiController controller, string controllerPrefix,
                        HttpMethod method, string requestUri)
{
    controller.Configuration = new HttpConfiguration();

    var route = controller.Configuration.Routes.MapHttpRoute(
                name: "DefaultApi",
                routeTemplate: "api/{controller}/{id}",
                defaults: new { id = RouteParameter.Optional }
    );

    var routeValues = new HttpRouteValueDictionary();
    routeValues.Add("controller", controllerPrefix);
    var routeData = new HttpRouteData(route, routeValues);
```

```
    controller.Request = new HttpRequestMessage(method, requestUri);
    controller.Request.Properties.Add(HttpPropertyKeys.HttpConfigurationKey,
                                              controller.Configuration);
    controller.Request.Properties.Add(HttpPropertyKeys.HttpRouteDataKey, routeData);
}
```

13. Add another test method, as shown in Listing 7-38, to test the action method for POST. This method does the following:

    a. We set the requestUri as http://localhost:8086/api/employees/. We then assert that the URI of the newly created resource is http://localhost:8086/api/employees/12345, where 12345 is the new ID.

    b. For the mock objects corresponding to IRepository and IUnitOfWork, we do not stub out the methods but set the expectation that the methods Insert and Save must be called once and only once. For the Insert method, we don't care about the input, so we call IgnoreArguments, and the input is ignored.

    c. In the Assert part, by calling the VerifyAllExpectations method on the mock objects, we assert the expectation we set earlier, which is that these methods must be called once.

    d. In addition, we also assert the status code to be 201 and the URI of the newly created resource.

Listing 7-38. The MustReturn201AndLinkForPost Test Method

```
[TestMethod]
public void MustReturn201AndLinkForPost()
{
    // Arrange
    int id = 12345;
    var employeeDto = new EmployeeDto() { Id = id, FirstName = "John", LastName = "Human" };
    string requestUri = "http://localhost:8086/api/employees/";
    Uri uriForNewEmployee = new Uri(new Uri(requestUri), id.ToString());

    IRepository<Employee> repository = MockRepository.GenerateMock<IRepository<Employee>>();
    repository.Expect(x => x.Insert(null)).IgnoreArguments().Repeat.Once();

    IUnitOfWork uow = MockRepository.GenerateMock<IUnitOfWork>();
    uow.Expect(x => x.Save()).Return(1).Repeat.Once();

    Mapper.CreateMap<EmployeeDto, Employee>();

    var controller = new EmployeesController(uow, repository, Mapper.Engine);
    controller.SetRequest("employees", HttpMethod.Post, requestUri);

    // Act
    HttpResponseMessage response = controller.Post(employeeDto);
```

```
        // Assert
        repository.VerifyAllExpectations();
        uow.VerifyAllExpectations();

        Assert.AreEqual(HttpStatusCode.Created, response.StatusCode);
        Assert.AreEqual(uriForNewEmployee, response.Headers.Location);
    }
```

14. Rebuild the solution. From Visual Studio, select TEST ➤ Run ➤ All Tests.

15. Visual Studio displays the results in the Test Explorer window, as shown in Figure 7-5.

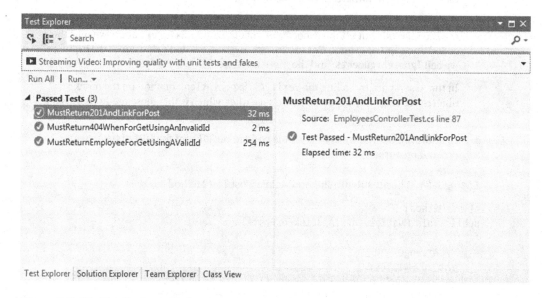

Figure 7-5. *The Test Explorer window*

16. If there are failures, the Test Explorer window shows the failure with more information, as illustrated in Figure 7-6.

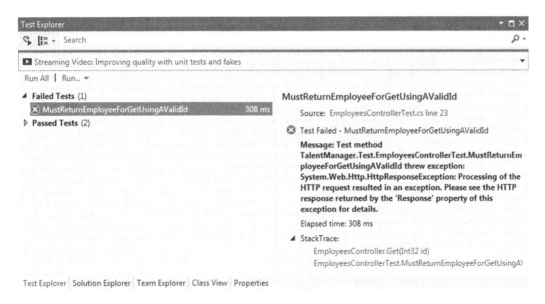

Figure 7-6. *The Test Explorer window displaying an error*

Summary

The term *dependency* or *coupling* is used to denote the degree to which a software component depends on another. The controller class that you create is one of the important components in ASP.NET Web API, since it is the business end where all the application-specific action happens. A common dependency that an ASP.NET Web API controller takes is the dependency on the classes related to persistence infrastructure such as a database. If your controller classes are tightly coupled to the database, unit tests you write will start exercising the database, and unit tests will no longer be unit tests but become integration tests.

One of the great things about ASP.NET MVC compared to ASP.NET Web Forms is the ease with which controller classes can be unit-tested without spinning the wheels of ASP.NET infrastructure. ASP.NET Web API is as testable as ASP.NET MVC. However, paying attention to the dependencies your controller classes take, as you design and construct your service, is important to ensure testability.

In object-oriented programming, dependency inversion is one of the SOLID design principles. According to this principle, high-level modules should not depend on low-level modules, and both should depend on abstractions. A high-level module such as a controller class can be designed to depend on an abstraction such as the IDbSet<T> interface instead of taking direct dependency on concrete classes related to the Entity Framework. However, IDbSet derives from IQueryable, which is considered a leaky abstraction.

Another option is to apply the repository pattern. The application of the repository pattern over an ORM is a topic for debate, and there are arguments for and against the usage of the repository pattern. The major argument against using the repository pattern with an ORM is that an ORM itself is an abstraction over the database, so why do we need another abstraction over ORM? While having a repository per-entity simplifies design and keeps the abstraction tight, this approach could result in proliferation of repository classes in larger projects. In such a case, a generic repository could be used, but this approach also typically uses IQueryable. This aspect of a generic repository using IQueryable makes the repository so generic that it becomes possible to write any kind of queries, thereby making the abstraction loose or leaky.

Once the controller becomes dependent only on abstractions (interfaces), it becomes easy to inject the dependencies through a container like StructureMap. It also becomes easy to mock these abstractions through a mocking framework like Rhino Mocks for automated unit-testing.

CHAPTER 8

■ ■ ■

Extending the Pipeline

ASP.NET Web API is a framework. The key defining attribute of a framework is that it controls the execution flow and calls the application-specific code written by a developer like you at the appropriate time. You don't call the framework but it calls your code, in line with the Hollywood principle of "don't call us, we'll call you." The most fundamental lever that you use to harness the power of the ASP.NET Web API framework in building a service is the controller, the `ApiController` subclass that you write. It is the business end where all the application-specific action happens.

ASP.NET Web API framework receives an HTTP request and goes about processing it. At some point during the processing, it calls the action method you have implemented in the `ApiController` subclass, passing in the parameters, and formats the output returned by your method to ultimately send an HTTP response back to the client. The sequence of steps from the time a request is received to the time the response is sent back defines the processing architecture of ASP.NET Web API. See Figure 8-1.

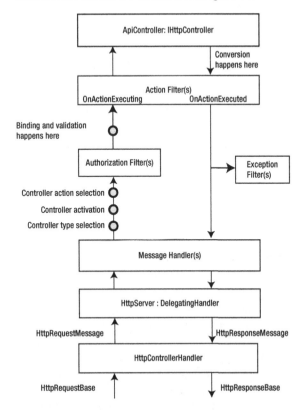

Figure 8-1. *The ASP.NET Web API pipeline*

ASP.NET Web API, being a framework, has various points of extensibility built in for us to hook our code in and extend the processing. We have already seen some of them in the preceding chapters: creating a new media type formatter deriving from MediaTypeFormatter, creating a new model binder implementing IModelBinder, creating a new value provider implementing IValueProvider, and creating a new parameter binding by deriving from HttpParameterBinding. There are other extensibility points available as well, but in this chapter I cover the message handlers, filters, and controller selectors. For a detailed illustration of the pipeline and extensibility points, refer to the chart from Microsoft available for download at http://www.microsoft.com/en-us/download/details.aspx?id=36476.

8.1 Creating a Message Handler

In this exercise, you will create a message handler that simply reads a request header and adds a response header. In the ASP.NET Web API pipeline, the first message handler to run is HttpServer. All of the other, custom message handlers run after HttpServer. A custom message handler is a class that inherits from the class DelegatingHandler. HttpServer gets to look at the request before any other message handler. For the outgoing response, the last handler in the chain gets to see the output first and HttpServer gets to see the response last.

This is a great model because your important handlers get to see the request first, and they are the last ones to do anything with the response. If a bad request (whatever the criteria are for the request to be classified bad) comes in, your important handlers see it first, and they can decide whether the inner handlers should be allowed to see the request or it should be stopped at that point in the pipeline. Similarly, on the way out, the important handlers get to decide as late as possible in the pipeline whether to send the response out, stop it, or make a last-minute alteration to the response. See Figure 8-2 for an illustration of the call sequence.

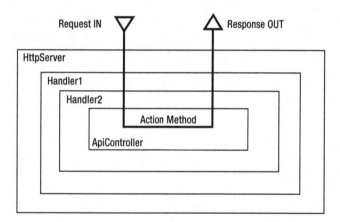

Figure 8-2. *The levels of message handlers can be compared to Chinese boxes*

1. You will use the same solution containing the four TalentManager.* projects from Chapter 7 for this exercise. For this reason, a prerequisite to working on this chapter is that you complete all the exercises in Chapter 7.

2. If you prefer, you can make a copy of the entire folder containing the solution and other files from Chapter 7 and start making changes for this chapter. Open the solution in Visual Studio.

3. Create a message handler class named MyImportantHandler in the project TalentManager.Web, as shown in Listing 8-1. The lines of code shown in bold type are run as part of the request handling. When the execution hits await, this message handler yields control to the next handler in the pipeline, and so on until control goes to the action method of the controller,

which runs and creates the response and returns it to the pipeline. The response flows in the reverse order and ultimately reaches the response-handling part of our handler (all the lines below the await line), and the response variable is set to the response. We can do what we want with the response, such as inspecting headers and adding our own headers and so on, and return the response to the next component in the pipeline.

Listing 8-1. The MyImportantHandler Class

```csharp
using System;
using System.Linq;
using System.Net;
using System.Net.Http;
using System.Threading;
using System.Threading.Tasks;

public class MyImportantHandler : DelegatingHandler
{
    private const string REQUEST_HEADER = "X-Name";
    private const string RESPONSE_HEADER = "X-Message";
    private const string NAME = "Voldemort";

    protected override async Task<HttpResponseMessage> SendAsync(HttpRequestMessage request,
                                                        CancellationToken cancellationToken)
    {
        // Inspect and do your stuff with request here
        string name = String.Empty;

        if (request.Headers.Contains(REQUEST_HEADER))
        {
            name = request.Headers.GetValues(REQUEST_HEADER).First();
        }

        // If you are not happy for a reason,
        // you can reject the request right here like this
        if (NAME.Equals(name, StringComparison.OrdinalIgnoreCase))
            return request.CreateResponse(HttpStatusCode.Forbidden);

        var response = await base.SendAsync(request, cancellationToken);

        // Inspect and do your stuff with response here
        if (response.StatusCode == HttpStatusCode.OK &&
                                !String.IsNullOrEmpty(name))
        {
            response.Headers.Add(RESPONSE_HEADER,
                String.Format("Hello, {0}. Time is {1}",
                        name,
                            DateTime.Now.ToString("MM/dd/yyyy hh:mm:ss.fff tt")));
        }

        return response;
    }
}
```

4. Create another handler class that is the duplicate of the MyImportantHandler class. Name it MyNotSoImportantHandler.

5. In the message handler MyNotSoImportantHandler, change REQUEST_HEADER to X-Name2, RESPONSE_HEADER to X-Message2, and the hard-coded name Voldemort to Potter, as shown in Listing 8-2.

Listing 8-2. Changes to MyNotSoImportantHandler

```
public class MyNotSoImportantHandler : DelegatingHandler
{
    private const string REQUEST_HEADER = "X-Name2";
    private const string RESPONSE_HEADER = "X-Message2";
    private const string NAME = "Potter";

    // The rest of the code is the same as MyImportantHandler
}
```

6. Put breakpoints in the lines string name = String.Empty; and if (response. StatusCode == HttpStatusCode.OK && ... in both the handlers, as shown in Figure 8-3. The first breakpoint is for the request part and the second one is for the response part.

```
protected override async Task<HttpResponseMessage> SendAsync(HttpRequestMessage request,
{
    // Inspect and do your stuff with request here
    string name = String.Empty;

    if (request.Headers.Contains(REQUEST_HEADER))
    {
        name = request.Headers.GetValues(REQUEST_HEADER).First();
    }

    // If you are not happy for a reason,
    // you can reject the request right here like this
    if (NAME.Equals(name, StringComparison.OrdinalIgnoreCase))
        return request.CreateResponse(HttpStatusCode.Forbidden);

    var response = await base.SendAsync(request, cancellationToken);

    // Inspect and do your stuff with response here
    if (response.StatusCode == HttpStatusCode.OK && !String.IsNullOrEmpty(name))
    {
        response.Headers.Add(RESPONSE_HEADER,
            String.Format("Hello, {0}. Time is {1}",
                    name,
                        DateTime.Now.ToString("MM/dd/yyyy hh:mm:ss.fff tt")));
    }

    return response;
}
```

Figure 8-3. Breakpoints in the message handler

7. Register the handlers in the Register method of WebApiConfig in the App_Start folder.
   The order *does* matter. MyImportantHandler must be added to the MessageHandlers
   collection before MyNotSoImportantHandler, as shown in Listing 8-3.

   Listing 8-3. Registering the Message Handlers

```
public static class WebApiConfig
{
    public static void Register(HttpConfiguration config)
    {
        config.Routes.MapHttpRoute(
            name: "DefaultApi",
            routeTemplate: "api/{controller}/{id}",
            defaults: new { id = RouteParameter.Optional }
        );

        config.MessageHandlers.Add(new MyImportantHandler());
        config.MessageHandlers.Add(new MyNotSoImportantHandler());
    }
}
```

8. Add a breakpoint in the starting brace of the action method public HttpResponseMessage
   Get(int id) {} in EmployeesController.

9. Rebuild the solution and run the TalentManager.Web project in Visual Studio by pressing F5.

10. Make a GET request from Fiddler to the URI http://localhost:39188/api/employees/1.
    Remember to replace port 39188 with the actual port that your application runs on.
    Do include two request headers, X-Name: Badri and X-Name2: Badri, in the Request
    Headers textbox in Fiddler. The request message will be as follows:

```
GET http://localhost:39188/api/employees/1 HTTP/1.1
X-Name: Badri
X-Name2: Badri
Host: localhost:39188
```

11. The first breakpoint to be hit is the one on the request-handling part of the
    MyImportantHandler class. Press F5.

12. The second breakpoint to be hit is in the request-handling part of the
    MyNotSoImportantHandler class. Again press F5.

13. The third breakpoint to be hit is the one on the action method of the controller.

14. The fourth breakpoint to be hit is in the response-handling part of the
    MyNotSoImportantHandler class. Press F5.

15. Finally, the last breakpoint to be hit is in the response-handling part of the
    MyImportantHandler class.

16. Thus, the request is first seen by MyImportantHandler, followed by MyNotSoImportantHandler
    before the action method runs. On the way out, the response is first seen by
    MyNotSoImportantHandler, followed by MyImportantHandler. As you can see from the
    following response message, the X-Message2 header was added by MyNotSoImportantHandler
    before X-Message was added by MyImportantHandler.

```
HTTP/1.1 200 OK
X-Message2: Hello, Badri. Time is 04/18/2013 07:41:22.864 PM
X-Message: Hello, Badri. Time is 04/18/2013 07:41:23.723 PM
Date: Thu, 18 Apr 2013 14:11:24 GMT
Content-Length: 91

{"Id":1,"FirstName":"John","LastName":"Human","DepartmentId":1,
"RowVersion":"AAAAAAAAF3U="}
```

17. It is clear now that MyImportantHandler sees the request first and sees the response last. This way, it has the ultimate control over the proceedings. If MyImportantHandler deems that MyNotSoImportantHandler must not see the request, it can stop the execution at that point itself. Let us now see how MyImportantHandler can stop a request from being processed further in the pipeline. When the value coming in the header X-Name is Voldemort, MyImportantHandler sends a status code of 403 - Forbidden and short-circuits the pipeline execution.

18. Issue a GET to http://localhost:39188/api/employees/1 with two request headers: X-Name: Voldemort and X-Name2: Badri.

19. The breakpoint on the request-handling part of the MyImportantHandler class is hit.

20. Press F5 now. No other breakpoints will be hit. Since MyImportantHandler returns a 403 - Forbidden because the name matches Voldemort, pipeline execution is short-circuited and neither MyNotSoImportantHandler nor the controller action has an opportunity to see the request.

21. Issue a GET to http://localhost:39188/api/employees/1 with two request headers: X-Name: Badri and X-Name2: Potter.

22. The first breakpoint to be hit is in the request-handling part of the MyImportantHandler class. Press F5.

23. The second breakpoint to be hit is in the request-handling part of the MyNotSoImportantHandler class. Again press F5.

24. The third breakpoint to be hit is in the response-handling part of the MyImportantHandler class. Press F5.

25. Other breakpoints, including that in the action method, are not hit.

26. Since MyImportantHandler allows the request through and MyNotSoImportantHandler short-circuits the pipeline this time by sending a 403 status code, the response-handling part of MyImportantHandler, which occurs before MyNotSoImportantHandler in the pipeline, still runs. However, none of the components after MyNotSoImportantHandler in the pipeline, such as the controller, will be able to see the request.

We have registered our handlers as global handlers, so they will be plugged into the pipeline for all the routes. It is possible to configure the handlers specifically for a route, as per-route message handlers.

27. Modify the Register method of WebApiConfig in the App_Start folder. Comment out the registration of handlers as global handlers. To hook these handlers specifically to a route, pass them into MapHttpRoute, as shown in Listing 8-4.

Listing 8-4. Registering the Per-Route Handlers

```
using System.Web.Http;
using System.Web.Http.Dispatcher;

public static class WebApiConfig
{
    public static void Register(HttpConfiguration config)
    {
        var handler = new MyImportantHandler()
        {
            InnerHandler = new MyNotSoImportantHandler()
            {
                InnerHandler = new HttpControllerDispatcher(config)
            }
        };

        config.Routes.MapHttpRoute(
            name: "premiumApi",
            routeTemplate: "premium/{controller}/{id}",
            defaults: new { id = RouteParameter.Optional },
            constraints: null,
            handler: handler
        );

        config.Routes.MapHttpRoute(
            name: "DefaultApi",
            routeTemplate: "api/{controller}/{id}",
            defaults: new { id = RouteParameter.Optional }
        );

        //config.MessageHandlers.Add(new MyImportantHandler());
        //config.MessageHandlers.Add(new MyNotSoImportantHandler());
    }
}
```

28. Rebuild the solution and then run the TalentManager.Web project from Visual Studio.

29. With the breakpoints on, make a GET to http://localhost:39188/api/employees/1 with two request headers: X-Name: Badri and X-Name2: Badri. Remember to replace port 39188 with the actual port that your application runs on. None of the breakpoints in the message handlers will be hit this time, since the handlers are configured for a different route. Of course, the breakpoint in the action method does get hit.

30. Make a GET to http://localhost:39188/premium/employees/1 with two request headers: X-Name: Badri and X-Name2: Badri. All five breakpoints will be hit, just like when we configured the handlers as global message handlers. Since the two message handlers are configured as per-route handlers for the premium route, the breakpoints on the two message handlers are hit, and only for the requests on the premium route.

8.2 Creating an Exception Filter

An *exception filter* runs when a controller method throws any unhandled exception. To create an exception filter, you must implement the IExceptionFilter interface or derive from the ExceptionFilterAttribute abstract class (which implements the IExceptionFilter interface) and override the OnException method. In this exercise, you will create an exception filter.

1. We will continue to use the project from Exercise 8.1 for this exercise.

2. EmployeesController has an action method to handle PUT, as shown in Listing 8-5.

    Listing 8-5. The PUT Action Method

    ```
    public void Put(int id, Employee employee)
    {
        repository.Update(employee);
        uow.Save();
    }
    ```

3. If you do not have the JSON representation of Employee handy, make a GET to http://localhost:39188/api/employees/1 and get the JSON like so:

    {"Id":1,"FirstName":"John","LastName":"Human","DepartmentId":1,"RowVersion":"AAAAAAAAB9Q="}

4. Issue a PUT to http://localhost:39188/api/employees/1 with a request header of Content-Type: application/json and a request body of {"Id":1,"FirstName":"Johnny", "LastName":"Human","DepartmentId":1}. Note the missing RowVersion field.

5. You will get a 500 - Internal Server Error status code and a concurrency exception.

{"Message":"An error has occurred.","ExceptionMessage":"Store update, insert, or delete statement affected an unexpected number of rows (0). Entities may have been modified or deleted since entities were loaded. Refresh ObjectStateManager entries.","ExceptionType":"**System.Data.Optimist icConcurrencyException**","StackTrace":" at System.Data.Mapping.Update.Internal.UpdateTranslator. ValidateRowsAffected(Int64 rowsAffected, UpdateCommand source)\r\n at System.Data.Mapping.Update. Internal.UpdateTranslator.Update(IEntityStateManager stateManager, IEntityAdapter adapter)\r\n at System.Data.EntityClient.EntityAdapter.Update(IEntityStateManager entityCache)\r\n at System. Data.Objects.ObjectContext.SaveChanges(SaveOptions options)\r\n at System.Data.Entity.Internal. InternalContext.SaveChanges()"}

6. Though the exception details are very useful for debugging, you will not want to send this information in production. You can disable it by including the following line in the Register method of WebApiConfig in the App_Start folder:

    config.IncludeErrorDetailPolicy = IncludeErrorDetailPolicy.Never;

7. Repeat the PUT and you will still get a 500 status code, but the message will not include the stack trace: {"Message":"An error has occurred."}.

8. This is not very useful to the consumer, since it just says that an error has occurred, which is already obvious because of the 500 status code.

9. Create a class ConflictExceptionHandlerAttribute in the TalentManager.Web project deriving from ExceptionFilterAttribute, as shown in Listing 8-6. This exception filter runs when an Entity framework call results in DbUpdateConcurrencyException. It creates an error response with a status code of 409 - Conflict and a nice message.

Listing 8-6. The ConflictExceptionHandlerAttribute Class

```
using System.Data.Entity.Infrastructure;
using System.Net;
using System.Net.Http;
using System.Web.Http.Filters;

public class ConflictExceptionHandlerAttribute : ExceptionFilterAttribute
{
    public override void OnException(HttpActionExecutedContext context)
    {
        string message = "Changes not saved because of missing or stale ETag. ";
        message += "GET the resource and retry with the new ETag";

        if (context.Exception is DbUpdateConcurrencyException)
        {
            context.Response = context.Request.CreateErrorResponse(
                                    HttpStatusCode.Conflict,
                                        message);
        }
    }
}
```

10. You can use this as a global filter, but let us apply it to the PUT action method in the EmployeesController class of TalentManager.Web, as shown in Listing 8-7.

Listing 8-7. A PUT Action Method with an Exception Filter

```
[ConflictExceptionHandler]
public void Put(int id, Employee employee)
{
    repository.Update(employee);
    uow.Save();
}
```

11. Rebuild the solution and issue a PUT to http://localhost:39188/api/employees/1 with a request header of Content-Type: application/json and a request body of {"Id":1,"FirstName":"Johnny","LastName":"Human","DepartmentId":1}.

12. The response is as follows. This is better than a generic 500 status code.

```
HTTP/1.1 409 Conflict
Cache-Control: no-cache
Content-Type: application/json; charset=utf-8
Date: Fri, 19 Apr 2013 04:50:07 GMT
Content-Length: 110

{"Message":"Changes not saved because of missing or stale ETag. GET the resource and
retry with the new ETag"}
```

8.3 Creating an Action Filter to Handle Concurrency

In this exercise, you will create an action filter. Building on Exercise 8.2, you will use ETags to implement optimistic concurrency. ETags are typically associated with web caching, but they can also be used for optimistic concurrency management.

Concurrency management is essential to ensure data integrity in multiuser environments such as the web. Since HTTP is stateless, locking a resource before the update, as we do in pessimistic locking, is not a feasible option. A better approach is to be optimistic that there will be no intermediate changes between the time of the read and the subsequent update, and failing the update if there is an intermediate change.

As part of the GET response, the web API sends an ETag in the ETag response header. Subsequently, if the same resource has to be updated through a PUT, the client sends the same ETag in the If-Match request header. If the ETag sent by the client matches the ETag in the database (the row_version column of type timestamp), the table is updated. If there is a mismatch, a status code of 409 - Conflict is sent back to the client. The client can follow this with a fresh GET and retry the update. See Figure 8-4.

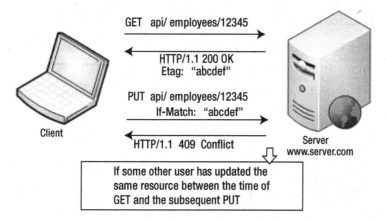

Figure 8-4. *The ETag for optimistic locking*

In this exercise, you will create an action filter that sets the ETag response header based on the row_version column of the employee table. We have been sending the version information as part of the response message body, but the standard way of doing that is to use the ETag response header. Also, when we issue a PUT from Fiddler, we send the version information in the request message body. The standard way of doing this is to send the same information in the If-Match request header.

The action filter you create as part of this exercise will take the version information from the RowVersion property of the EmployeeDto on the way out and copy that data into the ETag response header, immediately after the controller completes executing the action method for GET. Also, the filter will take the version information from the If-Match request header and copy that to the RowVersion property of the EmployeeDto parameter on the way in, just before the controller starts executing the action method for PUT.

1. We will continue to use the project from Exercise 8.2 for this.

2. In the TalentManager.Domain, create an interface IVersionable, as shown in Listing 8-8. Any domain and DTO class that would need to be concurrency-checked will implement this interface.

Listing 8-8. The IVersionable Interface

```
public interface IVersionable
{
        byte[] RowVersion { get; set; }
}
```

3. In the project `TalentManager.Domain`, modify the classes `Department` and `Employee` so that they implement this interface. Since we already have the `RowVersion` property, we just need to indicate that these classes implement `IVersionable`, as shown in Listing 8-9.

Listing 8-9. The Department and Employee Classes Implementing IVersionable

```
public class Employee : IIdentifiable, IVersionable
{
    public int Id { get; set; }

    public string FirstName { get; set; }

    public string LastName { get; set; }

    // Foreign key association
    public int DepartmentId { get; set; }

    // Independent association
    public virtual Department Department { get; set; }

    public byte[] RowVersion { get; set; }
}

public class Department : IIdentifiable, IVersionable
{
    public int Id { get; set; }

    public string Name { get; set; }

    public byte[] RowVersion { get; set; }
}
```

4. As in the previous step, make the `EmployeeDto` class in the `Models` folder of the `TalentManager.Web` project implement `IVersionable`: `public class EmployeeDto: IVersionable { ... }`. You will need to add the using `TalentManager.Domain`; directive to the `EmployeeDto` class, since the `IVersionable` interface is part of `TalentManager.Domain`.

5. Create a class named `OptimisticLockAttribute` deriving from `ActionFilterAttribute` in the `TalentManager.Web` project, as shown in Listing 8-10. This code does the following:

    a. The overridden `OnActionExecuted` method runs in the pipeline after the action method of the controller executes. Thus, it has access to the object returned by the action method.

    b. This method checks whether the HTTP method is GET.

c. If so, it retrieves the object returned by action method, which is in Response.Content. An assumption I make here is that Response.Content will be only ObjectContent and not anything else, such as StringContent. The Value property holds the actual object.

d. If this object implements the IVersionable interface, we take the value from the rowVersion property and set that in the ETag header after wrapping it with double quotes.

Listing 8-10. The OptimisticLockAttribute with OnActionExecuted

```
using System;
using System.Linq;
using System.Net.Http;
using System.Net.Http.Headers;
using System.Web.Http.Controllers;
using System.Web.Http.Filters;
using TalentManager.Domain;

public class OptimisticLockAttribute : ActionFilterAttribute
{
    // OnActionExecuting method goes here

    public override void OnActionExecuted(HttpActionExecutedContext context)
    {
        var request = context.Request;

        if (request.Method == HttpMethod.Get)
        {
            object content = (context.Response.Content as ObjectContent).Value;

            if (content is IVersionable)
            {
                byte[] rowVersion = ((IVersionable)content).RowVersion;

                var etag = new EntityTagHeaderValue("\"" +
                                        Convert.ToBase64String(rowVersion) + "\"");

                context.Response.Headers.ETag = etag;
            }
        }
    }
}
```

6. Complete the action filter, overriding the OnActionExecuting method, as shown in Listing 8-11. This method works as follows:

a. The overridden OnActionExecuting method runs in the pipeline before the action method of the controller executes. It has access to the action method parameter, since model binding happens before this method.

b. This method checks whether the HTTP method is PUT.

c. If so, it checks whether the request has the If-Match header.

d. We retrieve the value from the header and set it in the RowVersion property of the parameter of the action method, provided the parameter object implements IVersionable.

Listing 8-11. The OptimisticLockAttribute with OnActionExecuting

```
public override void OnActionExecuting(HttpActionContext context)
{
    var request = context.Request;
    if (request.Method == HttpMethod.Put)
    {
        EntityTagHeaderValue etagFromClient = request.Headers.IfMatch.FirstOrDefault();
        if (etagFromClient != null)
        {
            var rowVersion = Convert.FromBase64String(
                                   etagFromClient.Tag.Replace("\"", String.Empty));

            foreach (var x in context.ActionArguments.Values.Where(v => v is IVersionable))
            {
                ((IVersionable)x).RowVersion = rowVersion;
            }
        }
    }
}
```

7. EmployeesController has action methods to handle GET for employee by ID and PUT. Modify the methods by applying the OptimisticLock attribute on these two methods, as shown in Listing 8-12. Also, the PUT method is modified to have EmployeeDto as the parameter, and AutoMapper is used to map EmployeeDto to Employee before saving it to the database.

Listing 8-12. The GET by ID and PUT Action Methods

```
[OptimisticLock]
public HttpResponseMessage Get(int id)
{
    var employee = repository.Find(id);
    if (employee == null)
    {
        var response = Request.CreateResponse(HttpStatusCode.NotFound,
                                              "Employee not found");

        throw new HttpResponseException(response);
    }

    return Request.CreateResponse<EmployeeDto>(
                      HttpStatusCode.OK,
                      mapper.Map<Employee, EmployeeDto>(employee));
}
```

```
[OptimisticLock]
[ConflictExceptionHandler]
public void Put(int id, EmployeeDto employeeDto)
{
    var employee = mapper.Map<EmployeeDto, Employee>(employeeDto);

    repository.Update(employee);
    uow.Save();
}
```

8. Rebuild the solution and issue a GET to `http://localhost:39188/api/employees/1`. Remember to replace port 39188 with the actual port that your application runs on. The request and response are as follows. Some of the headers are removed for brevity. The response has the ETag header with a value the same as the RowVersion property. Note the ETag value somewhere, since you will need the value a few steps later.

Request
```
GET http://localhost:39188/api/employees/1 HTTP/1.1
Host: localhost:39188
```

Response
```
HTTP/1.1 200 OK
Content-Type: application/json; charset=utf-8
ETag: "AAAAAAAAF44="
Content-Length: 93
```

```
{"Id":1,"FirstName":"Johnny","LastName":"Human","DepartmentId":1,"RowVersion":"AAAAAAAAF44="}
```

9. Issue a PUT to `http://localhost:39188/api/employees/1`. Do not include the If-Match header in the request. The request and response are as follows. They are the same as the output we got in Exercise 8.2.

Request
```
PUT http://localhost:39188/api/employees/1 HTTP/1.1
Host: localhost:39188
Content-Type: application/json
Content-Length: 65
```

```
{"Id":1,"FirstName":"Johnny","LastName":"Human","DepartmentId":1}
```

Response
```
HTTP/1.1 409 Conflict
Content-Type: application/json; charset=utf-8
Date: Fri, 19 Apr 2013 17:13:20 GMT
Content-Length: 110
```

```
{"Message":"Changes not saved because of missing or stale ETag. GET the resource and
retry with the new ETag"}
```

10. Issue a PUT to `http://localhost:39188/api/employees/1`. This time, include the `If-Match` header in the request and use the value you got in the `ETag` header in the response to GET. The resource (employee) is successfully updated. The request and response are as follows. You can query the table and verify that the update is successful.

Request
```
PUT http://localhost:39188/api/employees/1 HTTP/1.1
Host: localhost:39188
Content-Type: application/json
Content-Length: 65
If-Match: "AAAAAAAAF44="

{"Id":1,"FirstName":"Johnny","LastName":"Human","DepartmentId":1}
```

Response
```
HTTP/1.1 204 No Content
```

11. In Fiddler, go back to the Composer tab and click Execute. Basically, you are repeating the request in the previous step. Your request will fail this time with a `409 - Conflict` and a message that Changes not saved because of missing or stale ETag. GET the resource and retry with the new ETag. This occurs because the earlier ETag you used to successfully update the employee is stale now.

12. To update again, you will need to do a GET and get the current ETag and perform the update. Thus, we have implemented optimistic concurrency checking using ETags.

8.4 Creating a Controller Selector for Versioning

In this exercise, you will create a custom controller selector to implement a simple versioning system for your web API. As part of the ASP.NET Web API pipeline processing, a controller is selected to handle the request. The controller selection logic is implemented in the `SelectController` method of the `DefaultHttpControllerSelector` class. This class implements the `IHttpControllerSelector` interface. The `SelectController` method calls another public `virtual` method, named `GetControllerName`. This method simply returns the controller name from the route data. You will override this method to implement your own logic.

You have `EmployeesController`, which is selected when the request comes to the URI such as this: `http://localhost:39188/api/employees/1`. As you make changes to the action methods, some client applications may stop working if the changes you made are breaking changes. Versioning your web API is a technique that helps prevent this situation. In our case, you will leave the base version of `EmployeesController` untouched and make the breaking changes to the next version of `EmployeesController`, say 2.0. The older clients will work off version 1.0, while the newer clients that need the enhanced version with new functionality can work off version 2.0. There are multiple ways versioning can be done. Some of them are as follows:

- Include the version information in the URI, for example `/api/v2/employees`.

- Use a request header, for example `X-Version: 2`.

- Use a query string, for example `/api/employees?v=2`.

- Use media types with the client asking for a version through the `Accept` header.

- Use a field in the request body.

- Tie the end user identity (or client identity) to a specific version.

In this exercise, we will use the header approach. Versioning is a complex topic, and all of the preceding options have pros and cons that you must weigh for the requirements you have at hand. I do not intend to give you a production-strength versioning solution through this exercise. The objective here is just to demonstrate how you can select a controller class on the fly by implementing a custom controller selector.

1. As with the other exercises in this chapter, you will continue to use the same project—the project from Exercise 8.3—for this exercise.

2. Create a copy of EmployeesController by copying and pasting EmployeesController to the Controller folder in Visual Studio. Rename the file to EmployeesV2Controller. Ensure that the class and the constructor are appropriately named as EmployeesV2Controller. Set a breakpoint in the action method handling GET, which is public HttpResponseMessage Get(int id) {...}, in both the controller classes: EmployeesController and EmployeesV2Controller.

3. In TalentManager.Web, create a class with a name of MyControllerSelector, deriving from DefaultHttpControllerSelector, as shown in Listing 8-13. At this point, it does nothing more than return the controller name returned by the base class, and you will get the same behavior as with the out-of-the-box controller selector.

    Listing 8-13. MyControllerSelector (Incomplete)

```
using System;
using System.Linq;
using System.Net;
using System.Net.Http;
using System.Web.Http;
using System.Web.Http.Controllers;
using System.Web.Http.Dispatcher;

public class MyControllerSelector : DefaultHttpControllerSelector
{
    public MyControllerSelector(HttpConfiguration configuration) : base(configuration) {}

    public override string GetControllerName(HttpRequestMessage request)
    {
        string controllerName = base.GetControllerName(request);

        // Our customization Step 1 goes here

        // Our customization Step 2 goes here

        return controllerName;
    }
}
```

4. Since we have a controller with a name containing the version (EmployeesV2Controller), a request can be made directly to it: http://localhost:39188/api/employeesv2/1. We will first ensure that those requests fail by adding the code shown in Listing 8-14 to the GetControllerName method. Copy and paste Listing 8-14 to replace the comment // Our customization Step 1 goes here.

Listing 8-14. The GetControllerName Method

```
// Having controllers like EmployeesV2Controller or EmployeesV3Controller is
// our internal business. // A client must not make a request directly like /api/employeesv2.

int version;
int length = controllerName.Length;
if (Int32.TryParse(controllerName.Substring(length - 1, 1), out version))
{
    if (controllerName.Substring(length - 2, 1).Equals("V", StringComparison.OrdinalIgnoreCase))

    {
        string message = "No HTTP resource was found that matches the request URI {0}";

        throw new HttpResponseException(
                request.CreateErrorResponse(
                    HttpStatusCode.NotFound,
                        String.Format(message, request.RequestUri)));
    }
}
```

5. Add the logic to format the controller name corresponding to the version requested in the header, as shown in Listing 8-15. Copy and paste Listing 8-15 to replace the comment `// Our customization Step 2 goes here`. This code does the following:

   a. It checks for the request header X-Version. If present, it takes the version from the value contained in this header.

   b. The controller name we have formatted is set in the `controllerName` variable, which is returned as the output of this method.

   c. Finally, it ensures that the controller name we have come up with exists in the mapping created by the base class. The `GetControllerMapping` method returns the mapping. There is no real need for this step, since if you send an invalid controller name, it will fail anyway. By doing this check, however, we can send a better error message to the end user.

Listing 8-15. The GetControllerName Method (Continuation)

```
// If client requests a specific version through the request header, we entertain it
if (request.Headers.Contains("X-Version"))
{
    string headerValue = request.Headers.GetValues("X-Version").First();

    if (!String.IsNullOrEmpty(headerValue) &&
                        Int32.TryParse(headerValue, out version))
    {
        controllerName = String.Format("{0}v{1}", controllerName, version);

        HttpControllerDescriptor descriptor = null;
        if (!this.GetControllerMapping().TryGetValue(controllerName, out descriptor))
        {
            string message = "No HTTP resource was found that matches the request URI {0} and version {1}";
```

```
        throw new HttpResponseException(
                request.CreateErrorResponse(
                    HttpStatusCode.NotFound,
                        String.Format(message, request.RequestUri, version)));
        }
    }
}
```

6. Plug in our custom implementation, replacing the out-of-box implementation in the Register method of WebApiConfig in the App_Start folder:

```
config.Services.Replace(typeof(IHttpControllerSelector), new MyControllerSelector(config));
```

7. There will be other lines of code in the Register method, but those lines will not alter the outcome of this exercise. You can just add this line to the end of the Register method.

8. Rebuild the solution.

9. Make a GET request to http://localhost:39188/api/employeesv2/1. Notice the suffix v2 in the URI. Remember to replace port 39188 with the actual port that your application runs on. You will get a 404 - Not Found withthe message No HTTP resource was found that matches the request URI http://localhost:39188/api/employeesv2/1. Thus, we have prevented the requests coming in directly to our version-suffixed controller classes.

10. Run the project TalentManager.Web in Visual Studio.

11. Set a breakpoint in the line return controllerName; in the class MyControllerSelector in TalentManager.Web.

12. Make a GET request to http://localhost:39188/api/employees/1 without any headers. When the breakpoint in MyControllerSelector is hit, inspect the controllerName variable, which is about to be returned. It will be "employees". Press F5 to continue.

13. The breakpoint in the action method of EmployeesController will be hit, indicating that EmployeesController is selected. Press F5 to finish execution.

14. Make another GET to http://localhost:39188/api/employees/1 with a request header of X-Version: 2. When the breakpoint in MyControllerSelector is hit, inspect the controllerName variable, which is about to be returned. It will be "employeesv2" this time. Press F5 to continue. The breakpoint in the action method of EmployeesV2Controller will be hit, indicating that EmployeesV2Controller is selected this time. Press F5 to finish execution.

15. Make another GET to http://localhost:39188/api/employees/1 with a request header of X-Version: 3. We don't have a controller for this version, and so there will be no entry for the corresponding controller, EmployeesV3Controller in the mapping returned by the GetControllerMapping method of the base class. An exception is thrown. Press F5 to continue, and we get a 404 and the message No HTTP resource was found that matches the request URI http://localhost:39188/api/employees/1 and version 3.

■ **Note** When a nonnumeric value appears in the X-Version request header, our selector switches to EmployeesController. This is just by design and can be changed to send back an error.

Summary

ASP.NET Web API, being a framework, is in control of the execution flow and calls the application-specific code written by a developer like you at the appropriate time. You don't call the framework code but it calls your code, in line with the Hollywood principle. The ASP.NET Web API framework receives an HTTP request and goes about processing it. At some point during the processing, it calls the action method you have implemented in the `ApiController` subclass, passing in the parameters, and formats the output returned by your method to ultimately send an HTTP response back to the client. The sequence of steps that happens from the time a request is received to the time the response is sent back defines the processing architecture of ASP.NET Web API.

Because it is a framework, ASP.NET Web API also has various points of extensibility built in, allowing us to hook our code in and extend the pipeline processing. In this chapter, I covered three of them: the message handlers, filters, and controller selectors. Message handlers run earlier in the pipeline and they run for all the requests. The lowest granularity possible is per-route. Filters run just before the execution of the action method. A filter can be applied to an action method or a controller (in which case it runs for all the action methods of that specific controller) or globally in the `WebApiConfig` class (in which case it runs for all requests). The controller selector runs before the filters. The default implementation of the controller selector is `DefaultHttpControllerSelector`, which implements the `IHttpControllerSelector` interface. The `SelectController` method selects the controller for a given request.

Summary

CHAPTER 9

Hosting ASP.NET Web API

Though ASP.NET Web API has ASP.NET in the name, it is not tied to ASP.NET. In fact, ASP.NET Web API is host-independent. There are three ways you can host your HTTP services built using ASP.NET Web API:

1. Using the ASP.NET infrastructure backed by the IIS (Internet Information Services) server, a technique called *web hosting*

2. Using any Windows process such as a console application or Windows service, a technique called *self-hosting*

3. Connecting a client to the Web API runtime, without hitting the network, a technique called *in-memory hosting*, used mainly for testing purposes

9.1 Web Hosting ASP.NET Web API

In this exercise, you will web-host your ASP.NET Web API in the local IIS server. You will create a new Visual Studio solution with all the related projects in such a way that this solution structure is as host-agnostic as possible. Table 9-1 lists the name of the projects you will create in this exercise with a brief description of the project contents.

Table 9-1. *Project Description*

Project Name	Description
Robusta.TalentManager.Domain	Contains the domain classes implementing the business rules pertaining to the domain. However, in this exercise, there are not a lot of business rules implemented, since the focus of this book is on ASP.NET Web API and not on solving a domain problem.
Robusta.TalentManager.Data	Contains the classes related to data access, specifically the classes related to the Entity Framework.
Robusta.TalentManager.WebApi.Core	Contains the core classes related to ASP.NET Web API, such as controllers, filters, message handlers, configuration files, and so on.
Robusta.TalentManager.WebApi.Dto	Contains the data transfer object class: the class that is formatted into a response and bound from a request. For this exercise, we will create just one DTO class.
Robusta.TalentManager.WebApi.WebHost	Contains just the Global.asax and Web.config file, and this is pretty much an empty web application that contains references to the other projects. This is the project that will be deployed in IIS for web hosting.

This is not the only way you can organize your projects to web-host your HTTP services based on ASP.NET Web API. You can equally well create an ASP.NET MVC 4 project based on the Web API template, as you have been doing so far. I use a slightly different organization here to demonstrate that there are various ways to create your ASP.NET Web API project. Also, by following this approach, we can reuse the projects for self-hosting.

1. Run Visual Studio 2012 as administrator.

2. Select File ➤ New ➤ Project and create a blank solution with a name of Robusta.TalentManager, by selecting Templates ➤ Other Project Types ➤ Visual Studio Solutions. I follow the convention of using the organization name, and the product or the application in the namespace. Assume the organization's name is Robusta, and your application is TalentManager.

3. In the Solution Explorer, right-click Solution 'Robusta.TalentManager' and choose Add ➤ New Project. Under Visual C# templates, select Windows and choose Class Library. Give it a name of Robusta.TalentManager.Domain. Delete the default generated class Class1.

4. Repeat the previous step and create three more Class Library projects with the following names: Robusta.TalentManager.Data, Robusta.TalentManager.WebApi.Core, and Robusta.TalentManager.WebApi.Dto. Delete the default Class1 in all these projects.

5. In the Solution Explorer, right-click Solution 'Robusta.TalentManager' and choose Add ➤ New Project. Under Visual C# templates, select Web and choose ASP.NET Empty Web Application. Give it a name of Robusta.TalentManager.WebApi.WebHost. Right-click this project in Solution Explorer and select Set As Startup Project.

6. Save the solution by pressing Ctrl+S and rebuild the solution just to ensure that it builds.

7. Add the following references to Robusta.TalentManager.Data:

    a. EntityFramework 5.0.0 (NuGet package)

    b. Robusta.TalentManager.Domain (Project reference: Solution ➤ Projects)

■ **Note** For NuGet packages, right-click References under the respective project and select Manage NuGet Packages. Search for and select the package, and click Install.

---

8. Add the following references to Robusta.TalentManager.WebApi.Core:

    a. Robusta.TalentManager.Domain (Project reference)

    b. Robusta.TalentManager.Data (Project reference)

    c. Robusta.TalentManager.WebApi.Dto (Project reference)

    d. Microsoft.AspNet.WebApi.Core (NuGet package)

    e. AutoMapper (NuGet package)

    f. StructureMap (NuGet package)

9. Add the following references to Robusta.TalentManager.WebApi.WebHost:

   a. Robusta.TalentManager.Domain (Project reference)

   b. Robusta.TalentManager.WebApi.Dto (Project reference)

   c. Robusta.TalentManager.WebApi.Core (Project reference)

   d. Microsoft.AspNet.WebApi.WebHost (NuGet package)

10. Rebuild the solution and make sure everything compiles at this point.

We will incorporate some of the features we implemented in Chapter 7. There will be some code repetition, but the objective is to get a working application on top of which we will add more functionality, as we progress through the exercises. We will reuse the same database, talent_manager.

11. In the Robusta.TalentManager.Domain project, create the Employee class along with two interfaces, IIdentifiable and IVersionable, as shown in Listing 9-1.

   Listing 9-1. The Employee Class and the Related Interfaces

```
public interface IIdentifiable
{
    int Id { get; }
}

public interface IVersionable
{
    byte[] RowVersion { get; set; }
}

public class Employee : IIdentifiable, IVersionable
{
    public int Id { get; set; }

    public string FirstName { get; set; }

    public string LastName { get; set; }

    public int DepartmentId { get; set; }

    public byte[] RowVersion { get; set; }
}
```

12. In the Robusta.TalentManager.Data project, create a folder named Configuration. Under this folder, create a class EmployeeConfiguration, as shown in Listing 9-2.

   Listing 9-2. The EmployeeConfiguration Class

```
using System.ComponentModel.DataAnnotations.Schema;
using System.Data.Entity.ModelConfiguration;
using Robusta.TalentManager.Domain;
```

```
public class EmployeeConfiguration : EntityTypeConfiguration<Employee>
{
    public EmployeeConfiguration()
    {
        HasKey(k => k.Id);

        Property(p => p.Id)
            .HasColumnName("employee_id")
                .HasDatabaseGeneratedOption(DatabaseGeneratedOption.Identity);

        Property(p => p.FirstName).HasColumnName("first_name");
        Property(p => p.LastName).HasColumnName("last_name");
        Property(p => p.DepartmentId).HasColumnName("department_id");

        Property(p => p.RowVersion).HasColumnName("row_version").IsRowVersion();
    }
}
```

13. In the Robusta.TalentManager.Data project, create three interfaces, IContext, IRepository, and IUnitOfWork, as shown in Listing 9-3. You can create three separate .cs files for these interfaces.

   Listing 9-3. The IContext, IRepository, and IUnitOfWork Interfaces

   ```
   using System;
   using System.Linq;
   using System.Linq.Expressions;
   using Robusta.TalentManager.Domain;

   public interface IContext : IDisposable
   {
       int SaveChanges();
   }

   public interface IRepository<T> : IDisposable where T : class, IIdentifiable
   {
       IQueryable<T> All { get; }
       IQueryable<T> AllEager(params Expression<Func<T, object>>[] includes);
       T Find(int id);

       void Insert(T entity);

       void Update(T entity);

       void Delete(int id);
   }

   public interface IUnitOfWork : IDisposable
   {
       int Save();
       IContext Context { get; }
   }
   ```

14. Create the corresponding concrete classes, Context, Repository<T>, and UnitOfWork, in the Robusta.TalentManager.Data project, as shown in Listing 9-4.

Listing 9-4. The Context, Repository<T>, and UnitOfWork Concrete Classes

```
using System.Data.Entity;
using System.Data.Entity.ModelConfiguration.Conventions;
using Robusta.TalentManager.Data.Configuration;

public class Context : DbContext, IContext
{
    static Context()
    {
        Database.SetInitializer<Context>(null);
    }

    public Context() : base("DefaultConnection") { }

    protected override void OnModelCreating(DbModelBuilder modelBuilder)
    {
        modelBuilder.Conventions.Remove<PluralizingTableNameConvention>();

        modelBuilder.Configurations
            .Add(new EmployeeConfiguration());
    }
}

using System;
using System.Data;
using System.Data.Entity;
using System.Linq;
using System.Linq.Expressions;
using Robusta.TalentManager.Domain;

public class Repository<T> : IRepository<T> where T : class, IIdentifiable
{
    private readonly Context context;

    public Repository(IUnitOfWork uow)
    {
        context = uow.Context as Context;
    }

    public IQueryable<T> All
    {
        get
        {
            return context.Set<T>();
        }
    }
}
```

```csharp
        public IQueryable<T> AllEager(params Expression<Func<T, object>>[] includes)
        {
            IQueryable<T> query = context.Set<T>();

            foreach (var include in includes)
            {
                query = query.Include(include);
            }

            return query;
        }

        public T Find(int id)
        {
            return context.Set<T>().Find(id);
        }

        public void Insert(T item)
        {
            context.Entry(item).State = EntityState.Added;
        }

        public void Update(T item)
        {
            context.Set<T>().Attach(item);
            context.Entry(item).State = EntityState.Modified;
        }

        public void Delete(int id)
        {
            var item = context.Set<T>().Find(id);
            context.Set<T>().Remove(item);
        }

        public void Dispose()
        {
            context.Dispose();
        }
    }

    public class UnitOfWork : IUnitOfWork
    {
        private readonly IContext context;

        public UnitOfWork()
        {
            context = new Context();
        }
```

```
        public UnitOfWork(IContext context)
        {
            this.context = context;
        }
        public int Save()
        {
            return context.SaveChanges();
        }

        public IContext Context
        {
            get
            {
                return context;
            }
        }

        public void Dispose()
        {
            context.Dispose();
        }
    }
```

15. In the Robusta.TalentManager.WebApi.Dto project, create a class EmployeeDto, as shown in Listing 9-5.

Listing 9-5. The EmployeeDto Class

```
public class EmployeeDto
{
    public int Id { get; set; }

    public string FirstName { get; set; }

    public string LastName { get; set; }

    public int DepartmentId { get; set; }

    public byte[] RowVersion { get; set; }
}
```

16. In the Robusta.TalentManager.WebApi.Core project, create a folder Infrastructure and under this folder, create two classes, StructureMapContainer and StructureMapDependencyScope, as shown in Listing 9-6. These classes are straight from Chapter 7. However, if you plan to copy and paste from the project corresponding to Chapter 7, ensure that the namespace of these classes is correct after the copy-paste: Robusta.TalentManager.WebApi.Core.Infrastructure.

Listing 9-6. StructureMapContainer and StructureMapDependencyScope

```
using System;
using System.Collections.Generic;
using System.Linq;
using System.Web.Http.Dependencies;
using StructureMap;

namespace Robusta.TalentManager.WebApi.Core.Infrastructure
{
    public class StructureMapDependencyScope : IDependencyScope
    {
        private readonly IContainer container = null;

        public StructureMapDependencyScope(IContainer container)
        {
            this.container = container;
        }

        public object GetService(Type serviceType)
        {
            bool isConcrete = !serviceType.IsAbstract && !serviceType.IsInterface;

            return isConcrete ?
                        container.GetInstance(serviceType):
                            container.TryGetInstance(serviceType);
        }

        public IEnumerable<object> GetServices(Type serviceType)
        {
            return container.GetAllInstances<object>()
                        .Where(s => s.GetType() == serviceType);
        }

        public void Dispose()
        {
            if (container != null)
                container.Dispose();
        }
    }
}

using System.Web.Http.Dependencies;
using StructureMap;

namespace Robusta.TalentManager.WebApi.Core.Infrastructure
{
    public class StructureMapContainer : StructureMapDependencyScope, IDependencyResolver
    {
        private readonly IContainer container = null;
```

```
        public StructureMapContainer(IContainer container)
            : base(container)
        {
            this.container = container;
        }

        public IDependencyScope BeginScope()
        {
            return new StructureMapDependencyScope(container.GetNestedContainer());
        }
    }
}
```

17. In the Robusta.TalentManager.WebApi.Core project, create a folder Configuration and under this folder, create three configuration classes, WebApiConfig, DtoMapperConfig, and IocConfig, as shown in Listing 9-7.

Listing 9-7. The WebApiConfig, DtoMapperConfig, and IocConfig Classes

```
using System.Web.Http;

public static class WebApiConfig
{
    public static void Register(HttpConfiguration config)
    {
        config.Routes.MapHttpRoute(
            name: "DefaultApi",
            routeTemplate: "api/{controller}/{id}",
            defaults: new { id = RouteParameter.Optional }
        );
    }
}

using System;
using System.Linq;
using System.Web.Http;
using AutoMapper;
using Robusta.TalentManager.Data;
using Robusta.TalentManager.WebApi.Core.Infrastructure;
using StructureMap;

public static class IocConfig
{
    public static void RegisterDependencyResolver(HttpConfiguration config)
    {
        ObjectFactory.Initialize(x =>
        {
            x.Scan(scan =>
            {
                scan.WithDefaultConventions();
```

```
                AppDomain.CurrentDomain.GetAssemblies()
                    .Where(a => a.GetName().Name.StartsWith("Robusta.TalentManager"))
                        .ToList()
                            .ForEach(a => scan.Assembly(a));
        });

        x.For<IMappingEngine>().Use(Mapper.Engine);
        x.For(typeof(IRepository<>)).Use(typeof(Repository<>));

    });

    config.DependencyResolver = new StructureMapContainer(ObjectFactory.Container);
    }
}


using AutoMapper;
using Robusta.TalentManager.Domain;
using Robusta.TalentManager.WebApi.Dto;

public static class DtoMapperConfig
{
    public static void CreateMaps()
    {
        Mapper.CreateMap<EmployeeDto, Employee>();
        Mapper.CreateMap<Employee, EmployeeDto>();
    }
}
```

18. In the project Robusta.TalentManager.WebApi.WebHost, create a new Global Application
    Class and accept the default name of Global.asax. Remove all the methods except
    Application_Start. Add the code in Listing 9-8 to this method.

    Listing 9-8. Global.asax.cs

    ```
    using System;
    using System.Web.Http;
    using Robusta.TalentManager.WebApi.Core.Configuration;

    public class Global : System.Web.HttpApplication
    {
        protected void Application_Start(object sender, EventArgs e)
        {
            IocConfig.RegisterDependencyResolver(GlobalConfiguration.Configuration);
            WebApiConfig.Register(GlobalConfiguration.Configuration);
            DtoMapperConfig.CreateMaps();
        }
    }
    ```

19. Edit Web.Config in the project Robusta.TalentManager.WebApi.WebHost to add the
    configSections and connectionStrings entries shown in Listing 9-9. Edit the connection
    to string and supply the appropriate server name and the connection credentials of user
    ID and password.

Listing 9-9. Web.Config

```
<configuration>
        <configSections>
                <section name="entityFramework"
                        type="System.Data.Entity.Internal.ConfigFile.EntityFrameworkSection,
                            EntityFramework, Version=5.0.0.0, Culture=neutral,
                                PublicKeyToken=b77a5c561934e089"
                        requirePermission="false" />
        </configSections>
        <connectionStrings>
                <add name="DefaultConnection"
                        providerName="System.Data.SqlClient"
                        connectionString="Server=server;Database=talent_manager;
                        User Id=uid;Password=pwd;" />
        </connectionStrings>
...
</configuration>
```

20. In the project Robusta.TalentManager.WebApi.Core, create a folder named Controllers and under this folder, add a class EmployeesController, as shown in Listing 9-10.

Listing 9-10. EmployeesController

```
using System;
using System.Net;
using System.Net.Http;
using System.Web.Http;
using AutoMapper;
using Robusta.TalentManager.Data;
using Robusta.TalentManager.Domain;
using Robusta.TalentManager.WebApi.Dto;

public class EmployeesController : ApiController
{
    private readonly IUnitOfWork uow = null;
    private readonly IRepository<Employee> repository = null;
    private readonly IMappingEngine mapper = null;

    public EmployeesController(IUnitOfWork uow,
                                    IRepository<Employee> repository,
                                        IMappingEngine mapper)
    {
        this.uow = uow;
        this.repository = repository;
        this.mapper = mapper;
    }
```

```
public HttpResponseMessage Get(int id)
{
    var employee = repository.Find(id);
    if (employee == null)
    {
        var response = Request.CreateResponse(HttpStatusCode.NotFound, "Employee not found");

        throw new HttpResponseException(response);
    }

    return Request.CreateResponse<EmployeeDto>(
                        HttpStatusCode.OK,
                                mapper.Map<Employee, EmployeeDto>(employee));
}

public HttpResponseMessage Post(EmployeeDto employeeDto)
{
    var employee = mapper.Map<EmployeeDto, Employee>(employeeDto);

    repository.Insert(employee);
    uow.Save();

    var response = Request.CreateResponse<Employee>(
                                HttpStatusCode.Created,
                                    employee);

    string uri = Url.Link("DefaultApi", new { id = employee.Id });
    response.Headers.Location = new Uri(uri);
    return response;
}

protected override void Dispose(bool disposing)
{
    if (repository != null)
        repository.Dispose();

    if (uow != null)
        uow.Dispose();

    base.Dispose(disposing);
}
}
```

21. Rebuild the solution and make a GET to http://localhost:7387/api/employees/1 from Fiddler. Adjust the port in the URI to reflect the port used by your application.

It works and returns the JSON representation of the employee resource. Thus, we have created the Visual Studio solution with all the projects from scratch without using the Web API template. The project Robusta.TalentManager.WebApi.WebHost is what you will deploy to IIS to web-host the Web API. You will follow the same process you typically follow to deploy any ASP.NET application, and we will now use local IIS to run our application.

22. Ensure that you have launched Visual Studio as administrator. If not, close and run as administrator.

23. Double-click Properties under `Robusta.TalentManager.WebApi.WebHost` in the Solution Explorer and go to the Web tab.

24. In the Servers section, uncheck Use IIS Express. Give the Project URL of `http://localhost/TalentManager` and click Create Virtual Directory. Dismiss the success message dialog and save the changes.

■ **Note** If you do not have IIS installed in your computer, the checkbox Use IIS Express will be checked and disabled, and you will not be able to uncheck it. You can install IIS or leave the checkbox checked and use IIS Express, which comes with Visual Studio.

---

25. Rebuild the solution and make a GET to `http://localhost/talentmanager/api/employees/1`. You will get the JSON representation of the employee resource back, the same as last time. The only difference is that the application runs in IIS now.

26. Run the Internet Information Services (IIS) Manager application. The path to this application in Windows 7 is `%windir%\system32\inetsrv\InetMgr.exe`. In Windows 7, you can type **inetmgr** in the Run box and click OK to launch IIS manager. In Windows 8, type **inetmgr** in the Search box and press Enter.

I use IIS 7.5 and depending on the version, what you see in your machine could be different from the screenshots (See Figure 9-1).

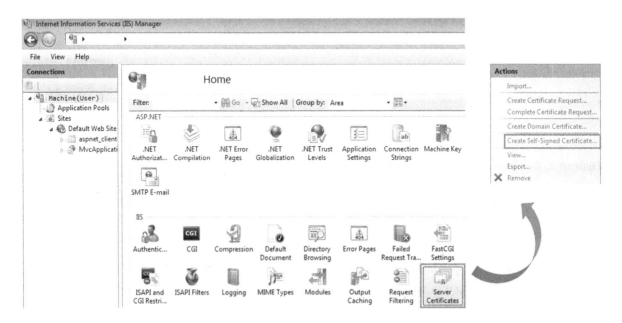

Figure 9-1. *IIS Manager—Server Certificate Generation*

27. Click on the root machine node in the tree view on the left pane and double-click the Server Certificates icon in the right pane.

28. In the resulting screen, click the Create Self-Signed Certificate link. Enter a friendly name such as **MyWebApiCert** in the pop-up and click OK to complete server certificate generation.

29. Now that we have the server certificate, we need to let IIS use it. Click the Default Web Site node of the tree view in the left pane.

30. In the Actions pane on the right, click Bindings. and then Add (see Figure 9-2). In the Add Site Binding dialog, select HTTPS as the Type and select the certificate we just generated, which is MyWebApiCert. Click OK to complete creating the binding.

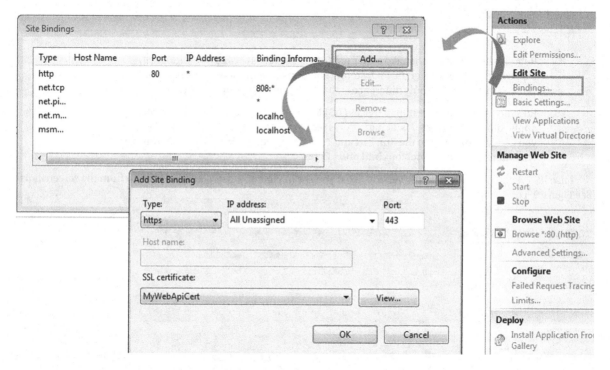

Figure 9-2. *IIS Manager—configuring HTTPS binding*

31. Now, you are all set to invoke the Web API using HTTPS. Open Internet Explorer and type `https://localhost/talentmanager/api/employees/1` in the address bar and press Enter.

32. Since this is a self-signed certificate, the browser will not be happy and will show the warning that the certificate is not something it trusts. Click the Continue To This Website (Not Recommended) link. It works, and the JSON representation is downloaded.

Thus, we have hosted our Web API in IIS and enabled HTTPS as well.

■ **Note** A self-signed certificate like the one we just created using IIS Manager is signed by the same entity for whose identity it stands. This is similar to you certifying yourself. In the real world, unless you are someone whom everyone else trusts, no one is going to believe the certificate you give to yourself. A third party that is trusted by both the first and second party is needed to complete the circle of trust. In the world of digital certificates, that trusted third party is a certification authority (CA) such as VeriSign. A certificate issued by a CA is trusted by all, but it does cost money. A self-signed certificate costs nothing but is trusted by no one. It can be used for testing purposes only.

9.2 Self-Hosting ASP.NET Web API

In this exercise, you will self-host your ASP.NET Web API. One of the great features of ASP.NET Web API is that it is host-independent. The same code we web-hosted in the previous exercise can be self-hosted. Self-hosting does not require IIS, and you can self-host a Web API in your own process. You will use a console application to self-host Web API in this exercise.

1. Run Visual Studio as administrator.

2. Open the Robusta.TalentManager solution from Exercise 9.1. In the Solution Explorer, right-click Solution 'Robusta.TalentManager' and choose Add ➤ New Project. Under Visual C# templates, select Windows and choose Console Application. Give it a name of Robusta.TalentManager.WebApi.SelfHost. Right-click this project in the Solution Explorer and select Set As Startup Project.

3. Right-click References under the Robusta.TalentManager.WebApi.SelfHost project. Select Manage NuGet Packages. Search for the package Microsoft.AspNet.WebApi. SelfHost, select the package in the search results, and click Install. We need references to the System.Web.Http.SelfHost, System.Net.Http, and System.Web.Http assemblies.

4. Add the following project references to Robusta.TalentManager.WebApi.SelfHost:

   a. Robusta.TalentManager.Domain

   b. Robusta.TalentManager.WebApi.Dto

   c. Robusta.TalentManager.WebApi.Core

5. In the Robusta.TalentManager.WebApi.SelfHost project, modify the Program class, as shown in Listing 9-11. Pay attention to the URI specified. We will use the same URI to make our Web API requests.

Listing 9-11. The Program Class

```
using System;
using System.Web.Http.SelfHost;
using Robusta.TalentManager.WebApi.Core.Configuration;

class Program
{
    static void Main(string[] args)
    {
        var configuration = new HttpSelfHostConfiguration("http://localhost:8086");
```

```
WebApiConfig.Register(configuration);
DtoMapperConfig.CreateMaps();
IocConfig.RegisterDependencyResolver(configuration);

using (HttpSelfHostServer server = new HttpSelfHostServer(configuration))
{
    server.OpenAsync().Wait();
    Console.WriteLine("Press Enter to terminate the server...");
    Console.ReadLine();
}
    }
}
```

6. In the `Robusta.TalentManager.WebApi.SelfHost` project, replace the contents of the `App.Config` file with the XML shown in Listing 9-12. Edit the connection string to supply the appropriate server name and connection credentials.

Listing 9-12. App.Config

```xml
<?xml version="1.0" encoding="utf-8" ?>
<configuration>
        <configSections>
                <section name="entityFramework"
                        type="System.Data.Entity.Internal.ConfigFile.EntityFrameworkSection,
                                EntityFramework, Version=5.0.0.0, Culture=neutral,
                                        PublicKeyToken=b77a5c561934e089"
                        requirePermission="false" />
        </configSections>
        <startup>
                <supportedRuntime version="v4.0" sku=".NETFramework,Version=v4.5" />
        </startup>
        <connectionStrings>
                <add name="DefaultConnection"
                        providerName="System.Data.SqlClient"
                        connectionString="Server=server;Database=talent_manager;
                        User Id=uid;Password=pwd;" />
        </connectionStrings>
</configuration>
```

7. Rebuild the solution, run the `Robusta.TalentManager.WebApi.SelfHost` Console Application project in Visual Studio, and make a GET to `http://localhost:8086/api/employees/1` from Fiddler. Unlike what you have been doing so far, you will not change the port 8086, since this URI is based on Listing 9-11, where we have the port specified.

8. You will get a JSON representation of the employee resource. You have just self-hosted the same Web API code you created in the Exercise 9.1. Close the console application hosting our Web API by pressing Enter on the command window.

We will now enable HTTPS. For this, we will use the same MyWebApiCert server certificate that we generated in Exercise 9.1.

9. Open Microsoft Management Console (MMC). In Windows 7 and Windows 8, you can search for *mmc* and run the program.

10. Select File ➤ Add/Remove Snap-In, followed by the Certificates snap-in on the left side under Available Snap-Ins.

11. Click Add and subsequently select Computer Account and click Next; then select Local Computer and click Finish to see the certificates on your computer.

12. In the left tree view, select Certificates (Local Computer) ➤ Personal ➤ Certificates. In the right list view, the certificates will be displayed. Select the one with the Friendly Name of MyWebApiCert. This certificate will be issued to your local machine name.

13. Double-click the certificate and go to the Details tab. Click the Thumbprint field. Copy the value, which will be something like this:

    a7 8f f5 7f 70 ce 4f a2 b1 07 41 0f b5 33 79 37 d2 d5 11 67

14. Open a DOS command prompt as administrator and run the following command:

    netsh http add sslcert ipport=0.0.0.0:**8086** certhash=a78ff57f70ce4fa2b107410fb5337937d2 d51167 appid={951B215B-DE1E-42AD-B82C-4F966867CE41}

    a. For ipport, the IP address 0.0.0.0 matches all IP addresses for the local machine, and 8086 is the port our self-host server listens on.

    b. For certhash, specify the thumbprint value you got from MMC, the value you copied from the Thumbprint field without any spaces.

    c. For appid, specify a GUID. It can be any GUID that will represent your application.

15. To the Robusta.TalentManager.WebApi.SelfHost project, add a reference to System.ServiceModel (Assemblies ➤ Framework).

16. Add a class MySelfHostConfiguration to the Robusta.TalentManager.WebApi.SelfHost project, deriving from HttpSelfHostConfiguration, as shown in Listing 9-13.

Listing 9-13. The MySelfHostConfiguration Class

```
using System.ServiceModel.Channels;
using System.Web.Http.SelfHost;
using System.Web.Http.SelfHost.Channels;

public class MySelfHostConfiguration : HttpSelfHostConfiguration
{
    public MySelfHostConfiguration(string baseAddress) : base(baseAddress) { }

    protected override BindingParameterCollection OnConfigureBinding(HttpBinding httpBinding)
    {
        httpBinding.Security.Mode = HttpBindingSecurityMode.Transport;

        return base.OnConfigureBinding(httpBinding);
    }
}
```

17. In the `Main` method of the `Program` class, comment out the line

    ```
    var configuration = new HttpSelfHostConfiguration("http://localhost:8086");
    ```

    and add the line

    ```
    var configuration = new MySelfHostConfiguration("https://localhost:8086");
    ```

18. Rebuild the solution and run the `Robusta.TalentManager.WebApi.SelfHost` Console Application project in Visual Studio.

19. Open Internet Explorer, type `https://localhost:8086/api/employees/1` in the address bar, and press Enter.

As in the case of web hosting, Internet Explorer will not be happy with the self-signed certificate and will show the warning that the certificate is not something it trusts.

20. Click the Continue To This Website link. It works, and the JSON representation is downloaded.

■ **Note** Our console application listens on port 8086 for HTTP traffic. This requires administrator privileges. This is the reason we run Visual Studio as administrator. You will not be able to run in the elevated level all the time, and it is not a good practice, anyway. But if you do not run as administrator, you will get the error `HTTP could not register URL` `http://+:8086/`. To resolve this problem, use `Netsh.exe` to reserve the URL for non-administrator accounts. Open a command prompt as administrator and run the following command: `netsh http add urlacl url=http://+:8086/` `user=<your account>`. You can delete the URL reservation for non-administrator accounts by running the following command: `netsh http delete urlacl url=http://+:8086/`.

9.3 In-Memory Hosting ASP.NET Web API

In this exercise, you will use in-memory hosting to integration-test your ASP.NET Web API. In the case of in-memory hosting, nothing goes over the wire. Hence it does not require a port or an IP address, and everything runs in memory. This attribute makes in-memory hosting very useful for testing the ASP.NET Web API pipeline. In Chapter 7, we unit-tested controllers in isolation. There are scenarios where you will want to test the controller along with some other components running in the pipeline, say a filter and a message handler. In-memory hosting makes it possible to test those cases quickly at the same pace that an isolated unit test runs.

1. In the `Robusta.TalentManager.WebApi.Core` project, apply the `Authorize` filter on the `Get(int)` action method of `EmployeesController`, as shown in Listing 9-14.

Listing 9-14. The GET Action Method with the Authorize Filter

```
[Authorize]
public HttpResponseMessage Get(int id)
{
    var employee = repository.Find(id);
    if (employee == null)
```

```
    {
        var response = Request.CreateResponse(HttpStatusCode.NotFound, "Employee not found");

        throw new HttpResponseException(response);
    }

    return Request.CreateResponse<EmployeeDto>(
                        HttpStatusCode.OK,
                        mapper.Map<Employee, EmployeeDto>(employee));
}
```

2. Rebuild the solution and make a GET to our web-hosted API (`http://localhost/` `talentmanager/api/employees/1`) from Fiddler. You will receive a `401 - Unauthorized` status code back.

The `Authorize` filter is not allowing the action method to run, since the user identity is not authenticated. I cover security in Chapter 10, but for the sake of this exercise, let us create a message handler that simply sets a hard-coded but authenticated identity, as long as the request contains the custom header X-PSK.

3. In the `Robusta.TalentManager.WebApi.Core` project, create a folder named `Handlers` and under this folder, create a class with a name of `AuthenticationHandler`, as shown in Listing 9-15.

Listing 9-15. The Authentication Message Handler

```
using System.Collections.Generic;
using System.Net.Http;
using System.Security.Claims;
using System.Threading;
using System.Threading.Tasks;

public class AuthenticationHandler : DelegatingHandler
{
    protected async override Task<HttpResponseMessage> SendAsync(
                                    HttpRequestMessage request,
                                        CancellationToken cancellationToken)
    {
        if (request.Headers.Contains("X-PSK"))
        {
            var claims = new List<Claim>
            {
                new Claim(ClaimTypes.Name, "jqhuman")
            };

            var principal = new ClaimsPrincipal(new[] { new ClaimsIdentity(claims, "dummy") });

            Thread.CurrentPrincipal = principal;
        }

        return await base.SendAsync(request, cancellationToken);
    }
}
```

4. In the `WebApiConfig` class under the `Configuration` folder in the project `Robusta.TalentManager.WebApi.Core`, add the following line of code in the `Register` method:

```
config.MessageHandlers.Add(new AuthenticationHandler());
```

5. This will add the handler to the handler collection so that the handler runs in the pipeline. You will need to add the directive to the `WebApiConfig` class.

```
using Robusta.TalentManager.WebApi.Core.Handlers;
```

6. Rebuild the solution and make a GET to the web-hosted API (`http://localhost/talentmanager/api/employees/1`) from Fiddler with a request header `X-PSK: somekey`. It starts working again, and you will receive a JSON representation.

Now, let us in-memory host our Web API to integration-test all these three classes together: controller, filter, and message handler.

7. In the Solution Explorer, right-click Solution 'Robusta.TalentManager' and choose Add ➤ New Project. Under Visual C# templates, select Test and choose Unit Test Project. Give it a name of `Robusta.TalentManager.WebApi.Test`.

8. Right-click References under the `Robusta.TalentManager.WebApi.Test` project and select `Manage NuGet Packages`. Search for the package `Microsoft.AspNet.WebApi.Core`, select the package in the search results, and click `Install`.

9. Add the following project references to `Robusta.TalentManager.WebApi.Test`:

   a. `Robusta.TalentManager.Domain`

   b. `Robusta.TalentManager.WebApi.Dto`

   c. `Robusta.TalentManager.WebApi.Core`

10. Right-click the `Robusta.TalentManager.WebApi.Test` project and select Add ➤ New Item and create a new Application Configuration File. Accept the default name of `App.Config`. Copy and paste the code in Listing 9-16 to the `App.Config` file. We need the Entity Framework–related information in the config file, because these are integration tests and they do touch the actual database. Also, edit the connection string to supply the appropriate server name and connection credentials.

Listing 9-16. App.Config

```xml
<?xml version="1.0" encoding="utf-8" ?>
<configuration>
    <configSections>
        <section name="entityFramework"
            type="System.Data.Entity.Internal.ConfigFile.EntityFrameworkSection,
                EntityFramework, Version=5.0.0.0, Culture=neutral,
                    PublicKeyToken=b77a5c561934e089"
            requirePermission="false" />
    </configSections>
    <connectionStrings>
        <add name="DefaultConnection"
```

```
                    providerName="System.Data.SqlClient"
                    connectionString="Server=server;Database=talent_manager;
                    User Id=uid;Password=pwd;" />
            </connectionStrings>
</configuration>
```

11. Rename UnitTest1 to EmployeesControllerIntegrationTest. Add the code from
    Listing 9-17 to this class. It does the following:

    a. In the Initialize method (decorated with TestInitialize) that runs before the test,
       we create a new instance of HttpConfiguration and call our config classes. We then
       create a new instance of HttpServer to be used in the test method. We also clear the
       Thread.CurrentPrincipal, since it has the Windows identity—the Windows account
       under which Visual Studio runs.

    b. In the Cleanup method that runs after the test, we just call Dispose on the HttpServer
       instance.

Listing 9-17. The EmployeesControllerIntegrationTest Class (Incomplete)

```
using System;
using System.Net;
using System.Net.Http;
using System.Security.Principal;
using System.Threading;
using System.Web.Http;
using Microsoft.VisualStudio.TestTools.UnitTesting;
using Robusta.TalentManager.WebApi.Core.Configuration;
using Robusta.TalentManager.WebApi.Dto;

[TestClass]
public class EmployeesControllerIntegrationTest
{
    private HttpServer server = null;

    [TestInitialize()]
    public void Initialize()
    {
        var configuration = new HttpConfiguration();

        IocConfig.RegisterDependencyResolver(configuration);
        WebApiConfig.Register(configuration);
        DtoMapperConfig.CreateMaps();

        server = new HttpServer(configuration);

        // This test runs under the context of my user
        // account (Windows Identity) and hence I clear that
        Thread.CurrentPrincipal = new GenericPrincipal(
                                        new GenericIdentity(String.Empty),
                                                null);
    }
```

```
    // Test methods go here

    [TestCleanup]
    public void Cleanup()
    {
        if (server != null)
            server.Dispose();
    }
}
```

12. Add the test method that checks for 401 - Unauthorized, when the credential is not sent in the request, as shown in Listing 9-18. Here we create an instance of `HttpMessageInvoker` using the `HttpServer` instance and make a request. The URI in the request is used only to extract the route data, and a real endpoint need not exist, since we use the in-memory–hosted Web API here. In this test, we have not set the request header for the handler to create the identity. The `Authorize` filter catches it and returns a 401.

Listing 9-18. The MustReturn401WhenNoCredentialsInRequest Test Method

```
[TestMethod]
public void MustReturn401WhenNoCredentialsInRequest()
{
    using (var invoker = new HttpMessageInvoker(server))
    {
        using (var request = new HttpRequestMessage(HttpMethod.Get,
                                        "http://localhost/api/employees/1"))
        {
            using (var response = invoker.SendAsync(request,
                                        CancellationToken.None).Result)
            {
                Assert.AreEqual(HttpStatusCode.Unauthorized, response.StatusCode);
            }
        }
    }
}
```

13. Add the test method that checks for 200 - OK, when the credential is sent in the request, as shown in Listing 9-19. In this test, we set the request header for the handler to create the identity. Thus, the `Authorize` filter is happy and it lets the action method run, which returns the employee data.

Listing 9-19. The MustReturn200AndEmployeeWhenCredentialsAreSupplied Test Method

```
[TestMethod]
public void MustReturn200AndEmployeeWhenCredentialsAreSupplied()
{
    using (var invoker = new HttpMessageInvoker(server))
    {
        using (var request = new HttpRequestMessage(HttpMethod.Get,
                                        "http://localhost/api/employees/1"))
```

```
        {
            request.Headers.Add("X-PSK", "somekey"); // Credentials

            using (var response = invoker.SendAsync(request,
                                        CancellationToken.None).Result)
            {
                Assert.IsNotNull(response);
                Assert.IsNotNull(response.Content);
                Assert.IsInstanceOfType(response.Content, typeof(ObjectContent<EmployeeDto>));
                Assert.AreEqual(HttpStatusCode.OK, response.StatusCode);

                var content = (response.Content as ObjectContent<EmployeeDto>);
                var result = content.Value as EmployeeDto;

                Assert.AreEqual(1, result.Id);
                Assert.AreEqual("Johnny", result.FirstName);
                Assert.AreEqual("Human", result.LastName);
            }
        }
    }
}
```

14. Rebuild the solution and run the tests from Test Explorer in Visual Studio
    (TEST menu ➤ Run ➤ All Tests).

Summary

ASP.NET Web API is host-independent, regardless of what the name suggests. ASP.NET infrastructure with IIS is not mandatory. There are three ways you can host your HTTP services built using ASP.NET Web API: web hosting, self-hosting, and in-memory hosting.

Web hosting uses the ASP.NET infrastructure backed by the IIS, and this is similar to hosting any ASP.NET application in IIS. Setting up transport security (HTTPS) is also similar to the way you set up HTTPS for any other ASP.NET application.

ASP.NET Web API can be self-hosted using any Windows process, such as a console application or Windows service. This option is useful when you do not or cannot have IIS. To enable HTTPS or reserve the URL for your Web API, you will need to use the netsh utility.

In the case of in-memory hosting, the clients connect directly to the Web API runtime, without hitting the network. This is used mainly for integration testing purposes, where you want to test the integration of multiple components running in the ASP.NET Web API pipeline.

■ ■ ■

CHAPTER 10

Securing ASP.NET Web API

According to US law, the term *information security* means protecting information and information systems from unauthorized access, use, disclosure, disruption, modification, or destruction in order to provide *confidentiality*, *integrity*, and *availability*, referred to as the CIA triad. *Confidentiality* is about preventing the disclosure of information to unauthorized entities. *Integrity* is about preventing modifications to the data by unauthorized entities. *Availability* is about the data and hence the information system that owns the data being available for legitimate users.

An entity, in this sense, refers to a user or an external system that uses an information system. To prevent the disclosure of information to unauthorized entities and to prevent modifications to the data by unauthorized entities, a system must be able to differentiate between authorized and unauthorized entities. In order to do that, a system must be able to identify an entity in the first place. Once the entity is identified, a system must be able to verify that identity by validating the credentials presented by the entity against an authority. Once a system is able to identify and authenticate an entity, it is in a position to control the access to the data it owns and hence to ensure confidentiality and integrity of data.

Availability, the third aspect of the CIA triad, from a security standpoint is mostly attributed to IT administration and operation activities involving specialized hardware and software, and is typically related to application programming in a limited sense. Though security is a team effort among the IT administration, operations, and development teams, this book is for programmers and hence the focus of this chapter is on the integrity and confidentiality aspects of the CIA triad from a programming perspective.

The topic of ASP.NET Web API security is very broad. I cover the security techniques related to ASP.NET Web API in-depth in my book *Pro ASP.NET Web API Security: Securing ASP.NET Web API* (Apress, 2013). This chapter covers the fundamentals and the key topics important for securing your ASP.NET Web API in order to provide a basic but solid understanding of the security concepts related to ASP.NET Web API.

10.1 Implementing Direct Authentication

In this exercise, you will implement the direct authentication pattern, in which a client application submits its credentials directly to your ASP.NET Web API. As an example, you will use the basic authentication scheme defined in Request for Comments (RFC) 2617, *HTTP Authentication: Basic and Digest Access Authentication* for this exercise.

Authentication is the process of an application such as your web API discovering the identity of a user through an identifier and verifying that identity by validating the credentials provided by the user against an authority (such as the membership store). Direct authentication is a common security pattern in which a client presents its credentials to a service directly. There is a trust relationship between the client application and your web API. Building a trust relationship is typically done out-of-band. For example, before using your web API, a user registers with the entity hosting your service and uses the credentials created in that process to authenticate from the client application.

Basic authentication is a simple scheme and works as follows:

1. The client makes a request to the service, ASP.NET Web API in our case.

2. If the resource requires the client to be authenticated, the service sends back a `401 - Unauthorized` status code in the response, setting the response header to `WWW-Authenticate: Basic`. This response header can also contain a *realm*, which is a string that uniquely identifies an area within the server for which the server needs a valid credential to successfully process the request.

3. The client now sends an authorization header like `Authorization: Basic YmFkcmmk6U2VjcmV0U2F1Y2U=`, which contains the credentials. The authorization request header value is just a base64-encoded string of the user ID and password, separated by a colon, and is not encrypted in any way.

4. If the credentials are valid, the service sends back the response and a `200 - OK` status code, as illustrated in Figure 10-1.

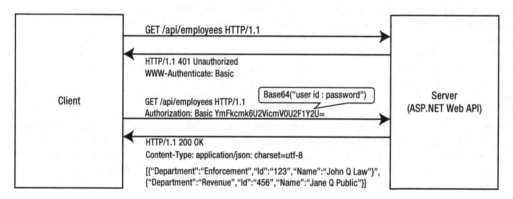

Figure 10-1. *HTTP basic authentication*

Take the following steps to implement basic authentication:

1. You will use the solution from Chapter 9 for this exercise. For this reason, a prerequisite to start working on this chapter is that you complete all the exercises in Chapter 9.

2. If you prefer, you can make a copy of the entire folder containing the solution and other files from Chapter 9 and start making changes for this chapter. Open the `Robusta.TalentManager` solution in Visual Studio 2012.

3. In the `Robusta.TalentManager.Domain` project, create a class User, as shown in Listing 10-1. This class has three properties, `UserName`, `Password`, and `Salt`, respectively storing the username, the hashed password, and the salt used to hash the password. *Hashing* is the process by which arbitrary data (the password in this case) is converted into a fixed-length string. The fundamental problem with plain hashing is that the mapping of a specific output to the corresponding input can be precomputed, stored, and looked up to determine the original data given a hash. An easy solution to this problem is *salting*. A salt is just a random string that is added to the data before hashing so that the output cannot be mapped back to the input using precomputed mappings. We store the hashed password and the corresponding salt at the user level. The `IsAuthentic` method takes in a password and determines if it is a valid password for that user.

Listing 10-1. The User Domain Class

```
using System.Linq;
using System.Security.Cryptography;

public class User : IIdentifiable
{
    public int Id { get; set; }
    public string UserName { get; set; }
    public byte[] Password { get; set; }
    public byte[] Salt { get; set; }

    public bool IsAuthentic(string password)
    {
        byte[] storedPassword = this.Password;
        byte[] storedSalt = this.Salt;

        var pbkdf2 = new Rfc2898DeriveBytes(password, storedSalt);
        pbkdf2.IterationCount = 1000;
        byte[] computedPassword = pbkdf2.GetBytes(32);

        return storedPassword.SequenceEqual(computedPassword);
    }
}
```

4. In the Robusta.TalentManager.Data project, create a new mapping for User, as shown in Listing 10-2. Create the UserConfiguration class in the Configuration folder.

Listing 10-2. The UserConfiguration Class

```
using System.ComponentModel.DataAnnotations.Schema;
using System.Data.Entity.ModelConfiguration;
using Robusta.TalentManager.Domain;

public class UserConfiguration : EntityTypeConfiguration<User>
{          .
    public UserConfiguration()
    {
        HasKey(k => k.Id);

        Property(p => p.Id)
            .HasColumnName("user_id")
                .HasDatabaseGeneratedOption(DatabaseGeneratedOption.Identity);

        Property(p => p.UserName).HasColumnName("user_name");
        Property(p => p.Password).HasColumnName("password");
        Property(p => p.Salt).HasColumnName("salt");
    }
}
```

5. Modify the OnModelCreating method of the Context class in the Robusta.TalentManager. Data project, as shown in Listing 10-3.

Listing 10-3. The OnModelCreating Method of the Context Class

```
protected override void OnModelCreating(DbModelBuilder modelBuilder)
{
    modelBuilder.Conventions.Remove<PluralizingTableNameConvention>();

    modelBuilder.Configurations
        .Add(new EmployeeConfiguration())
        .Add(new UserConfiguration());
}
```

6. Open SQL Server Management Studio and create a new table named user in the
    talent_manager database. Locate the talent_manager database in the tree view on the
    left (choose Your Server ➤ Databases ➤ talent_manager). Right-click talent_manager and
    select New Query. Copy and paste the CREATE SQL statement in Listing 10-4 and press F5 to
    run the SQL statement. The column user_id is the primary key and is an identity column.

Listing 10-4. The CREATE SQL Statement for the User Table

```
CREATE TABLE [dbo].[user](
    [user_id] [int] IDENTITY(1,1) NOT NULL,
    [user_name] [char](8) NOT NULL,
    [password] [binary](32) NOT NULL,
    [salt] [binary](32) NOT NULL,
 CONSTRAINT [PK_Table_1] PRIMARY KEY CLUSTERED
(
    [user_id] ASC
) WITH (PAD_INDEX = OFF, STATISTICS_NORECOMPUTE = OFF, IGNORE_DUP_KEY = OFF, ALLOW_ROW_
LOCKS = ON, ALLOW_PAGE_LOCKS = ON) ON [PRIMARY]
) ON [PRIMARY]
```

7. Also run the INSERT SQL statement in Listing 10-5 from SQL Server Management Studio,
    to seed the table with a record.

Listing 10-5. The INSERT SQL Statement

```
INSERT INTO [talent_manager].[dbo].[user] (user_name, password, salt) values
('jqhuman',
0x012E7C7B70462B9AF3C109E7CF565189D82D5697DD8645AEF67CA87F2B5795A7,
0x18E086233B60F812B41916A2D7F2EC73E76D26E980CD56F83606687EC778E89A)
```

8. The C# code that I used to come up with these 0x values is shown in Listing 10-6, just for
    your reference. You do not need to use this listing anywhere in this exercise. At the time
    the user ID is created, possibly as part of the user registration process, a salt is generated
    and the password entered by the user is hashed and stored. This typically happens in an
    application outside of ASP.NET Web API. For that purpose, code similar to Listing 10-6 can
    be used to insert the record in the user table.

Listing 10-6. C# Code to Insert a User Record

```
string data = "p@ssw0rd!"; // User-entered password
byte[] salt = new Byte[32];
using (var provider = new System.Security.Cryptography.RNGCryptoServiceProvider())
```

```
    {
        provider.GetBytes(salt); // Generated salt
    }

    var pbkdf2 = new System.Security.Cryptography.Rfc2898DeriveBytes(data, salt);
    pbkdf2.IterationCount = 1000;
    byte[] hash = pbkdf2.GetBytes(32); // Hashed and salted password

    var user = new User() { UserName = "jqhuman", Password = hash, Salt = salt };
    var repository = new Repository<User>(uow);
    repository.Insert(user);
    uow.Save();
```

9. In the Robusta.TalentManager.WebApi.Core project, we created a message handler named AuthenticationHandler, as part of Exercise 9-3. The class is located in the Handlers folder. Comment out the class definition. We will reuse the handler to implement basic authentication. Replace the class with the one shown in Listing 10-7.

Listing 10-7. The Basic Authentication Message Handler (Incomplete)

```
using System;
using System.Collections.Generic;
using System.Linq;
using System.Net;
using System.Net.Http;
using System.Net.Http.Headers;
using System.Security.Claims;
using System.Text;
using System.Threading;
using System.Threading.Tasks;
using System.Web;
using Robusta.TalentManager.Data;
using Robusta.TalentManager.Domain;

public class AuthenticationHandler : DelegatingHandler
{
    private const string SCHEME = "Basic";
    private readonly IRepository<User> repository = null;

    public AuthenticationHandler(IRepository<User> repository)
    {
        this.repository = repository;
    }

    protected async override Task<HttpResponseMessage> SendAsync(
                                    HttpRequestMessage request,
                                            CancellationToken cancellationToken)
```

259

```
    {
        try
        {
            // Perform request processing - Code from Listing 10-8 goes here

            var response = await base.SendAsync(request, cancellationToken);

            // Perform response processing - Code from Listing 10-9 goes here

            return response;
        }
        catch (Exception)
        {
            // Perform error processing - Code from Listing 10-10 goes here
        }
    }
}
```

We will now add code to the three appropriate places in the listing to handle the request, response, and error.

10. First, for the request processing part, retrieve the user ID and password from the HTTP Authorization header and perform the authentication, as shown in Listing 10-8. Following are the steps:

   a. Get the payload of the HTTP Authorization request header, if the header is present.

   b. Split the payload by semicolon and take the trimmed first part as the user ID and the second part as the password.

   c. Perform the actual authentication by calling the IsAuthentic method on the domain object.

   d. Gather the claims, create a principal, and set it in Thread.CurrentPrincipal. If you web-host, you must also set the principal in HttpContext.Current.User.

   e. Up until this point, the project Robusta.TalentManager.WebApi.Core is a pure ASP.NET Web API project with no dependencies on hosting. Now, we must create a dependency on the System.Web assembly, since we access HttpContext.

   f. Add a reference to System.Web (choose Assemblies ➤ Framework). This is needed because when our web API runs in the ASP.NET pipeline, as in the case of web hosting, Thread.CurrentPrincipal will be overwritten at times and we must set HttpContext.Current as well. Do a null check before setting it, because it will be null in the case of self-hosting.

Listing 10-8. Request Processing

```
var headers = request.Headers;
if (headers.Authorization != null && SCHEME.Equals(headers.Authorization.Scheme))
{
    Encoding encoding = Encoding.GetEncoding("iso-8859-1");
    string credentials = encoding.GetString(
    Convert.FromBase64String(headers.Authorization.Parameter));
```

```
            string[] parts = credentials.Split(':');
            string userName = parts[0].Trim();
            string password = parts[1].Trim();

            User user = repository.All.FirstOrDefault(u => u.UserName == userName);
            if (user != null && user.IsAuthentic(password))
            {
                var claims = new List<Claim>
                {
                    new Claim(ClaimTypes.Name, userName)
                };

                var principal = new ClaimsPrincipal(new[] {
                                                    new ClaimsIdentity(claims, SCHEME) });

                Thread.CurrentPrincipal = principal;

                if (HttpContext.Current != null)
                    HttpContext.Current.User = principal;
            }
        }
    }
```

11. For the response processing part, check whether the HTTP status code is 401 - Unauthorized.
    If so, add the corresponding WWW-Authenticate response header, as shown in Listing 10-9.
    Per the HTTP specification, when a 401 status code is sent back to the client, the response
    must include the WWW-Authenticate header specifying the schemes the server supports for
    the client to authenticate itself.

    Listing 10-9. Response Processing

```
if (response.StatusCode == HttpStatusCode.Unauthorized)
{
        response.Headers.WwwAuthenticate.Add(
                            new AuthenticationHeaderValue(SCHEME));
}
```

12. For the error processing part, if there is any exception in the message handler flow, set the
    status code to 401 - Unauthorized, and set the WWW-Authenticate header just as in the
    previous step, and return the response, short-circuiting the pipeline. See Listing 10-10.

    Listing 10-10. Error Processing

```
var response = request.CreateResponse(HttpStatusCode.Unauthorized);
response.Headers.WwwAuthenticate.Add(
                                    new AuthenticationHeaderValue(SCHEME));
return response;
```

The preceding code is a great example for illustrating the power of message handlers. The HTTP status code
can be set to 401 - Unauthorized by any component in the pipeline, including the Authorize filter. By registering
AuthenticationHandler as the first handler to execute after HttpServer, we get the opportunity to inspect the
response as late as possible and add the necessary WWW-Authenticate header(s).

13. Configure the message handler in the `Register` method of `WebApiConfig` class in the Configuration folder of the `Robusta.TalentManager.WebApi.Core` project, as shown in Listing 10-11. Comment out the line from the previous chapter where we added `AuthenticationHandler` to the `MessageHandlers` collection.

Listing 10-11. The Configure Message Handler

```
using System.Web.Http;
using Robusta.TalentManager.Data;
using Robusta.TalentManager.Domain;
using Robusta.TalentManager.WebApi.Core.Handlers;

public static class WebApiConfig
{
    public static void Register(HttpConfiguration config)
    {
        config.Routes.MapHttpRoute(
            name: "DefaultApi",
            routeTemplate: "api/{controller}/{id}",
            defaults: new { id = RouteParameter.Optional }
        );

        //config.MessageHandlers.Add(new AuthenticationHandler());

        var repository = config.DependencyResolver
                    .GetService(typeof(IRepository<User>))
                                        as IRepository<User>;

        config.MessageHandlers.Add(new AuthenticationHandler(repository));

    }
}
```

14. In the `Robusta.TalentManager.WebApi.Core` project, the `Get` method of `EmployeesController` must have the `Authorize` attribute applied to it, like so:

```
[Authorize] public HttpResponseMessage Get(int id) { ... }
```

from the previous chapter. Just ensure that the `Authorize` attribute is still applied on the action method.

15. Rebuild the solution and make a GET request from Fiddler to the URI `http://localhost/talentmanager/api/employees/1`. This code uses the endpoint corresponding to the web host, but you can use the self-host endpoint as well. It makes no difference, since the same message handler is exercised. You will get a 401 status code. Since you have the `Authorize` filter applied on the Get method, the filter returns the 401 status code on seeing that the identity is not authenticated. The request and response messages are shown in Listing 10-12 (messages edited for brevity). Notice the `WWW-Authenticate: Basic` response header part of the response; this is how our web API indicates the authentication scheme to the client.

Listing 10-12. The Request and Response Messages (Failure Scenario)

Request
```
GET http://localhost/talentmanager/api/employees/1 HTTP/1.1
Host: localhost
```

Response
```
HTTP/1.1 401 Unauthorized
Content-Type: application/json; charset=utf-8
WWW-Authenticate: Basic
Date: Mon, 22 Apr 2013 13:27:35 GMT
Content-Length: 61
```

```
{"Message":"Authorization has been denied for this request."}
```

16. Make another GET request from Fiddler to the URI `http://localhost/talentmanager/api/employees/1`, this time including the Authorization header: `Authorization: Basic anFodW1hbjpwQHNzdzByZCE=`. This is just the user ID and password separated by a colon, which is the string `jqhuman:p@ssw0rd!` in the base64-encoded format.

17. This time, you get the JSON representation of the employee resource back. Since you have configured to run `AuthenticationHandler` in the pipeline, it is setting `Thread.CurrentPrincipal` with an authenticated identity, and that makes the `Authorize` filter on the `Get` method happy. It lets the execution proceed to the action method, and you get the JSON back. The request and response messages are shown in Listing 10-13 (some of the headers removed for brevity).

   Listing 10-13. The Request and Response Messages (Success Scenario)

   Request
   ```
   GET http://localhost/talentmanager/api/employees/1 HTTP/1.1
   Authorization: Basic anFodW1hbjpwQHNzdzByZCE=
   Host: localhost
   ```

   Response
   ```
   HTTP/1.1 200 OK
   Content-Type: application/json; charset=utf-8
   Content-Length: 93
   ```

   ```
   {"Id":1,"FirstName":"Johnny","LastName":"Human","DepartmentId":1,"RowVersion":"AAAAAAAAF3E="}
   ```

18. Open Internet Explorer and type `http://localhost/talentmanager/api/employees/1` in the address bar.

You have just made a GET request. If you have Fiddler running, it will have captured a request and response exactly the same as in Listing 10-12.

19. Internet Explorer, on receiving the `WWW-Authenticate: Basic` response header, pops up a dialog box and collects the username and password. Enter some username and password.

20. Internet Explorer packages the credential in the basic scheme and retries the earlier GET. The message handler will receive the same user ID and password entered, and you can verify this by breaking the flow in the message handler.

■ **Caution**   In a real-world application, do not use basic authentication without SSL/TLS. HTTPS is a must for this scheme, without which anyone can sniff the traffic and get the credentials. Also, if your client is browser-based and you let the browser pop up the dialog box and collect the credentials from the end user, the credentials will be cached by the browser until you close it. If you make a request to a URI for which you are already authenticated, the browser automatically sends the credentials in the Authorize header, making this mechanism susceptible to cross-site request forgery (CSRF) attacks. For this reason, try to avoid basic authentication with browser-based clients.

10.2 Implementing Brokered Authentication

In this exercise, you will implement the brokered authentication pattern, in which a client application submits the username-and-password credential to a broker, gets a JSON Web Token (JWT), and ultimately presents that token to your ASP.NET Web API as the credential for authentication.

The brokered authentication pattern introduces a broker or a centralized entity for authentication. Even if no trust is established between the client and the service, trust relationships are established between the client and the broker and between the service and the broker. In those cases where a client will be unable or unwilling to authenticate directly to a web API using the credentials, the client can authenticate against the central broker and receive a token and submit it to the web API as the credential for authentication.

For this exercise, the broker will be just an ASP.NET handler that implements IHttpHandler. The broker takes in a username and password from the request body, authenticates them, and returns a JWT. In practice, when you deal with an entity like a broker, which is external to your application, you will resort to some kind of standard protocol to communicate with the broker and get the token. In SOAP-based services, WS-Trust is one such specification used, and the broker in that case will be a Security Token Service (STS). In the case of REST-based services, the OAuth 2.0 protocol can be used. However, for the sake of brevity, we will not implement OAuth 2.0 or an STS based on WS-Trust in this exercise. We'll just use the ASP.NET handler that responds to HTTP POST. You can find more information related to OAuth 2.0 in my other book: *Pro ASP.NET Web API Security: Securing ASP.NET Web API* (Apress, 2013).

■ **Note**   If you need a prebuilt implementation that issues tokens through OAuth 2.0, Thinktecture.IdentityServer v2 (https://github.com/thinktecture/Thinktecture.IdentityServer.v2) is a good open source option to evaluate. IdentityServer is a lightweight STS built with .NET 4.5, MVC 4, Web API, and WCF. It supports multiple protocols (both WS-Trust and OAuth 2.0). IdentityServer can mint tokens of different formats (SAML 1.1/2.0, JWT) and integrates with ASP.NET membership, roles, and profile out-of-the-box.

1.   Run another instance of Visual Studio 2012 as administrator.

2.   Create a new ASP.NET Empty Web Application with a name of Robusta.Broker.

3.   Right-click References under the Robusta.Broker project and select Manage NuGet Packages. Search for System.IdentityModel.Tokens.Jwt, locate the package, and click Install. This package, named JSON Web Token Handler for the Microsoft .Net Framework 4.5, provides an assembly that contains the classes to validate, read, and mint JWT tokens.

4.   Add a reference to System.IdentityModel.

5. Create a class BrokerHandler, deriving from IHttpHandler, as shown in Listing 10-14. The following steps show the logic implemented in the ProcessRequest method:

   a. We get the username and password from the request.

   b. For the sake of brevity, we do not authenticate the credentials. We simply assume the credentials are valid, if the username matches password. If so, we create a JWT using JwtSecurityTokenHandler part of the System.IdentityModel.Tokens.Jwt NuGet package.

   c. If authentication fails, that is, if the username does not match password, we send back a 401 status code.

   d. For signing the token, we use a shared symmetric key. As the name indicates, a shared symmetric key is shared between the sender and the receiver. The same key is used to sign the token and validate the signature. For the purpose of this exercise, we just use a hard-coded key but in practice, this will be the key corresponding to the audience.

   e. We create the token with only one claim: the name claim.

   f. Finally, the token is written into the HTTP response.

Listing 10-14. The BrokerHandler Class

```
using System;
using System.IdentityModel.Protocols.WSTrust;
using System.IdentityModel.Tokens;
using System.Security.Claims;
using System.Web;

public class BrokerHandler : IHttpHandler
{
    private const string ISSUER = "Robusta.Broker";
    private const string AUDIENCE = "http://localhost/talentmanager/api";

    public bool IsReusable
    {
        get { return true; }
    }

    public void ProcessRequest(HttpContext context)
    {
        HttpRequest request = context.Request;

        string userName = request["username"];
        string password = request["password"];

        bool isAuthentic = !String.IsNullOrEmpty(userName) && userName.Equals(password);

        if (isAuthentic)
        {
            // I use a hard-coded key
            byte[] key = Convert.FromBase64String(
                                        "qqO5yXcbijtAdYmS2Otyzeze2XQedqy+Tp37wQ3sgTQ=");
```

```
        var signingCredentials = new SigningCredentials(
                                            new InMemorySymmetricSecurityKey(key),
                                            SecurityAlgorithms.HmacSha256Signature,
                                            SecurityAlgorithms.Sha256Digest);


        var descriptor = new SecurityTokenDescriptor()
        {
            TokenIssuerName = ISSUER,
            AppliesToAddress = AUDIENCE,
            Lifetime = new Lifetime(DateTime.UtcNow, DateTime.UtcNow.AddMinutes(5)),
            SigningCredentials = signingCredentials,
            Subject = new ClaimsIdentity(new Claim[]
            {
                new Claim(ClaimTypes.Name, userName)
            })
        };

        var tokenHandler = new JwtSecurityTokenHandler();

        var token = tokenHandler.CreateToken(descriptor);

        context.Response.Write(tokenHandler.WriteToken(token));
    }
    else
        context.Response.StatusCode = 401;
}
}
```

6. Register the handler in Web.config, as shown in Listing 10-15, by creating the <system. webServer> element. We use IIS 7.5 and an integrated pipeline for this exercise, and hence the Web.config entry is all that is needed to register the handler. The handler is registered to handle only POST requests.

Listing 10-15. The Web.Config File

```xml
<?xml version="1.0"?>
<configuration>
    <system.web>
        <compilation debug="true" targetFramework="4.5" />
        <httpRuntime targetFramework="4.5" />
    </system.web>
    <system.webServer>
        <handlers>
            <add name="BrokerHandler"
                 path="jwt" verb="POST"
                    type="Robusta.Broker.BrokerHandler, Robusta.Broker" />
        </handlers>
    </system.webServer>
</configuration>
```

7. If you do not have the Robusta.TalentManager solution open, run another instance of Visual Studio as administrator and open the Robusta.TalentManager solution from Exercise 10.1.

8. Right-click References under the Robusta.TalentManager.WebApi.Core project. Select Manage NuGet Packages. Search for the package System.IdentityModel.Tokens.Jwt, select the package in the search results, and click Install.

9. To the Robusta.TalentManager.WebApi.Core project, add a reference to the .NET libraries System.ServiceModel and System.IdentityModel.

10. In the Robusta.TalentManager.WebApi.Core project, create a new class in the Handlers folder with a name of JwtHandler, as shown in Listing 10-16.

   a. This handler expects the JWT to come in the bearer scheme in the Authorization request header.

   b. It retrieves the token from the header and uses JwtSecurityTokenHandler to validate the token. Validation includes checking for the audience: the entity to which the token has been issued, who the issuer is, and the integrity of the token. In this case, the audience in the token must be http://localhost/talentmanager/api and the issuer must be Robusta.Broker for the validation to succeed. For the integrity check, the signature is validated through the shared symmetric key. Here also, we use the same hard-coded key.

   c. If the token is valid, claims are extracted and a ClaimsPrincipal object is returned; we set this to Thread.CurrentPrincipal. If we are web hosting, the same object is set in HttpContext.Current.User as well.

Listing 10-16. The JwtHandler Class

```
using System;
using System.Collections.Generic;
using System.IdentityModel.Tokens;
using System.Net;
using System.Net.Http;
using System.Net.Http.Headers;
using System.ServiceModel.Security.Tokens;
using System.Threading;
using System.Threading.Tasks;
using System.Web;

public class JwtHandler : DelegatingHandler
{
    private const string ISSUER = "Robusta.Broker";
    private const string AUDIENCE = "http://localhost/talentmanager/api";

    protected async override Task<HttpResponseMessage> SendAsync(
                                    HttpRequestMessage request,
                                        CancellationToken cancellationToken)
    {
        byte[] key = Convert.FromBase64String(
                            "qqO5yXcbijtAdYmS2Otyzeze2XQedqy+Tp37wQ3sgTQ=");
```

```
    try
    {
        var headers = request.Headers;
        if (headers.Authorization != null)
        {
            if (headers.Authorization.Scheme.Equals("Bearer"))
            {
                string jwt = request.Headers.Authorization.Parameter;

                JwtSecurityTokenHandler tokenHandler = new JwtSecurityTokenHandler();
                TokenValidationParameters parms = new TokenValidationParameters()
                {
                    AllowedAudience = AUDIENCE,
                    ValidIssuers = new List<string>() { ISSUER },
                    SigningToken = new BinarySecretSecurityToken(key)
                };

                var principal = tokenHandler.ValidateToken(jwt, parms);

                Thread.CurrentPrincipal = principal;

                if (HttpContext.Current != null)
                    HttpContext.Current.User = principal;
            }
        }

        var response = await base.SendAsync(request, cancellationToken);
        if (response.StatusCode == HttpStatusCode.Unauthorized)
        {
            response.Headers.WwwAuthenticate.Add(
            new AuthenticationHeaderValue("Bearer",
            "error=\"invalid_token\""));
        }
        return response;
    }
    catch (Exception)
    {
        var response = request.CreateResponse(HttpStatusCode.Unauthorized);
        response.Headers.WwwAuthenticate.Add(
        new AuthenticationHeaderValue("Bearer", "error=\"invalid_token\""));
        return response;
    }
  }
}
```

11. Configure the message handler in the `Register` method of the `WebApiConfig` class in the Configuration folder, as shown in Listing 10-17.

Listing 10-17. Registering JwtHandler

```
public static class WebApiConfig
{
    public static void Register(HttpConfiguration config)
    {
        config.Routes.MapHttpRoute(
            name: "DefaultApi",
            routeTemplate: "api/{controller}/{id}",
            defaults: new { id = RouteParameter.Optional }
        );

        //config.MessageHandlers.Add(new AuthenticationHandler());

        var repository = config.DependencyResolver
                    .GetService(typeof(IRepository<User>))
                                    as IRepository<User>;

        config.MessageHandlers.Add(new AuthenticationHandler(repository));
        config.MessageHandlers.Add(new JwtHandler());
    }
}
```

12. Rebuild both the Robusta.TalentManager and Robusta.Broker solutions.

13. Make a POST request to the broker URI http://localhost:24890/handler/jwt from Fiddler. Adjust the port number to reflect the port Robusta.Broker project uses. Use Content-Type: application/x-www-form-urlencoded in the request header and usernam e=jqhuman&password=jqhuman as the request body. You get back the JWT. The request and response messages are shown in Listing 10-18.

Listing 10-18. Request and Response Messages (Broker)

Request
```
POST http://localhost:24890/handler/jwt HTTP/1.1
Content-Type: application/x-www-form-urlencoded
Host: localhost:24890
Content-Length: 33

username=jqhuman&password=jqhuman
```

Response
```
HTTP/1.1 200 OK
Content-Length: 311
```

eyJ0eXAiOiJKV1QiLCJhbGciOiJIUzI1NiJ9.eyJhdWQiOiJodHRwOi8vbG9jYWxob3N0L3RhbGVudG1hbmFnZXIvYXBpIiwia
XNzIjoiUm9idXNOYS5Ccm9rZXIiLCJuYmYiOjEzNjY3MDc2MTQsImV4cCI6MTM2NjcwNzkxNCwiaHR0cDovL3NjaGVtYX
MueG1sc29hcC5vcmcvd3MvMjAwNS8wNS9pZGVudGl0eS9jbGFpbXMvbmFtZSI6ImpxaHVtYW4ifQ.3jMam6VRXlDTspZfDtvwQM
vdAopA4vqiqYOhdPhZgMI

14. The response message body is the JWT. You will need to send this in the `Authorization` header in the bearer scheme to the web API as the credential to authenticate.

15. Make a GET to `http://localhost/TalentManager/api/employees/1` with a request header of `Authorization: Bearer <entire jwt string goes here>` from Fiddler by copying and pasting the token from the response of the previous call to the broker endpoint.

16. The message handler validates this token and establishes the identity based on the claims in this token. Since it establishes an authenticated identity, the `Authorize` filter on the `Get` action method is happy and lets the action method run, and you get the response back. The request and response messages are in Listing 10-19.

Listing 10-19. Request and Response Messages (Web API)

Request
```
GET http://localhost/TalentManager/api/employees/1 HTTP/1.1
Authorization: Bearer
eyJ0eXAiOiJKV1QiLCJhbGciOiJIUzI1NiJ9.eyJhdWQiOiJodHRwOi8vbG9jYWxob3N0L3RhbGVudG1hbmFnZXIvYXBp
IiwiaXNzIjoiUm9idXN0ZXN55Ccm9rZXIiLCJuYmYiOjEzNjY3MDc2MTQsImV4cCI6MTM2NjcwNzkxNCwiaHR0cDovL3Nja
GVtYXMueG1sc29hcC5vcmcvd3MvMjAwNS8wNS9pZGVudGl0eS9jbGFpbXMvbmFtZSI6ImpxaHVtYW4ifQ.3j
Mam6VRXlDTspZfDtvwQMvdAopA4vqiqYOhdPhZgMI
```

Response
```
HTTP/1.1 200 OK
Content-Type: application/json; charset=utf-8
Date: Tue, 23 Apr 2013 09:06:02 GMT
Content-Length: 93

{"Id":1,"FirstName":"Johnny","LastName":"Human","DepartmentId":1,"RowVersion":"AAAAAAAAF48="}
```

■ **Note** Since we have given a lifetime of 5 minutes for the token, you will need to make the preceding request to the web API within this time period from when the token was issued. Otherwise, the request will fail because of the expired token.

Thus, you were able to exchange your username and password for a JWT with the broker and submit the token to your web API as the credential, and you got the response back. You trust the broker, and your web API trusts the broker as well. The web API accepts the token you presented to it because it was issued by the broker the web API trusts.

Since we plugged in `JwtHandler` to the pipeline, in addition to the `AuthenticationHandler`, the web API at this point is capable of performing direct authentication based on the username and password you send through the basic scheme (shown in the previous exercise) as well as the authentication based on JWT.

HTTP MODULES VERSUS MESSAGE HANDLERS

By implementing your authentication code in an HTTP module, you can have that code execute even before your first all-route message handler runs. If you have a web API and other resources such as HTTP handlers, pages, or MVC controllers in the same application, and you want to establish an identity in one place and share it, an HTTP module is a great option. An HTTP module sees all requests that go through the ASP.NET pipeline. A message handler only sees requests that are routed to Web API.

The flip side of using an HTTP module is that your design is no longer host-agnostic, and you are creating a dependency on web hosting (IIS). I use message handlers throughout this chapter because they are host-agnostic, but you must be aware of the trade-offs involved in choosing between a message handler and an HTTP module.

10.3 Authorizing Requests

In this exercise, you will implement authorization for your web API. Authorization, sometimes abbreviated to *AuthZ*, is the process of an application determining whether an entity is allowed to perform a requested action. Once an authenticated identity is established for an entity, the application can control the entity's access to the application resources based on this identity. An extremely simple and trivial application might authorize resource access purely based on the identity. But most practical applications authorize access based on attributes, such as roles, that are associated with the identity.

1. In the Robusta.Broker project, modify the ProcessRequest method in BrokerHandler to return one more claim in addition to the name claim, as shown in Listing 10-20.

   Listing 10-20 The ProcessRequest Method with an Additional Claim

   ```
   public void ProcessRequest(HttpContext context)
   {
       ...

           var descriptor = new SecurityTokenDescriptor()
           {
               TokenIssuerName = ISSUER,
               AppliesToAddress = AUDIENCE,
               Lifetime = new Lifetime(DateTime.UtcNow, DateTime.UtcNow.AddMinutes(5)),
               SigningCredentials = signingCredentials,
               Subject = new ClaimsIdentity(new Claim[]
               {
                   new Claim(ClaimTypes.Name, userName),
                   new Claim(ClaimTypes.Role, "HRManager")
               })
           };

       ...

   }
   ```

2. In the Robusta.TalentManager.WebApi.Core project, modify the EmployeesController GET action method, as shown in Listing 10-21.

Listing 10-21. The EmployeesController GET Action Method

```
[Authorize(Roles="HRManager")]
public HttpResponseMessage Get(int id)
{
    var employee = repository.Find(id);
    if (employee == null)
    {
        var response = Request.CreateResponse(HttpStatusCode.NotFound, "Employee not found");

        throw new HttpResponseException(response);
    }

    return Request.CreateResponse<EmployeeDto>(
                    HttpStatusCode.OK,
                    mapper.Map<Employee, EmployeeDto>(employee));
}
```

3. Rebuild both the solutions and make a POST request to the broker URI
   `http://localhost:24890/handler/jwt` from Fiddler. Adjust the port number
   to reflect the port `Robusta.Broker` project uses. Use `Content-Type:`
   `application/x-www-form-urlencoded` in the request header and
   `username=jqhuman&password=jqhuman` as the request body. You'll get back the JWT. Copy
   the entire token string.

4. Make a GET to `http://localhost/TalentManager/api/employees/1` with a request
   header of `Authorization: Bearer <entire jwt string goes here>` from Fiddler by
   pasting the token you copied in the previous step.

You will get the JSON response back, the same as the last time. What is different now is that we are authorizing
the action method `Get` based on the role, using the `Authorize` attribute. We allow access only if the user is in the role
of `HRManager`.

5. Modify the `Authorize` attribute applied on the `Get` action method in `EmployeesController`
   so that it looks for the role of `HRDirector`:

   `[Authorize(Roles="HRDirector")] public HttpResponseMessage Get(int id) { ... }`

6. Rebuild `Robusta.TalentManager` and repeat the previous GET before JWT expires. (You
   can always get a fresh JWT from the broker and retry the GET request, when in doubt.)
   Even with a fresh JWT, you will get `401 - Unauthorized`, because `Authorize` will not allow
   the `Get` action method to run. It is configured to look for a user in the role of `HRDirector`,
   but the current user is in the role of `HRManager`.

7. The current role check we do is simple. Suppose you want to extend the logic to allow
   access to the `Get` method, if the user is in a role of `HRManager` between the hours of
   3 PM and 5 PM only. That may be a weird rule, but its purpose is only to demonstrate
   implementing something more complex than a simple role-based check.

8. In the `Robusta.TalentManager.WebApi.Core` project, create a folder named `Filters`.
   Within this, create a class `AuthorizeByTimeSlot`, as shown in Listing 10-22.

Listing 10-22. The AuthorizeByTimeSlot Filter

```
using System;
using System.Web.Http;
using System.Web.Http.Controllers;

public class AuthorizeByTimeSlot : AuthorizeAttribute
{
    public int SlotStartHour { get; set; }
    public int SlotEndHour { get; set; }

    protected override bool IsAuthorized(HttpActionContext context)
    {
        if (DateTime.Now.Hour >= this.SlotStartHour &&
                DateTime.Now.Hour <= this.SlotEndHour &&
                    base.IsAuthorized(context))
            return true;

        return false;
    }
}
```

9. Apply the filter on the Get method of EmployeesController, as shown in Listing 10-23.
    Also add the directive

    ```
    using Robusta.TalentManager.WebApi.Core.Filters;
    ```

    to EmployeesController.

Listing 10-23. The AuthorizeByTimeSlot Filter Applied to GET

```
[AuthorizeByTimeSlot(Roles="HRManager", SlotStartHour=15, SlotEndHour = 17)]
public HttpResponseMessage Get(int id)
{
    // Action method logic goes here
}
```

10. Rebuild the Robusta.TalentManager solution and make the GET request between the
    hours of 3 and 5 PM. The request will go through. At any other time of the day, it will be
    rejected with a 401.

Summary

Information security means protecting information and information systems from unauthorized access, use, disclosure, disruption, modification, or destruction in order to provide confidentiality, integrity, and availability, referred to as the CIA triad. Confidentiality is about preventing the disclosure of information to unauthorized entities. Integrity is about preventing modifications to the data by unauthorized entities. Availability is about the data and hence the information system that owns the data being available for legitimate users.

To prevent the disclosure of information to unauthorized entities and to prevent modifications to the data by such entities, a system must be able to differentiate between authorized and unauthorized entities. In order to do that, a system must be able to identify an entity in the first place. Once identified, a system must be able to verify the identity of the entity by validating the credentials presented by the entity against an authority; this process is called *authentication*. Once a system is able to identify and authenticate an entity, it is in a position to control the access to the data it owns, and this process is called *authorization*. Authentication and authorization are fundamental to ensure confidentiality and integrity.

Direct authentication is a common security pattern in which a client presents its credentials to a service directly. There is a trust relationship between the client and the service. Brokered authentication, on the other hand, is a pattern that introduces a central authentication entity, called the broker. Even if no trust is established between the client and the service, trust relationships are established between the client and the broker and between the service and the broker.

In the area of direct authentication, HTTP authentication schemes are commonly used. Request for Comments (RFC) 2617, *HTTP Authentication: Basic and Digest Access Authentication,* provides the specification for the HTTP authentication framework. The basic authentication scheme is based on the model that the client must authenticate itself with a user ID and a password. In the case of the brokered authentication pattern, in which a broker issues a token to a client application based on a protocol such as OAuth 2.0 or WS-Trust, the token with the claims set is presented to the service as the credential. In this chapter, we looked at one token format, which is JSON Web Token (JWT).

CHAPTER 11

■ ■ ■

Consuming ASP.NET Web API

One of the greatest benefits of ASP.NET Web API is its reachability. A broad range of clients in disparate platforms can consume your web API, leveraging the support HTTP enjoys across platforms and devices. In this chapter, I cover the topic of client applications consuming your web API. I've limited the coverage to .NET clients—a console application, a Windows Presentation Foundation (WPF) application, and a JavaScript client running in the context of a browser.

11.1 Calling a Web API from a Console Application

In this exercise, you will call your web API from a C# console application. To call the web API, you can use `System.Net.WebClient`, or even `WebRequest` and `WebResponse` classes, or for that matter any other library you are familiar with. You just need HTTP capabilities to call a web API. However, this example will use `HttpClient`, the modern HTTP client that is available from the .NET framework version 4.5 (ported to .NET 4.0 as well). You can issue more than one request through a single `HttpClient` instance, and you get the `async` features of .NET 4.5 by default, helping you manage and coordinate multiple requests.

1. You will use the solution from Chapter 10 for this exercise. For this reason, a prerequisite to start working on this chapter is that you complete all the exercises in Chapter 10.

2. If you prefer, you can make a copy of the entire folder containing both the solutions (`Robusta.TalentManager` and `Robusta.Broker`) and other files from Chapter 10 and start making changes for this chapter.

3. Open the `Robusta.TalentManager` solution in Visual Studio 2012.

4. In the `Robusta.TalentManager.WebApi.Core` project, open `EmployeesController` and comment out the `AuthorizeByTimeSlot` attribute on the `Get(int)` action method.

5. In the Solution Explorer, right-click Solution 'Robusta.TalentManager' and choose Add ➤ New Project. Under Visual C# templates, select Windows and choose Console Application. Give it a name of `Robusta.TalentManager.WebApi.Client.ConsoleApp`. Right-click this project in the Solution Explorer and select Set As Startup Project.

6. Right-click References under the `Robusta.TalentManager.WebApi.Client.ConsoleApp` project and select Manage NuGet Packages. Search for the package `Microsoft.AspNet.WebApi.Client`, select the package in the search results, and click Install.

7. Add the following project reference to `Robusta.TalentManager.WebApi.Client.ConsoleApp`:

   a. `Robusta.TalentManager.WebApi.Dto`

8. Add the code in Listing 11-1 to the Main method in the Program class of the Robusta.TalentManager.WebApi.Client.ConsoleApp project. Add a breakpoint in the closing brace of the Main method.

Listing 11-1. The Console Application Main Method

```
using System;
using System.Net.Http;
using System.Net.Http.Headers;
using Robusta.TalentManager.WebApi.Dto;

class Program
{
    static void Main(string[] args)
    {
        HttpClient client = new HttpClient();
        client.BaseAddress = new Uri("http://localhost/TalentManager/api/");

        HttpResponseMessage response = client.GetAsync("employees/1").Result;

        Console.WriteLine("{0} - {1}", (int)response.StatusCode, response.ReasonPhrase);

        if (response.IsSuccessStatusCode)
        {
            var employee = response.Content.ReadAsAsync<EmployeeDto>().Result;
            Console.WriteLine("{0}\t{1}\t{2}",
                            employee.Id,
                                employee.FirstName,
                                    employee.LastName,
                                        employee.DepartmentId);

        }
    } // Add a breakpoint on this line
}
```

9. Rebuild the solution and press F5.

10. It works and returns a 200 - OK and the employee data.

11. We read the response as response.Content.ReadAsAsync<EmployeeDto>().Result;. Since the web API returns EmployeeDto and this class is part of a separate assembly, Robusta.TalentManager.WebApi.Dto, we are able to just reference the assembly and use the same type in both the server and the client side.

12. Also, by getting the Result property of the Task object, we block the Main method. The main thread waits for the response to come back and resumes processing.

13. Add the code from Listing 11-2 to the end of the existing Main method.

Listing 11-2. POSTing an Employee

```
EmployeeDto newEmployee = new EmployeeDto()
{
    FirstName = "Julian",
    LastName = "Heineken",
    DepartmentId = 2
};

response = client.PostAsJsonAsync<EmployeeDto>
                            ("http://localhost/TalentManager/api/employees", newEmployee)
                                .Result;

if (response.IsSuccessStatusCode)
{
    Console.WriteLine(response.Content.ReadAsStringAsync().Result);

    if (response.Headers != null)
        Console.WriteLine(response.Headers.Location);
}

Console.WriteLine("{0} - {1}", (int)response.StatusCode, response.ReasonPhrase);
```

14. Rebuild the solution and press F5. The code we just added makes a POST and adds a new employee resource.

HttpClient makes it easy to add the request headers using strongly typed APIs instead of having to work with strings all the time.

15. Add the code from Listing 11-3 to the end of the Main method. It requests an XML representation of the employee resource and writes the XML to the console.

Listing 11-3. Adding Accept Headers

```
client.DefaultRequestHeaders.Accept.Add(
                            new MediaTypeWithQualityHeaderValue("application/json", 0.8));

client.DefaultRequestHeaders.Accept.Add(
                            new MediaTypeWithQualityHeaderValue("application/xml", 0.9));

response = client.GetAsync("employees/1").Result;

Console.WriteLine("{0} - {1}", (int)response.StatusCode, response.ReasonPhrase);

if (response.IsSuccessStatusCode)
{
    Console.WriteLine(response.Content.ReadAsStringAsync().Result);
}
```

16. In the Robusta.TalentManager.WebApi.Core project, open EmployeesController and apply the Authorize attribute on the Get and Post action methods, like so:

[Authorize]
```
public HttpResponseMessage Get(int id) { ... }
```

[Authorize]
```
public HttpResponseMessage Post(EmployeeDto employeeDto) { ... }
```

17. Rebuild the solution and press F5 to run the console client application. You get 401 - Unauthorized for all three calls from the Main method.

The Authorize attribute expects authenticated identity, and we are not passing any credentials for the message handlers to establish identity. To send the credentials, we could add the code directly in the Main method. Instead, let us use a client-side message handler. Just as on the server side, you can have message handlers on the client side as well.

18. Add a class named CredentialsHandler to the Robusta.TalentManager.WebApi.Client.ConsoleApp project, as shown in Listing 11-4.

Listing 11-4. The Client Message Handler

```csharp
using System;
using System.Net.Http;
using System.Net.Http.Headers;
using System.Text;
using System.Threading;
using System.Threading.Tasks;

public class CredentialsHandler : DelegatingHandler
{
    protected override async Task<HttpResponseMessage> SendAsync(
                                  HttpRequestMessage request,
                                      CancellationToken cancellationToken)
    {
        var headers = request.Headers;
        if (headers.Authorization == null)
        {
            string creds = String.Format("{0}:{1}", "jqhuman", "p@ssw0rd!");
            byte[] bytes = Encoding.Default.GetBytes(creds);

            var header = new AuthenticationHeaderValue("Basic", Convert.ToBase64String(bytes));
            headers.Authorization = header;
        }

        return await base.SendAsync(request, cancellationToken);
    }
}
```

19. Comment out the line `HttpClient client = new HttpClient();` in the `Main` method of the `Program` class in the `Robusta.TalentManager.WebApi.Client.ConsoleApp` project and add the following line:

    `HttpClient client = HttpClientFactory.Create(new CredentialsHandler());`

    We use `HttpClientFactory` to create the client instance in order to specify the handler to be run in the client pipeline.

20. Rebuild the solution and press F5 to run the console client application. All three web API calls work now.

■ **Note**   Because we set the header from the message handler, the header is set for every request, with the handler being called every time we make a web API call. If you set the header using the `DefaultRequestHeaders` property of `HttpClient`, setting it once is enough.

11.2 Calling a Web API from a WPF Application

In this exercise, you will call your web API from a WPF application using `HttpClient`. The code you will write for calling the web API will be very similar to Exercise 11.1. However, you will see how to write non-blocking code to take advantage of the `async` features of .NET 4.5.

If you are not familiar with the Model-View-View-Model (MVVM) pattern typically followed with WPF applications, the code in this exercise might appear different from what you are used to, but the idea is to separate the concerns and make the view models completely unit-testable. So you will not find any code in the view (the code-behind file of the XAML) except the call to the `InitializeComponent` method. We use MVVM mainly to keep the code clean, and the MVVM pattern is not mandatory for consuming ASP.NET Web API from your WPF application.

1. We will continue to use the solution from the previous exercise. Run Visual Studio as administrator and open the `Robusta.TalentManager` solution from Exercise 11.1.

2. In the Solution Explorer, right-click Solution 'Robusta.TalentManager' and choose Add ➤ New Project. Under Visual C# templates, select Windows and choose WPF Application. Give it a name of `Robusta.TalentManager.WebApi.Client.WinApp`. Right-click this project in the Solution Explorer and select Set As Startup Project.

3. Right-click References under the `Robusta.TalentManager.WebApi.Client.WinApp` project. Select Manage NuGet Packages. Search for the package `Microsoft.AspNet.WebApi.Client`, select the package in the search results, and click Install.

4. Add the following project reference to `Robusta.TalentManager.WebApi.Client.WinApp`:

   a.   `Robusta.TalentManager.WebApi.Dto`

5. Create a folder named `ViewModels` in the `Robusta.TalentManager.WebApi.Client.WinApp` project.

6. Within this folder, create an abstract `ViewModelBase` class, as shown in Listing 11-5.

Listing 11-5. The ViewModelBase Class

```
using System;
using System.ComponentModel;
using System.Linq.Expressions;

public abstract class ViewModelBase : INotifyPropertyChanged
{
    public event PropertyChangedEventHandler PropertyChanged;

    protected void RaisePropertyChanged<T>(Expression<Func<T>> propertyExpresssion)
    {
        string propertyName = GetPropertyName(propertyExpresssion);

        if (this.PropertyChanged != null)
            this.PropertyChanged(this, new PropertyChangedEventArgs(propertyName));
    }

    private string GetPropertyName<T>(Expression<Func<T>> propertyExpresssion)
    {
        string propertyName = String.Empty;

        MemberExpression expression = propertyExpresssion.Body as MemberExpression;
        if (expression != null)
        {
            propertyName = expression.Member.Name;
        }

        return propertyName;
    }
}
```

7. Create a folder named `Commands` in the `Robusta.TalentManager.WebApi.Client.WinApp` project.

8. In this folder, create a new class named `RelayCommand`, as shown in Listing 11-6.

Listing 11-6. The RelayCommand Class

```
using System;
using System.Windows.Input;

public class RelayCommand : ICommand
{
    private readonly Action<object> action;
    private readonly Predicate<object> canExecute;

    public RelayCommand(Action<object> execute) : this(execute, null) { }

    public RelayCommand(Action<object> execute, Predicate<object> canExecute)
    {
        action = execute;
        this.canExecute = canExecute;
    }
```

```
    public bool CanExecute(object parameter)
    {
        return canExecute == null ? true : canExecute(parameter);
    }

    public event EventHandler CanExecuteChanged
    {
        add { CommandManager.RequerySuggested += value; }
        remove { CommandManager.RequerySuggested -= value; }
    }

    public void Execute(object parameter)
    {
        action(parameter);
    }
}
```

9.   Delete MainWindow.xaml.

10. Create a folder named Views in the Robusta.TalentManager.WebApi.Client.WinApp project.

11. In this folder, create a new Window (WPF) with a name of EmployeeFind. Figure 11-1 shows the window as it appears in the designer.

Figure 11-1. *The EmployeeFind window*

12. The XAML for this window is shown in Listing 11-7.

Listing 11-7. The EmployeeFind XAML

```xml
<Window x:Class="Robusta.TalentManager.WebApi.Client.WinApp.Views.EmployeeFind"
        xmlns="http://schemas.microsoft.com/winfx/2006/xaml/presentation"
        xmlns:x="http://schemas.microsoft.com/winfx/2006/xaml"
        Title="Find Employee" Height="300" Width="300">
    <Grid>
        <StackPanel>
            <WrapPanel>
                <TextBlock Text="ID:" Width="50"/>
                <TextBox Text="{Binding EmployeeId}" Width="100"/>
                <Button Content="Find" HorizontalAlignment="Left"
                        Command="{Binding FindCommand}" Name="btnFind"
                        VerticalAlignment="Top" Width="100" FontWeight="Normal"/>
            </WrapPanel>
            <TextBlock Name="txbResult">
                <Run Text="Employee ID: "/>
                <Run Text="{Binding EmployeeFound.Id}" />
                <LineBreak/>
                <Run Text="Employee Name: "/>
                <Run Text="{Binding EmployeeFound.FirstName}" />
                <Run Text="{Binding EmployeeFound.LastName}" />
            </TextBlock>
        </StackPanel>
    </Grid>
</Window>
```

13. In the ViewModels folder, create a new class named EmployeeFindViewModel, deriving
    from ViewModelBase, as shown in Listing 11-8. The Find button is bound to the
    FindCommand property of the view model, which just relays to the method FindEmployee,
    which implements the logic to call the web API. Pay attention to the Result property used,
    which blocks the thread.

Listing 11-8. The EmployeeFindViewModel Class

```csharp
using System;
using System.Net.Http;
using System.Net.Http.Headers;
using System.Text;
using System.Windows.Input;
using Robusta.TalentManager.WebApi.Client.WinApp.Commands;
using Robusta.TalentManager.WebApi.Dto;

public class EmployeeFindViewModel : ViewModelBase
{
    private int employeeId;
    private EmployeeDto employeeFound;
```

```csharp
    public EmployeeFindViewModel()
    {
        this.FindCommand = new RelayCommand(p => FindEmployee());
    }

    public ICommand FindCommand { get; private set; }

    public int EmployeeId
    {
        get
        {
            return employeeId;
        }
        set
        {
            employeeId = value;
            RaisePropertyChanged(() => this.EmployeeId);
        }
    }

    public EmployeeDto EmployeeFound
    {
        get
        {
            return employeeFound;
        }
        set
        {
            employeeFound = value;
            RaisePropertyChanged(() => this.EmployeeFound);
        }
    }

    private void FindEmployee()
    {
        HttpClient client = new HttpClient();
        string creds = String.Format("{0}:{1}", "jqhuman", "p@ssw0rd!");
        byte[] bytes = Encoding.Default.GetBytes(creds);

        var header = new AuthenticationHeaderValue("Basic", Convert.ToBase64String(bytes));
        client.DefaultRequestHeaders.Authorization = header;

        // GET
        HttpResponseMessage response = client
                    .GetAsync("http://localhost/TalentManager/api/employees/" + this.EmployeeId)
                        .Result;

        if (response.IsSuccessStatusCode)
        {
            this.EmployeeFound = response.Content.ReadAsAsync<EmployeeDto>().Result;
        }
    }
}
```

14. Open App.xaml and remove the attribute StartupUri="MainWindow.xaml" from the Application element.

15. Right-click App.xaml in Solution Explorer and select View Code. Override the OnStartup method in App.xaml.cs, as shown in Listing 11-9.

Listing 11-9. The Startup Method

```
using System.Windows;
using Robusta.TalentManager.WebApi.Client.WinApp.ViewModels;
using Robusta.TalentManager.WebApi.Client.WinApp.Views;

public partial class App : Application
{
    protected override void OnStartup(StartupEventArgs e)
    {
        base.OnStartup(e);

        EmployeeFindViewModel viewModel = new EmployeeFindViewModel();

        EmployeeFind view = new EmployeeFind();
        view.DataContext = viewModel;
        view.Show();
    }
}
```

16. Open EmployeesContoller in the Robusta.TalentManager.WebApi.Core project and add a delay in the Get method, as shown in Listing 11-10.

Listing 11-10. Adding Delay in the Get Method of EmployeesController

```
[Authorize]
public HttpResponseMessage Get(int id)
{
    var employee = repository.Find(id);
    if (employee == null)
    {
        var response = Request.CreateResponse(HttpStatusCode.NotFound, "Employee not found");

        throw new HttpResponseException(response);
    }

    System.Threading.Thread.Sleep(5000);

    return Request.CreateResponse<EmployeeDto>(
                        HttpStatusCode.OK,
                            mapper.Map<Employee, EmployeeDto>(employee));
}
```

17. Rebuild the solution and press F5 to run the WPF application.

18. Type an employee ID, say **2**, in the text box and click Find.

19. Click the title bar of the window and try to move it. You will not be able to move, as the window will be frozen and not responding to your input.

20. After a few seconds, when the response is returned by the web API, the window starts responding to your input, and you can now move the window by dragging its title bar. This behavior occurs because of our call to the Result property on the Task object returned by the GetAsync method, which blocks the UI thread.

21. Solving this problem is very easy with ASP.NET Web API, especially in .NET 4.5. Modify the FindEmployee method in the EmployeeFindViewModel class in the Robusta. TalentManager.WebApi.Client.WinApp project, as shown in Listing 11-11. The changes are shown in bold type.

Listing 11-11. Asynchronous FindEmployee

```
private async Task FindEmployee()
{
    HttpClient client = new HttpClient();
    string creds = String.Format("{0}:{1}", "jqhuman", "p@ssw0rd!");
    byte[] bytes = Encoding.Default.GetBytes(creds);

    var header = new AuthenticationHeaderValue("Basic", Convert.ToBase64String(bytes));
    client.DefaultRequestHeaders.Authorization = header;

    // GET
    //HttpResponseMessage response = client
    //                .GetAsync("http://localhost/TalentManager/api/employees/" + this.EmployeeId)
    //                .Result;

    HttpResponseMessage response = await client
                .GetAsync(
                        "http://localhost/TalentManager/api/employees/"
                            + this.EmployeeId); // Not calling .Result now

    if (response.IsSuccessStatusCode)
    {
        this.EmployeeFound = response.Content.ReadAsAsync<EmployeeDto>().Result;
    }
}
```

22. Rebuild the solution and press F5 to run the WPF application. Type an employee ID, say **2**, in the text box and click Find. Click the title bar of the window and try to move it. Now, you will be able to move the window freely, and it will continue to respond to your mouse input, as you move your mouse over the controls, drag the title bar, or even minimize the window and restore it. Eventually, when the result comes back, the employee name and the ID are displayed.

23. When you are done, remove the delay we introduced in the Get action method of EmployeesController in the Robusta.TalentManager.WebApi.Core project by deleting this line:

```
System.Threading.Thread.Sleep(5000);
```

11.3 Calling a Web API from JavaScript

In this exercise, you will call your web API from JavaScript. ASP.NET Web API is a great technology choice to produce the JSON for your JavaScript application needs. Consuming a web API from JavaScript is a different process than in the preceding exercises, where you consumed the web API from .NET clients. Of course, you will use a JavaScript library such as jQuery (which we use in this exercise), but JavaScript runs under the context of a browser and there are limitations associated with this scenario.

In Chapter 3, we looked at the same-origin policy, which allows JavaScript running on a web page originating from a site (defined by a combination of scheme, hostname, and port number) to access the methods and properties of another page originating from the same site but prevents access to pages originating from different sites. For example, the URI for an employee resource that we have been using all along in this chapter is `http://localhost/TalentManager/api/employees/12345`. If you try to access this URI from the JavaScript running in a page from another ASP.NET MVC application, say `http://localhost:14126/Home/Index`, the browser will not allow the call. In Chapter 3, we worked around this problem by using JSONP, which is nothing more than a hack. JSONP will not work with HTTP methods other than GET, such as POST or PUT. A better alternative is Cross-Origin Resource Sharing (CORS), which I'll describe in this exercise.

The Web Applications Working Group within the W3C has proposed the Cross-Origin Resource Sharing (CORS) recommendation, which provides a way for the browser and the server to work together to determine whether to allow the cross-origin request through the use of HTTP headers. There are two types of cross-site requests:

1. **Simple requests:** GET or POST requests are simple requests. For POST requests, the `Content-Type` request header must be one of the following values: `application/x-www-form-urlencoded`, `multipart/form-data`, or `text/plain`. There must not be any custom headers in the request. In the case of simple requests, the `Origin` request header is sent to the server, which responds with the `Access-Control-Allow-Origin` header in the response, indicating that cross-site access is acceptable. A value of * means the resource can be accessed by any domain in a cross-site manner. If the access must be restricted to a specific domain, that domain can be sent in this header.

2. **Pre-flighted requests:** Any request that does not qualify to be a simple request is a pre-flighted request. Pre-flighted requests first send an HTTP OPTIONS request to the resource on the other domain, in order to determine whether the actual request is safe to send. An OPTIONS request has two request headers: `Access-Control-Request-Method` and `Origin`. The `Access-Control-Request-Method` header contains the HTTP method of the actual cross-site request. The server responds with `Access-Control-Allow-Methods`, `Access-Control-Allow-Origin`, and `Access-Control-Allow-Headers` (this is not an exhaustive list; check `http://www.w3.org/TR/cors/`). The first header contains the list of HTTP methods that are allowed. The second header denotes the allowed origin, and the third header contains the list of allowed headers (the header names) for the cross-site request.

Another aspect worthy of careful consideration is the security aspect of authentication, specifically how to present the credentials to the web API from JavaScript. The following are the possible scenarios.

- JavaScript gets the credentials from the user and presents them as-is to the web API. This is the simplest scenario of all. There are two sub-scenarios possible here: (1) the user enters the credentials in a window popped up by the browser and (2) the user enters the credentials in an HTML form, from which JavaScript picks up the credentials and uses them for subsequent requests. The former case is susceptible to attacks like cross-site request forgery (CSRF). The downside with the latter case is that the credentials are cached by JavaScript, and any security flaw with the client application can expose the web API credentials.

- JavaScript gets the credentials from the user and presents them to a broker, which validates and returns another credential such as a token, which has a finite lifetime. JavaScript presents the token as a credential to the web API. The token is cached by JavaScript but if it is compromised, the window of opportunity to exploit will be limited by the token expiry.

- JavaScript does not get the credential at all. It redirects the user to a page that is part of a broker or some entity that the user trusts. Here in this page, the user enters the credentials and is authenticated, and the broker page sends back a token to the JavaScript. This is similar to the previous scenario, except that the JavaScript running in the client application does not get access to the user credential at all. OAuth 2.0 implicit grant is a great candidate for this case. You can find more information about OAuth 2.0 in my other book, *Pro ASP.NET Web API Security: Securing ASP.NET Web API* (Apress, 2013; see `http://www.apress.com/microsoft/asp-net/9781430257820`).

In this exercise, you will implement a solution along the lines of the second scenario. You will use the broker that we created in Chapter 10 to obtain the token. JavaScript will POST the credentials to the broker and get back a JWT that it sends to the web API as credential. From the CORS perspective, the call to the broker will be a simple cross-site request, and the call to web API will be a pre-flighted request. For the simple request, we send the `Access-Control-Allow-Origin` header by manually adding it to the response. For the pre-flighted request, we use the library Thinktecture.IdentityModel.

■ **Note** `Thinktecture.IdentityModel` supports a rich configuration API to control the cross-site access. The CORS implementation of `Thinktecture.IdentityModel` will be part of the `System.Web.Cors` namespace in ASP.NET Web API VNext. At the time of writing, this is available only in the nightly builds and hence we use `Thinktecture.IdentityModel`. By the time you read this chapter, if the `System.Web.Cors` namespace is available in the stable release, you should make use of it.

---

1. We will continue to use the same solution—the solution we used in Exercise 11.2 for this exercise. Run Visual Studio as administrator. Open the `Robusta.TalentManager` solution from Exercise 11.2.

2. In the Solution Explorer, right-click Solution 'Robusta.TalentManager' and choose Add ➤ New Project. Under Visual C# templates, select Web and choose `ASP.NET MVC 4 Web Application`. Give it a name of `Robusta.TalentManager.WebApi.Client.Web`. Choose the Basic application template. Right-click this project in the Solution Explorer and select Set As Startup Project.

3. Run the Internet Information Services (IIS) Manager application. The path to this application in Windows 7 is `%windir%\system32\inetsrv\InetMgr.exe`. In Windows 7, you can type **inetmgr** in the Run box and click OK to launch IIS Manager. In Windows 8, type **inetmgr** in the Search box and press Enter.

4. In IIS Manager, go to Your Server ➤ Sites ➤ Default Web Site ➤ TalentManager. This is the web site of the project `Robusta.TalentManager.WebApi.WebHost` in IIS. Double-click Handler Mappings in the IIS section. Remove `OPTIONSVerbHandler` by right-clicking the handler and selecting Remove from the pop-up. Restart IIS. The reason for the removal is that we need to send precise response headers for OPTIONS requests as part of CORS. The out-of-box OPTIONS handler is not suitable for our needs.

5. In the `Robusta.TalentManager.WebApi.Client.Web` project, right-click the `Controllers` folder and select Add ➤ Controller. Select Empty MVC Controller from the Template dropdown in the Add Controller dialog and create a new MVC controller with a name of `HomeController`.

6. Visual Studio creates a default action method:

```
public ActionResult Index() { return View(); }
```

7. Right-click the `Index` action method code generated by Visual Studio in `HomeController` and select Add View.

8. Accept the default name of `Index` and the view engine of `Razor` (`CSHTML`). If the Create A Strongly-Typed View checkbox is checked, uncheck it and click Add.

9. Copy and paste the code from Listing 11-12 into the `/Home/Index` view created in the previous step. Change the port placeholder `<brokerport>` in the following listing to the port on which the `Robusta.Broker` application runs on your machine. To determine the port, open the `Robusta.Broker` solution in Visual Studio and press F5. Internet Explorer opens the home page. Ignore the `403 - Forbidden` status code and just note down the port displayed by IE in the URL bar. The code does the following:

   a. Using jQuery UI, we pop up a dialog based on the content of the DIV tag (`id="login-dialog"`).

   b. When the user clicks OK, we make a POST to the broker to get the JWT, passing in the credentials entered by the user.

   c. When the call to the broker successfully returns, we clear out the username and password from DOM.

   d. Then, we make a call to the web API, sending the JWT in the bearer scheme. Of course, we do not cache the token, either; but in a real application, you will need to store the token to use in the subsequent web API calls.

Listing 11-12. The /Home/Index View

```
@section scripts{
    <script type="text/javascript">
        $(function () {
            $("#login-dialog").dialog({
                modal: true,
                buttons: {
                    Ok: function () {
                        $(this).dialog("close");

                        $.post("http://localhost:<brokerport>/handler/jwt",
                            {
                                username: $('#username').val(),
                                password: $('#password').val()
                            })
                            .done(function (token) {
                                $('#username').val(null);
                                $('#password').val(null);
```

```
                        $.ajax({
                            type: 'GET',
                            url: 'http://localhost/talentmanager/api/employees/1',
                            headers: { 'Authorization': 'Bearer ' + token },
                            success: function (employee) {
                                var content = employee.Id + ' ' + employee.FirstName;
                                content = content + ' ' + employee.LastName;
                                $('#employee').append($('<li/>', { text: content }));
                            }
                        });
                    });
                }
            }
        });
    });

    </script>
}
<div>
    <div>
        <ul id="employee" />
    </div>
</div>

<div id="login-dialog" title="Please Login">
    <table>
        <tr>
            <td>User ID:</td>
            <td>@Html.TextBox("username")</td>
        </tr>
        <tr>
            <td>Password:</td>
            <td>@Html.Password("password")</td>
        </tr>
    </table>
</div>
```

10. Since we use the jQuery UI for the pop-up, we need the script library to be sent back. By default, BundleConfig.cs, in the App_Start folder in the Robusta.TalentManager. WebApi.Client.Web project, has jQuery UI script and style bundles created. We just need to reference the bundles. Change _Layout.cshtml under Views ➤ Shared, as shown in Listing 11-13. The lines shown in bold type are the new lines added.

Listing 11-13. The Master Layout

```
<!DOCTYPE html>
<html>
<head>
    <meta charset="utf-8" />
    <meta name="viewport" content="width=device-width" />
    <title>@ViewBag.Title</title>
```

```
    @Styles.Render("~/Content/css")
    @Styles.Render("~/Content/themes/base/css")
    @Scripts.Render("~/bundles/modernizr")
</head>
<body>
    @RenderBody()

    @Scripts.Render("~/bundles/jquery")
    @Scripts.Render("~/bundles/jqueryui")

    @RenderSection("scripts", required: false)
</body>
</html>
```

11. Right-click References under the Robusta.TalentManager.WebApi.Core project and select
     Manage NuGet Packages. Search for the package Thinktecture.IdentityModel, select the
     package in the search results, and click Install.

12. In the Robusta.TalentManager.WebApi.Core project, in the Configuration folder, create a
     class named CorsConfig, as shown in Listing 11-14. Change port 14126 to the port used by
     the Robusta.TalentManager.WebApi.Client.Web project in your machine.

Listing 11-14. The CorsConfig Class

```
using System.Web.Http;
using Thinktecture.IdentityModel.Http.Cors.WebApi;

public static class CorsConfig
{
    public static void RegisterCors(HttpConfiguration httpConfig)
    {
        WebApiCorsConfiguration corsConfig = new WebApiCorsConfiguration();

        corsConfig.RegisterGlobal(httpConfig);

        corsConfig
            .ForResources("Employees")
                .ForOrigins("http://localhost:14126")
                    .AllowRequestHeaders("Authorization")
                        .AllowMethods("GET");
    }
}
```

13. In the Robusta.TalentManager.WebApi.WebHost project, add the following line to the
     Application_Start method in Global.asax, as shown in Listing 11-15.

Listing 11-15. Registering CORS Configuration

```
public class Global : System.Web.HttpApplication
{
    protected void Application_Start(object sender, EventArgs e)
    {
        IocConfig.RegisterDependencyResolver(GlobalConfiguration.Configuration);
        WebApiConfig.Register(GlobalConfiguration.Configuration);
        DtoMapperConfig.CreateMaps();

        CorsConfig.RegisterCors(GlobalConfiguration.Configuration);
    }
}
```

14. Finally, we need one change to be done in the broker. Open the Robusta.Broker solution that copied over from the previous exercise into the folder you are working on.

15. Change the BrokerHandler class as shown in Listing 11-16. Lines shown in bold type are the additions. The changes are done to handle the simple CORS. That is, we send the Access-Control-Allow-Origin header in the response to ensure that the AJAX call to get the JWT succeeds. Change port 14126 to the port used by the Robusta.TalentManager.WebApi.Client.Web project in your machine.

Listing 11-16. BrokerHandler Supporting CORS

```
using System;
using System.Collections.Generic;
using System.IdentityModel.Protocols.WSTrust;
using System.IdentityModel.Tokens;
using System.Security.Claims;
using System.Web;

public class BrokerHandler : IHttpHandler
{
    private const string ISSUER = "Robusta.Broker";
    private const string AUDIENCE = "http://localhost/talentmanager/api";

    private ISet<string> allowedOrigins = new HashSet<string>()
                                                { "http://localhost:14126" };

    public bool IsReusable
    {
        get { return true; }
    }

    public void ProcessRequest(HttpContext context)
    {
        HttpRequest request = context.Request;

        string userName = request["username"];
        string password = request["password"];
```

```
            bool isAuthentic = !String.IsNullOrEmpty(userName) &&
                                            userName.Equals(password);

        if (isAuthentic)
        {
            // I use a hard-coded key
            byte[] key = Convert.FromBase64String(
                                "qqO5yXcbijtAdYmS2Otyzeze2XQedqy+Tp37wQ3sgTQ=");

            var signingCredentials = new SigningCredentials(
                            new InMemorySymmetricSecurityKey(key),
                                SecurityAlgorithms.HmacSha256Signature,
                                SecurityAlgorithms.Sha256Digest);

            var descriptor = new SecurityTokenDescriptor()
            {
                TokenIssuerName = ISSUER,
                AppliesToAddress = AUDIENCE,
                Lifetime = new Lifetime(DateTime.UtcNow, DateTime.UtcNow.AddMinutes(5)),
                SigningCredentials = signingCredentials,
                Subject = new ClaimsIdentity(new Claim[]
                {
                    new Claim(ClaimTypes.Name, userName),
                    new Claim(ClaimTypes.Role, "HRManager")
                })
            };

            var tokenHandler = new JwtSecurityTokenHandler();

            var token = tokenHandler.CreateToken(descriptor);

            var origin = context.Request.Headers["Origin"];

            if(origin != null && allowedOrigins.Contains(origin))
                context.Response.Headers.Add("Access-Control-Allow-Origin", origin);

            context.Response.Write(tokenHandler.WriteToken(token));
        }
        else
            context.Response.StatusCode = 401;
    }
}
```

16. Rebuild both solutions and run the Robusta.TalentManager.WebApi.Client.Web project using Google Chrome. To do that, click the down arrow next to Internet Explorer and select Google Chrome, as shown in Figure 11-2. We use Google Chrome because CORS is not supported in Internet Explorer version 9 and below. CORS is supported in IE 10[1], however.

---

[1] http://caniuse.com/cors

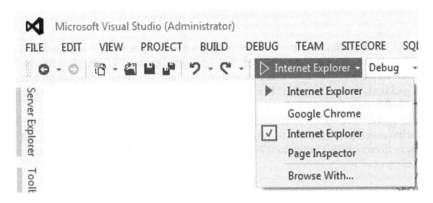

Figure 11-2. *Running with Google Chrome*

17. You will get a popup, as shown in Figure 11-3. Enter **jqhuman** for both user ID and password. The results of the web API call will be displayed in the browser window.

Figure 11-3. *The jQuery UI popup*

18. Here is the sequence of events as the user enters the user ID and password and clicks OK.

   a. We make an AJAX call to the broker `http://localhost:<brokerport>/handler/jwt`, sending the request message with the body of `username=jqhuman&password=jqhuman` and `Content-Type: application/x-www-form-urlencoded`. This is a simple cross-site request, and Google Chrome lets it go through since we send the `Access-Control-Allow-Origin` response header. The response message body contains JWT.

   b. Using that, we make the web API call, which is another AJAX call to `http://localhost/talentmanager/api/employees/1`. We send the `Authorization` request header, passing in the JWT in bearer scheme. Chrome sends an OPTIONS request to check if the cross-site request is acceptable with the web API. We have configured Thinktecture.IdentityModel to handle this request. Thinktecture. IdentityModel sends the required response headers (`Access-Control-Allow-Methods`, `Access-Control-Allow-Origin`, and `Access-Control-Allow-Headers`) to make Chrome happy. Chrome allows the GET with `Authorize` request header containing the JWT obtained from the broker, and jQuery pulls down the JSON response and renders the employee data.

Summary

A broad range of clients in disparate platforms—any software program or hardware device capable of making HTTP calls—can consume HTTP services built using ASP.NET Web API. Consuming your HTTP services from a .NET client is easier with HttpClient, the modern HTTP client that is available from the .NET framework version 4.5 (ported to .NET 4.0 as well). With HttpClient, you get the async benefit of .NET 4.5 by default, and it is quite easy to write non-blocking, responsive applications.

When it comes to JavaScript clients, you need to consider the unique aspects related to the client application running in the context of a browser. There could be restrictions related to the same-origin policy imposed by browsers. CORS is one way to overcome this limitation. The security requirements are also unique with JavaScript applications.

■ ■ ■

CHAPTER 12

Building a Performant Web API

Performance is one of the attributes of software quality. An application with performance levels meeting or exceeding the expectations of its end users can be called *performant*. Often the term *performance* is used synonymously with *scalability*, which is another software quality attribute.

Performance, an indication of the responsiveness of an application, can be measured in terms of latency or throughput. *Latency* is the time taken by an application to respond to an event, for example the number of seconds taken by a screen to show some search result, in response to a user clicking a search button. *Throughput* is the number of events that take place in a specified duration of time, for example number of orders processed by an order processing system in a minute.

Scalability is the ability of an application to handle increased usage load without any (or appreciable) degradation of the performance. Scalability also refers to the ability of an application to show improved performance in proportion to the addition of resources such as memory, CPU power, and so on. A performant application need not be scalable, and vice versa, but ideally your application should be both performant and scalable.

The topics of performance and scalability are vast, and when it comes to ASP.NET Web API, these topics typically cut across multiple technologies. For example, if your ASP.NET Web API uses SQL Server as the persistence store and Entity framework for object-relational mapping, and you host it in IIS (web hosting), you need to be performant on all the following areas: the .NET framework in general, ASP.NET, IIS, EF, SQL server and of course ASP.NET Web API. It is not possible to cover all these topics in a single book, let alone a single chapter. Hence, in this chapter I cover only a few important and must-know areas in ASP.NET Web API.

12.1 Creating Asynchronous Action Methods

In this exercise, you will create asynchronous action methods. The objective behind creating an asynchronous method is to handle more requests with the same number of threads in the thread pool. On the IIS server, the .NET framework maintains a thread pool. The threads from this pool are used to service the requests. The number of threads in a thread pool is finite. The number of threads can be increased to the physical limits, but additional threads do add overhead. The better approach will be to serve the requests with fewer threads, in an efficient manner.

When a request comes in, a thread from the thread pool is assigned to process the request. This thread busily works as the request is processed; and on completion of the request, the thread is returned to the pool to service some other request. This is similar to the operation of a post office or bank,[1] where you wait in line and are processed by an available teller. The teller is with you all the time during the transaction, irrespective of whether she is capable of handling someone else while she waits on some external entity to complete your request. Likewise, as the thread allocated from the thread pool services your request, there are times when a thread must wait for an external entity such as a result from a web service call becoming available. During this time, the thread does nothing but is still

---

[1]"C# 5, ASP.NET MVC 4, and asynchronous Web applications" by Steve Sanderson, Tech Days 2012.

allocated to your request because the service call is a blocking call. For this reason, the thread cannot return to the pool. As the number of incoming requests exceeds the number of threads that are free in the pool, requests start queuing up, as is the case when you visit your bank during the lunch break. If you somehow return the thread to the pool and take the same or another thread when the result from the web service is available to resume processing, you will be able to process more requests with the same number of threads. In a restaurant, by contrast, a waiter takes the order, puts it in for the chef to work on, and goes to some other table to take orders. Eventually, when the food is available, the waiter appears to serve you the food, but she does not stand there staring at you, while you eat! The waiter just works on some other table, until the time you are in need of something. In the case of ASP.NET Web API, a processing mechanism similar to the restaurant model is possible with the use of asynchronous controllers.

Asynchronous action methods allow you to start a long-running operation, return your thread to the pool, and then wake up on a different thread or the same thread depending on the availability of threads in the pool at that time, when the operation is complete, to resume the processing. The async and await keywords of C# 5.0 makes writing asynchronous methods easy.

However, asynchronous methods are not suitable for operations that are CPU-intensive, generally called CPU-bound. Using asynchronous action methods on such CPU-bound operations provides no benefits and actually results in overhead from switching the threads. Using asynchronous methods for the operations that are network-bound or I/O-bound, as in the case of calling an external service or reading or writing a large chunk of data from the hard disk, is typically beneficial. This basically means that we should start with normal synchronous methods and switch to asynchronous methods on a case-by-case basis.

1. Run Visual Studio and create a new ASP.NET MVC 4 Web Application. Give the project a name of **Performant** and click OK.

2. Select the Web API template and click OK. You can leave the Create A Unit Test Project checkbox unchecked and the Razor option selected in the View Engine dropdown.

3. Modify the ValuesController class generated by Visual Studio, as shown in Listing 12-1. Change the *<Path>* placeholder in the code to a valid path in your file system. Note the following about this code:

   a. The ReadFile method just reads a text file and returns the content to the action method, which returns it as the response content.

   b. I have added a delay of 500 milliseconds just for simulating a big file read.

Listing 12-1. The ValuesController Class

```
using System.IO;
using System.Threading;
using System.Web.Http;

public class ValuesController : ApiController
{
    public string Get(int id)
    {
        return ReadFile();
    }

    private string ReadFile()
    {
        using (StreamReader reader = File.OpenText(@"C:\<Path>\SomeFile.txt"))
```

```
        {
            Thread.Sleep(500);
            return reader.ReadToEnd();
        }
    }
}
```

4. Rebuild the solution and make a GET to `http://localhost:35535/api/values/1` using Fiddler. Remember to replace port 35535 with the actual port that your application runs on. Web API returns the text, as expected.

5. Now, let us simulate some load. For this purpose I use ApacheBench (`http://httpd.apache.org/docs/2.2/programs/ab.html`), the same tool used by Steve Sanderson in Tech Days 2012 in the talk I noted previously. ApacheBench is just a command-line tool.

6. Download and install Apache HTTP Server and you will find ApacheBench (`ab.exe`) in the `bin` folder. One of the popular options for downloading Apache for Windows is Apache Haus (`http://www.apachehaus.com/cgi-bin/download.plx`). You can download the zip of Apache server and take `ab.exe` from the zip under the `bin` folder. We need only the executable `ab.exe` and nothing else.

7. Run the following command in a command box: `ab -n 60 -c 60` `http://localhost:35535/api/values/1`. Basically, we ask ApacheBench to make 60 GET requests with a concurrency of 60 to our URI. The output is as follows (some parts removed for brevity).

```
C:\>ab -n 60 -c 60 http://localhost:35535/api/values/1
This is ApacheBench, Version 2.0.41-dev <$Revision: 1.121.2.12 $> apache-2.0
Copyright (c) 1996 Adam Twiss, Zeus Technology Ltd, http://www.zeustech.net/
Copyright (c) 2006 The Apache Software Foundation, http://www.apache.org/

Benchmarking localhost (be patient).....done

Server Software:        Microsoft-IIS/8.0
Server Hostname:        localhost

Document Path:          /api/values/1
Document Length:        771 bytes

Concurrency Level:      60
Time taken for tests:   7.154410 seconds
Requests per second:    8.39 [#/sec] (mean)
Time per request:       7154.410 [ms] (mean)
Time per request:       119.240 [ms] (mean, across all concurrent requests)
Transfer rate:          9.36 [Kbytes/sec] received

Percentage of the requests served within a certain time (ms)
    50%    3576
    66%    4593
    75%    5560
    80%    5628
    90%    6614
    95%    7079
    98%    7121
```

```
 99%    7134
100%    7134 (longest request)
```

8. You can run ab few more times to get a good handle on the response times as well as the throughput (requests per second).

9. Now, modify the ValuesController class, as shown in Listing 12-2. Change the *<Path>* placeholder in the code to the valid path in your file system.

Listing 12-2. The ValuesController Class Converted to Async

```
using System.IO;
using System.Threading.Tasks;
using System.Web.Http;

public class ValuesController : ApiController
{
    public async Task<string> Get(int id)
    {
        return await ReadFileAsync();
    }

    private async Task<string> ReadFileAsync()
    {
        using (StreamReader reader = File.OpenText(@"C:\<Path>\SomeFile.txt"))
        {
            await Task.Delay(500);
            return await reader.ReadToEndAsync();
        }
    }
}
```

Note the following about this code:

a. We now have the ReadFileAsync method, the asynchronous equivalent for the previously used method.

b. We do have the same amount of delay, 500 milliseconds, but here we use Task.Delay instead of Thread.Sleep. The main difference is that the former is non-blocking while the latter is a blocking delay.

c. Apart from these two differences, the code is functionally equivalent to the previous version in all aspects including the delay baked in.

d. Pay attention to the return type of the action method, which is Task<string>.

10. Rebuild the solution and make a GET to http://localhost:35535/api/values/1. Web API returns the same text, as expected. I've placed this step of making a GET from the browser immediately after a rebuild so that application is warmed up and ready to take the load generated by ab.

11. Run the following command in a command box: ab -n 60 -c 60 http://localhost:35535/api/values/1. This is the same command we ran to take the baseline. The output is as follows.

```
C:\>ab -n 60 -c 60 http://localhost:35535/api/values/1
This is ApacheBench, Version 2.0.41-dev <$Revision: 1.121.2.12 $> apache-2.0
Copyright (c) 1996 Adam Twiss, Zeus Technology Ltd, http://www.zeustech.net/
Copyright (c) 2006 The Apache Software Foundation, http://www.apache.org/

Benchmarking localhost (be patient).....done

Server Software:        Microsoft-IIS/8.0
Server Hostname:        localhost

Document Path:          /api/values/1
Document Length:        771 bytes

Concurrency Level:      60
Time taken for tests:   0.599034 seconds
Requests per second:    100.16 [#/sec] (mean)
Time per request:       599.034 [ms] (mean)
Time per request:       9.984 [ms] (mean, across all concurrent requests)
Transfer rate:          111.85 [Kbytes/sec] received

Percentage of the requests served within a certain time (ms)
  50%    560
  66%    570
  75%    575
  80%    577
  90%    579
  95%    583
  98%    583
  99%    584
 100%    584 (longest request)
```

12. Now, with the `async` action method, there is a significant improvement in response times as well as the throughput.

13. The numbers that you see in your run may be different from the ones you see here, based on the hardware configuration of your machine. But the important takeaway here is the overhead that is added on top of the 500 milliseconds baseline delay that we created. With an asynchronous action method the overhead is very small, and with a synchronous action method there is a huge overhead. 500 milliseconds delay is quite significant but as the delay tends to be smaller, the returns you get out of employing asynchronous action method tend to diminish. Also, if the long-running action is CPU-bound, `async` will not be very useful. Network-bound and I/O-bound long-running operations will be good candidates for asynchrony.

12.2 Pushing Real-time Updates to the Client

If the data returned by a service has the characteristic of changing rapidly over time, for example stock quotes, the traditional technique is for the client applications to poll the service repeatedly at regular interval. A client application makes a request, waits for the response to be returned by the service, inspects the response to see if it has gotten anything interesting and acts accordingly, and repeats this process again and again.

Server-Sent Events (SSEs), on the other hand, allows a unidirectional persistent connection between a client and service established as a result of the initial request made by the client, with the service continuing to push data to the client continuously through this connection, until the time the client drops the connection. This is more efficient than polling, but one consideration is the potentially higher number of open connections.

In the following exercise, you will use the PushStreamContent class to push real-time updates to the client. You will create a console application client as well as a JavaScript-based client to receive the updates from your web API. For the JavaScript client, you will use the Server-Sent Events (SSE) EventSource API, which is standardized as part of HTML5 by the W3C. All modern browsers support SSE, with Internet Explorer being a notable exception. We will use Google Chrome for this exercise.

SSEs have been around for a while but are somewhat eclipsed by later APIs like WebSockets that provide a richer protocol for bidirectional, full-duplex communication. Two-way channel is required for some scenarios but there are cases where a unidirectional push from the server to the client is sufficient. SSEs are better suited for this purpose. Also, SSEs just use the traditional HTTP. That means they do not require any special protocols or opening ports in the firewall and so on to implement your solution.

1. Run Visual Studio as administrator.

2. Open the solution Performant that we used in Exercise 12.1.

3. Create a class Quote, as shown in Listing 12-3. You can create this class in the Models folder.

Listing 12-3. The Quote Class

```
public class Quote
{
    public string Symbol { get; set; }
    public decimal Bid { get; set; }
    public decimal Ask { get; set; }
    public DateTime Time { get; set; }
}
```

4. Modify ValuesController, as shown in Listing 12-4. Add two static fields and an action method to handle GET. This code does the following:

   a. The first field is a timer that fires every two seconds. We will implement the callback method TimerCallback in the next step.

   b. The second field is a ConcurrentDictionary that stores the StreamWriter corresponding to each subscription. A client subscribes to the events by making a GET call to our controller. We use a ConcurrentDictionary so that the corresponding StreamWriter object can be removed from the dictionary when a client drops off.

   c. When a client makes a GET request, we create a new HttpResponseMessage using the PushStreamContent object and a text/event-stream media type. PushStreamContent takes in an Action as parameter to the constructor.

   d. To get around the same-origin policy, we send the Access-Control-Allow-Origin response header with a * but in production, you will need to be tighter and send only those origins that you want to allow access.

Listing 12-4. Changes to ValuesController

```
using System;
using System.Collections.Concurrent;
using System.IO;
using System.Net;
using System.Net.Http;
```

```
using System.Threading;
using System.Web.Http;
using Newtonsoft.Json;
using Performant.Models;

public class ValuesController : ApiController
{
    private static readonly Lazy<Timer> timer = new Lazy<Timer>(
                                            () => new Timer(TimerCallback, null, 0, 2000));
    private static readonly
                ConcurrentDictionary<StreamWriter, StreamWriter> subscriptions =
                                        new ConcurrentDictionary<StreamWriter, StreamWriter>();

    public HttpResponseMessage Get()
    {
        Timer t = timer.Value;

        Request.Headers.AcceptEncoding.Clear();

        HttpResponseMessage response = Request.CreateResponse();
        response.Headers.Add("Access-Control-Allow-Origin", "*");
        response.Content = new PushStreamContent(OnStreamAvailable, "text/event-stream");
        return response;
    }

    // More code goes here
}
```

5. Add the method shown in Listing 12-5 to ValuesController. The Action delegate passed to the PushStreamContent constructor will be this method. We create a StreamWriter using the incoming Stream and add it to the ConcurrentDictionary.

Listing 12-5. The Callback Method

```
private static void OnStreamAvailable(Stream stream, HttpContent headers,

TransportContext context)
{
            StreamWriter writer = new StreamWriter(stream);
            subscriptions.TryAdd(writer, writer);
}
```

6. Finally, we need to start sending events. How this can be done will depend on the business need. For example, you can implement a POST or a PUT action method, which can be called by some other entity to signal the controller to start pushing data to the clients. Or the controller can poll a source and on getting some interesting data, it can start pushing that data to all the clients. We will implement the latter approach, though I've just hard-coded the data; we do not poll an actual external source. The timer fires every two seconds to create a dummy Quote object, which is serialized to all the clients. Add the timer callback, as shown in Listing 12-6 to ValuesController. This code does the following:

    a.   We do not call any service but just create a Quote object simulating real data from a quote service. I serialize the object into a JSON string. Pay attention to the two trailing new lines and the field name of data, as needed by SSE.

    b.   We just loop through the StreamWriter objects available in the dictionary and write out the payload. If a client has dropped off, we get an exception and remove the subscription or the writer object from the dictionary and call Close on the writer.

Listing 12-6 The Timer Callback

```
private static void TimerCallback(object state)
{
    Random random = new Random();

    // Call the service to get the quote - hardcoding the quote here
    Quote quote = new Quote()
    {
        Symbol = "CTSH",
        Bid = random.Next(70, 72) + Math.Round((decimal)random.NextDouble(), 2),
        Ask = random.Next(71, 73) + Math.Round((decimal)random.NextDouble(), 2),
        Time = DateTime.Now
    };

    string payload = "data:" + JsonConvert.SerializeObject(quote) + "\n\n";

    foreach (var pair in subscriptions.ToArray())
    {
        StreamWriter writer = pair.Value;

        try
        {
            writer.Write(payload);
            writer.Flush();
        }
        catch
        {
            StreamWriter disconnectedWriter;
            subscriptions.TryRemove(writer, out disconnectedWriter);

            if (disconnectedWriter != null)
                disconnectedWriter.Close();
        }
    }
}
```

    7.   We are done with the server-side implementation. Rebuild the solution to make sure it compiles.

We will now create a console application client to receive events from our web API.

8.   In the Solution Explorer, right-click Solution 'Performant' and choose Add ➤ New Project. Under Visual C# templates, select Windows and choose Console Application. Give it a name of your choice. Right-click this project in the Solution Explorer and select Set As Startup Project.

9.   Add the following references to the console application project: System.Net, System.Net.Http, and System.Net.Http.Formatting. The version is 4.0.0.0 for all the three. The first two assemblies will be present in Assemblies ➤ Framework and the last one in Assemblies ➤ Extensions in the Reference Manager window that opens up, as you select Add Reference after right-clicking References under the project in Solution Explorer.

10. Modify the Program class of the console application, as shown in Listing 12-7. The Main method just calls the RunClient method, where all the action happens. Remember to replace port 35535 with the port used by your web API application. This code does the following:

    a.   It creates a new instance of HttpClient class and calls the GetAsync method. Pay attention to the option HttpCompletionOption.ResponseHeadersRead. This indicates to HttpClient that the operation can complete as soon as a response is available and the headers are read, even if the entire content is not read yet.

    b.   It then reads the bytes off the content stream and converts the bytes to a string and write it off to the console.

Listing 12-7. The Program Class

```csharp
using System;
using System.IO;
using System.Net.Http;
using System.Text;

class Program
{
    static async void RunClient()
    {
        HttpClient client = new HttpClient();

        HttpResponseMessage response = await client.GetAsync(
                                       "http://localhost:35535/api/values",
                                           HttpCompletionOption.ResponseHeadersRead);

        using (Stream stream = await response.Content.ReadAsStreamAsync())
        {
            byte[] buffer = new byte[512];
            int bytesRead = 0;

            while ((bytesRead = await stream.ReadAsync(buffer, 0, buffer.Length)) != 0)
            {
                string content = Encoding.UTF8.GetString(buffer, 0, bytesRead);
                Console.WriteLine(content);
            }
        }
    }

    static void Main(string[] args)
```

```
    {
        RunClient();

        Console.WriteLine("Press ENTER to Close");
        Console.ReadLine();
    }
}
```

11. Rebuild the solution. Right-click the Performant project in the Solution Explorer and select Debug ➤ Start New Instance.

12. With the Performant project running, right-click the console application project in the Solution Explorer and select Debug ➤ Start New Instance.

13. You will start getting the events in the form of JSON messages, pushed by our web API to the client, like so:

```
Press ENTER to Close
data:{"Symbol":"CTSH","Bid":71.44,"Ask":72.70,"Time":"2013-04-27T14:22:21.642857 2+05:30"}

data:{"Symbol":"CTSH","Bid":70.80,"Ask":72.15,"Time":"2013-04-27T14:22:23.654972 3+05:30"}

data:{"Symbol":"CTSH","Bid":70.15,"Ask":71.60,"Time":"2013-04-27T14:22:25.668087 5+05:30"}
```

14. Instead of the client polling the web API, as soon as a new message is available, it is pushed in real time to the client.

15. Let us now create a web application to receive these events. In the Solution Explorer, right-click 'Solution Performant' and choose Add ➤ New Project. Under Visual C# templates, select Web and choose ASP.MET MVC 4 Web Application. Choose the Basic template and give it a name of your choice. Right-click this project in the Solution Explorer and select Set as Startup Project.

16. Configure Visual Studio to use Google Chrome, as shown in Figure 12-1. SSE is not supported in IE.

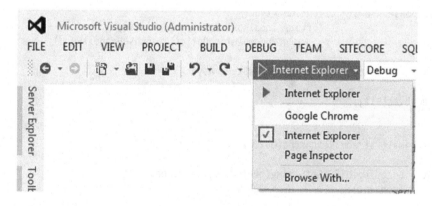

Figure 12-1. *Using Google Chrome to browse*

17. Create an empty MVC controller with a name of HomeController. Also, create the view for the default Index action method generated by Visual Studio. You can right-click the action method and choose Add View and click Add.

18. Copy and paste the code from Listing 12-8 into the view Index.cshtml (Views/Home). We use the EventSource JavaScript API to receive the server sent events. Remember to replace port 35535 with the port used by your web API application.

Listing 12-8. /Home/Index View

```
@section scripts{
    <script type="text/javascript">

        if (!!window.EventSource) {
            var source = new EventSource('http://localhost:35535/api/values');
            source.addEventListener('message', function (e) {
                var data = JSON.parse(e.data);

                var content = data.Symbol + ' Bid: ' + data.Bid +
                                        ' Ask: ' + data.Ask + ' ' + data.Time;

                $('#messages').html(content);
            }, false);

            source.addEventListener('error', function (e) {
                if (e.readyState == EventSource.CLOSED) {
                    console.log("error!");
                }
            }, false);
        }
        else {
            alert('It is almost time to upgrade your browser!');
        }

    </script>
}

<div id="messages"></div>
```

19. Rebuild the solution.

20. Right-click the Performant project in the Solution Explorer and select Debug ➤ Start New Instance. Repeat this step for the other two projects as well: console application and MVC project.

Now, we have both the console application and the web application running side by side and receiving server-sent events.

21. Place a break point in the catch block of the TimerCallback method in ValuesController in the Performant project.

22. Now close the console application by bringing it to focus and pressing Enter. Verify that the next time the web API tries to send the event down to this closed application, an exception is thrown and as part of the handling, the StreamWriter object is removed from the dictionary.

12.3 Implementing Simple Web Caching

In this exercise, you will implement a simple web-caching mechanism. The term *caching* has different connotations. If you have ASP.NET experience, you will know of output caching and application data caching. The former is about storing the resource representation in the server or intermediaries or the user agent, while the latter is about storing the frequently-used application data in the server. Web or HTTP caching is defined in the HTTP specification http://www.w3.org/Protocols/rfc2616/rfc2616-sec13.html#sec13.

A Web cache is a cache of the web server responses such as the web pages, the images, and the style sheets, for later use. The purpose of web caching is to reduce the number of round trips, the network bandwidth, and the web server resource utilization. End users also perceive better performance. The web cache can be in a web browser, if one is involved, or any of the intermediate servers such as that of the ISP or any proxy servers in between. Expiration and validation are the two primary mechanisms associated with the caching. The expiration mechanism allows a response to be reused without checking with the server, thereby reducing the round trip while the validation mechanism minimizes the bandwidth usage.

What is cached need not always be a file such as an image or a CSS. Even ASP.NET Web API responses can be cached. An example of such a scenario would be a web API returning a master list such as list of codes that changes infrequently. By default, the ASP.NET Web API framework marks the response not to be cached by setting the value of the Cache-Control header to no-cache. The Cache-Control: max-age directive specifies the duration in seconds a cache can be used before it expires.

1. Run Visual Studio and create a new ASP.NET MVC 4 Web Application. Give the project a name of **WebCaching** and click OK.

2. Select the Web API template and click OK. You can leave the Create A Unit Test Project checkbox unchecked and the Razor option selected in the View Engine dropdown.

3. Create a new model class Employee, as shown in Listing 12-9. Create this class in the Models folder.

Listing 12-9. The Employee Class

```
public class Employee
{
    public int Id { get; set; }
    public string FirstName { get; set; }
    public string LastName { get; set; }
}
```

4. Create an action filter with a name of CacheAttribute, as shown in Listing 12-10. This filter simply adds the Cache-Control response header like so: Cache-Control: must-revalidate, max-age=x, private. This basically means the response can be cached for 'x' seconds by the browser but not any intermediaries and that the web API requires revalidation of the cache on any subsequent use when the cache becomes stale.

Listing 12-10. The CacheAttribute Action Filter

```
using System;
using System.Net.Http.Headers;
using System.Web.Http.Filters;
```

```
public class CacheAttribute : ActionFilterAttribute
{
    public double MaxAgeSeconds { get; set; }

    public override void OnActionExecuted(HttpActionExecutedContext context)
    {
        if (this.MaxAgeSeconds > 0)
        {
            context.Response.Headers.CacheControl = new CacheControlHeaderValue()
            {
                MaxAge = TimeSpan.FromSeconds(this.MaxAgeSeconds),
                MustRevalidate = true,
                Private = true
            };
        }
    }
}
```

5. Create a new empty API controller with a name of EmployeesController, as shown in Listing 12-11. There is an action method to handle GET, and we return a couple of hard-coded employees. The cache filter we created in the previous step has been applied to the action method with MaxAgeSeconds of 6 so that cache becomes stale every 6 seconds. We specify a small number here for the purpose of testing; typical production implementations do not specify such a small expiry time for cache.

Listing 12-11. EmployeesController

```
using System.Collections.Generic;
using System.Net;
using System.Net.Http;
using System.Web.Http;
using WebCaching.Models;

public class EmployeesController : ApiController
{
    [Cache(MaxAgeSeconds=6)]
    public HttpResponseMessage GetAllEmployees()
    {
        var employees = new Employee[]
        {
                new Employee()
                {
                        Id = 1,
                        FirstName = "John",
                        LastName = "Human"
                },
                new Employee()
                {
                        Id = 2,
                        FirstName = "Jane",
                        LastName = "Taxpayer"
                }
        };
```

```
        var response = Request.CreateResponse<IEnumerable<Employee>>
                                        (HttpStatusCode.OK, employees);


        return response;
    }

}
```

6. Replace the code in the Index view (Views/Home/Index.cshtml) of the HomeController (MVC controller), which Visual Studio created by default, with the code shown in Listing 12-12. We use JavaScript to make an AJAX call to the GET action method of our API controller and render the resulting JSON in a DIV tag. I have included the time here to demonstrate that JavaScript runs and builds the unordered list items every time you click Get.

Listing 12-12. The /Home/Index View

```
@section scripts{
    <script type="text/javascript">
        $(document).ready(function () {
            $('#search').click(function () {
                $('#employees').empty();
                $.getJSON("/api/employees", function (data) {
                    $.each(data, function (i, employee) {
                        var now = new Date();
                        var ts = now.getHours() + ':' + now.getMinutes() + ':' + now.getSeconds();

                        var content = employee.Id + ' ' + employee.FirstName;
                        content = content + ' ' + employee.LastName + ' ' + ts;

                        $('#employees').append($('<li/>', { text: content }));
                    });
                });
            });
        });
    </script>
}
<div>
    <div>
        <h1>Employees Listing</h1>
        <input id="search" type="button" value="Get" />
    </div>
    <div>
        <ul id="employees" />
    </div>
</div>
```

7. Rebuild the solution. Open Fiddler and run the project from Visual Studio by pressing F5.

8. When the home page is displayed, click Get. The data for the two employees we hard-coded in the controller are rendered as the unordered list, along with a time stamp.

9. Keep clicking Get a few more times. Every time you click Get, the list is rebuilt with the timestamp changing every time.

10. Look at the Fiddler capture. There will be only one web API call, in spite of your three or four clicks.

11. Keep clicking Get a few more times. At this point, you will be able to see one more entry in the Fiddler capture. Since we have specified a cache expiry of 6 seconds, the GET call made by jQuery (internally XMLHttpRequest) is serviced from the browser cache itself for these six seconds. At the end of six seconds, the cache becomes stale and the browser allows the call to go through to the web API; and you will see an entry for this in Fiddler. For the cache hits, there will be no entry in Fiddler. This is web caching in action.

The greatest thing about web caching, unlike other caching techniques such as caching application data in the server, is that the server-side code is not doing any work at all. No work is clearly better than less work! Web caching can clearly give your web API a great performance boost, if done correctly. However, you must never cache sensitive data, especially in a public cache such as one maintained by a proxy.

12. Let us now implement the validation mechanism using ETags. An ETag is a unique identifier assigned by the web server to identify a specific version of a resource representation. If the representation changes any time, a new ETag is assigned. The server sends the ETag header along with the response (see Figure 12-2). The client caches the response and the ETag. Subsequently, when the client makes a request for the same resource, the server will send the previously saved ETag in the If-None-Match request header. If the resource has not changed in the server, the server can just respond with a status code of 304 - Not Modified without sending the full response back. When the resource representation has changed, the server sends the new representation with the new ETag corresponding to the changed representation.

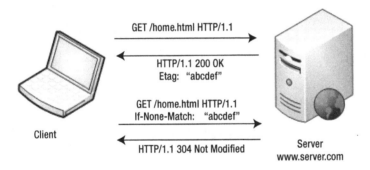

Figure 12-2. The ETag header and response

13. The basic idea behind sending the 304 - Not Modified status is to save network bandwidth. If the response has not changed, there is no need to resend the entire response back. The server can simply return the status code and tell the client that what it got the last time is still valid. The important thing here is that the response must be cached at the client side for this to work. Though it is possible to use the ETag without web caching (as in the case of implementing the optimistic concurrency that you saw in Chapter 8), the ETags and web caching go hand in hand.

14. Create an action filter with a name of EnableETag, as shown in Listing 12-13. This code does the following:

    a. The concurrent dictionary is used to store ETags generated. When it comes back in the If-None-Match request header, we can look up the dictionary to see if the resource representation cached is still valid. The drawback of using the dictionary is that it is stored at the AppDomain level. If your web API is load-balanced and you do not implement sticky session, this mechanism will not work. You might need to use a persistence store such as a database for this, but I use the dictionary because it keeps the code concise.

    b. In the OnActionExecuting method, check whether the method is GET and if so, look up the dictionary for the ETag in the If-None-Match request header. If the ETag is present in the dictionary, send back a 304 - Not Modified and short-circuit the pipeline processing. There is no need for the GET method to run. If ETag is not present, we do not short-circuit, and hence the action method will run.

    c. In the OnActionExecuted method, if the method is PUT or POST, just invalidate the ETags in the dictionary so that any subsequent GET with the If-None-Match request header containing the old ETag will result in the action method being run. If it is a GET, retrieve the ETag from the dictionary and send that in the ETag response header.

Listing 12-13. The EnableETag Action Filter

```
using System;
using System.Collections.Concurrent;
using System.Collections.Generic;
using System.Linq;
using System.Net;
using System.Net.Http;
using System.Net.Http.Headers;
using System.Web.Http.Controllers;
using System.Web.Http.Filters;

public class EnableETag : ActionFilterAttribute
{
    private static ConcurrentDictionary<string, EntityTagHeaderValue>
                                        etags = new ConcurrentDictionary
                                            <string, EntityTagHeaderValue>();

    public override void OnActionExecuting(HttpActionContext context)
    {
        var request = context.Request;

        if (request.Method == HttpMethod.Get)
        {
            var key = GetKey(request);

            ICollection<EntityTagHeaderValue> etagsFromClient = request.Headers.IfNoneMatch;

            if (etagsFromClient.Count > 0)
            {
```

```
            EntityTagHeaderValue etag = null;
            if (etags.TryGetValue(key, out etag)
                                && etagsFromClient.Any(t => t.Tag == etag.Tag))
            {
                context.Response = new HttpResponseMessage(HttpStatusCode.NotModified);
            }
        }
    }
}

public override void OnActionExecuted(HttpActionExecutedContext context)
{
    var request = context.Request;
    var key = GetKey(request);

    EntityTagHeaderValue etag = null;

    bool isGet = request.Method == HttpMethod.Get;
    bool isPutOrPost = request.Method == HttpMethod.Put ||
                                        request.Method == HttpMethod.Post;

    if ((isGet && !etags.TryGetValue(key, out etag)) || isPutOrPost)
    {
        etag = new EntityTagHeaderValue("\"" + Guid.NewGuid().ToString() + "\"");
        etags.AddOrUpdate(key, etag, (k, val) => etag);
    }

    if(isGet)
        context.Response.Headers.ETag = etag;
}

private string GetKey(HttpRequestMessage request)
{
    return request.RequestUri.ToString();
}
}
```

15. Apply the EnableETag filter on the GetAllEmployees action method of
EmployeesController. Also, create an action method to handle POST and apply the
EnableETag filter on that method as well, as shown in Listing 12-14.

Listing 12-14. Changes to EmployeesController

```
public class EmployeesController : ApiController
{
    [Cache(MaxAgeSeconds = 6)]
    [EnableETag]
    public HttpResponseMessage GetAllEmployees()
    {
        // Method is unchanged from the Listing 12-11
    }
```

```
    [EnableETag]
    public void Post(Employee employee)
    {
        // It is okay to do nothing here for this exercise
    }
}
```

16. Rebuild the solution. Open Fiddler and run the project from Visual Studio by pressing F5.

17. When the home page is displayed, click Get. Keep clicking Get a few more times. Every time you click Get, the list is rebuilt with the timestamp changing every time.

18. Look at the Fiddler capture. There will be only one web API call, as against your three or four clicks. As part of the response message of this GET, ETag header is returned.

19. After six seconds, that is, after the cache expiry, same as the last time, an HTTP GET is made. Unlike last time, the call does not return 200 - OK and the JSON response. It just returns a 304 - Not Modified. As part of the request message, If-None-Match header was sent with the value same as the ETag. See Listing 12-15 for the HTTP request and responses.

Listing 12-15. HTTP Request and Response Messages

Initial GET Transaction

REQUEST
```
GET http://localhost:57925/api/employees HTTP/1.1
Accept: application/json, text/javascript, */*; q=0.01
Host: localhost:57925
```

RESPONSE
```
HTTP/1.1 200 OK
Cache-Control: must-revalidate, max-age=6, private
Content-Type: application/json; charset=utf-8
ETag: "0488a8df-c021-4cfa-88a9-78aa782c9cba"
Content-Length: 98
```

```
[{"Id":1,"FirstName":"John","LastName":"Human"},{"Id":2,"FirstName":"Jane","LastName":"Taxpayer"}]
```

Subsequet GET Transaction (After the cache expiry)

REQUEST
```
GET http://localhost:57925/api/employees HTTP/1.1
Accept: application/json, text/javascript, */*; q=0.01
If-None-Match: "0488a8df-c021-4cfa-88a9-78aa782c9cba"
```

RESPONSE
```
HTTP/1.1 304 Not Modified
Cache-Control: must-revalidate, max-age=6, private
```

20. Thus, we implemented the validation mechanism. The AJAX calls are serviced from the cache until the time the cache expires. On expiry, a call is made to the web API with the ETag that was received the previous time to check if the data is still valid. If it is valid, the status code of 304 is returned and the client gets another lease of 6 seconds, during which no HTTP call is made.

21. From Fiddler, make a POST request to `http://localhost:57925/api/employees`. Adjust the port to reflect the port your application runs on. Use the request header of `Content-Length: 0` in the Request Headers text box in the Composer tab of Fiddler.

22. Since we have applied the `EnableETag` filter on the action method handling POST, the filter invalidates the ETag.

23. Click Get again and see the Fiddler capture. See Listing 12-16. It is no longer a `304 - Not Modified` but a `200 - OK`. The response contains a new ETag now and the JSON is sent back in the response. For the subsequent GET requests, this new ETag will be used.

Listing 12-16. A GET Transaction after Invalidation

Request
```
GET http://localhost:57925/api/employees HTTP/1.1
Accept: application/json, text/javascript, */*; q=0.01
If-None-Match: "0488a8df-c021-4cfa-88a9-78aa782c9cba"
```

Response
```
HTTP/1.1 200 OK
Cache-Control: must-revalidate, max-age=6, private
Content-Type: application/json; charset=utf-8
ETag: "ddc8000d-3170-44c4-b154-7961ccc594ba"
Content-Length: 98
```

```
[{"Id":1,"FirstName":"John","LastName":"Human"},{"Id":2,"FirstName":"Jane","LastName":"Taxpayer"}]
```

The `EnableETag` filter accesses the dictionary using the URI as the key . This is acceptable only for the most simplistic requirements. The resource identified by the URI of `http://localhost:57925/api/employees` can have multiple representations. We currently cache one and assume that is the only representation possible. For example, you can have an XML and JSON representation for this resource, based on the `Accept` header. Also, you can have multiple language-based representations using `Accept-Language`. Based on the `Accept-Encoding` header, you can have gzip and deflate representations, and with `Accept-Charset`, you can have UTF-16 and UTF-8. Most of these are out-of-box and you can have your own custom values as well. If you think about the permutations and combinations, caching can get really complex, provided your web API is leveraging all these features.

The HTTP specification defines another header, `Vary`, which can be used by the server to indicate the set of request header fields the resource representation in the response depends on. In other words, the key must be based on all the headers in the Vary header. For example, a web API that supports different media types will specify a `Vary` header like so: `Vary: Accept`. The intermediaries and the browser must cache multiple representations for this URI based on the value in the Accept header.

The objective of this exercise was to introduce you to web caching but not to produce a production-strength caching mechanism. CacheCow, an open source implementation of HTTP caching, available in GitHub (`https://github.com/aliostad/CacheCow`) will be a good start, if you are interested in implementing a full-blown mechanism.

Summary

Performance is an indication of the responsiveness of an application. It can be measured in terms of latency or throughput. Latency is the time taken by an application to respond to an event, while throughput is the number of events that take place in a specified duration of time. Another quality attribute that is often used interchangeably with performance is scalability, which is the ability of an application to handle increased usage load without any (or appreciable) degradation of the performance. The topics of performance and scalability are vast, and this chapter covered only a few important areas in ASP.NET Web API, namely asynchronous action methods, pushing real-time updates to the client, and web caching.

Asynchronous action methods allow you to start a long running operation, return your thread to the pool, and then wake up on a different thread or the same thread, to resume the processing. The `async` and `await` keywords of C# 5.0 makes writing asynchronous methods easy. However, asynchronous methods are not suitable for CPU-bound operations. Using asynchronous methods for the operations that are network-bound or I/O-bound, as in the case of calling an external service or reading or writing large chunk of data from the hard disk, is typically beneficial.

If the data returned by a service has the characteristic of changing rapidly over time, the traditional technique is for the client applications to poll the service repeatedly at regular intervals. Server-Sent Events (SSE), on the other hand, allows a unidirectional persistent connection between a client and service established as a result of the initial request made by the client, with service continuing to push data to the client continuously through this connection, until the time the client drops the connection. ASP.NET Web API supports the `PushStreamContent` class to push real-time updates to the client. The Server-Sent Events (SSE) EventSource API, which is standardized as part of HTML5 by the W3C can be used by a JavaScript client to receive the updates from web API. All the modern browsers except IE support SSE.

A Web cache is a cache of the web server responses for later use. The purpose of web caching is to reduce the number of round trips, the network bandwidth, and the web server resource utilization. End users also perceive better performance. The web cache can be in a web browser, or any of the intermediate servers such as that of ISP or any proxy servers in between. Expiration and validation are the two primary mechanisms associated with the caching, making use of the `Cache-Control` and `ETag` response headers. The expiration mechanism allows a response to be reused without checking with the server, thereby reducing the round trips while the validation mechanism minimizes the bandwidth usage.

Index

■ W, X, Y, Z